# C: An Advanced Introduction

# PRINCIPLES OF COMPUTER SCIENCE SERIES

Series Editors
**ALFRED V. AHO,** *Bell Telephone Laboratories, Murray Hill, New Jersey*
**JEFFREY D. ULLMAN,** *Stanford University, Stanford, California*

**Narain Gehani**
*C: An Advanced Introduction*

**David Maier**
*The Theory of Relational Databases*

**Theo Pavlidis**
*Algorithms for Graphics and Image Processing*

**Arto Salomaa**
*Jewels of Formal Language Theory*

**Jeffrey D. Ullman**
*Computational Aspects of VLSI*


## ANOTHER BOOK OF INTEREST

**Jeffrey D. Ullman**
*Principles of Database Systems, Second Edition*

# C: An Advanced Introduction

**Narain Gehani**
AT & T Bell Laboratories
Murray Hill, New Jersey

COMPUTER SCIENCE PRESS

*Computer Science Press*
*11 Taft Court*
*Rockville, Maryland 20850*
1 2 3 4 5 6  Printing                                              Year  89 88 87 86 85


**Library of Congress Cataloging in Publication Data**

Gehani, Narain, 1947-
    C : an advanced introduction.

    Bibliography: p.
    Includes index.
    1. C (Computer program language)    I. Title.
QA76.73.CL5G44      1984        001.64'24         84-12145
ISBN 0-88175-053-0

To
my friends and colleagues
at
AT&T Bell Labs

# Contents

# Preface

## 1. Introduction

The C programming language was designed and implemented by Dennis Ritchie in 1972 at AT&T Bell Laboratories. Despite a late start, the popularity of C has been increasing rapidly. C compilers are now available for many machines and the list of available C compilers is growing fast [Halfant 1983, Kern 1983, Phraner 1983]. Two important reasons for this increasing popularity are the

1. *Flexibility of the C Language*: It can be used for a wide variety of application domains with relative ease.

2. *Popularity of the UNIX*™ *System*: Most of the software in the UNIX System is written in C and C is the primary language supported by the UNIX system.

Ever since its design, C has been evolving, particularly in the areas of type checking and mechanisms to improve program portability. For example, a project to transport the UNIX operating system to an Interdata 8/32 computer led to several additions to C, notably, unions, casts and type definitions [Bourne 82]. More recently, an effort has been under way to incorporate data abstraction facilities in C [Stroustrup 1983]; data abstraction is an area in which the current version of C has only limited facilities. C is currently in the process of being adopted as an ANSI standard; it is likely that this process will result in further changes to C, several of which are under consideration. ANSI standardization of C is scheduled for late 1985.

I would have liked to base this book on the ANSI version of C, which is currently in preliminary form. However, I decided against doing this because the ANSI version of C is likely to undergo many changes before it is adopted as a standard and because existing compilers do not implement this version. I will discuss C as it is described in *The C Programming Language—Reference Manual* [Ritchie 1980], which is the latest version of the C reference manual. The anticipated differences between this version of C and the preliminary

---

™  UNIX is a trademark of AT&T Bell Laboratories.

ANSI version are summarized in Appendix C.

C is a flexible programming language that gives a great deal of freedom to the programmer. This freedom is the source of much expressive power and one of the main strengths of C, making it powerful, versatile and easy to use in a variety of application areas. However, undisciplined use of this freedom can lead to errors. Consequently, in this book I shall, without loss of generality, restrict discussion to a disciplined use of C. For example, I shall discuss only a restricted version of the *switch* statement in which the code for the different alternatives does not overlap. Although overlapping alternatives can sometimes be used to advantage, such code can be hard to read, modify and maintain, and can be a potential source of errors. Likewise, I shall not rely on default initial values for variables because only a subset of variables is initialized by default; I will explicitly initialize all variables in the example programs.

No C compiler will check and warn of all violations of the disciplined use of C advocated in this book. However, many undisciplined uses will be detected by the C program checker *lint* [AT&T UNIX (Release 5.0) 1982, AT&T UNIX (System V) 1983]; the programmer is urged to check programs with *lint* before compiling and executing them.

C is an evolving language—new features have been added to it in response to perceived needs and to correct deficiencies. Some of the old features have been retained to keep the language upwards compatible with the earlier versions of the language. Consequently, there are some facilities in C that are redundant or obsolete. I shall not discuss these facilities except when necessary.

## 2. About This Book

I have written this book especially for readers with a good knowledge of at least one procedural programming language such as Pascal, PL/I, ALGOL 60, Simula 67, ALGOL 68, FORTRAN or Ada®. I have emphasized the advanced aspects of C: type declarations, data abstraction, exceptions, concurrent programming, the C preprocessor and tools designed for use with C programs.

Some of the advanced aspects of C require support from the underlying operating system such as the UNIX system. Consequently, their availability and use may depend upon the operating system being used. For the operating system dependent aspects, I will assume that the programmer is writing C programs on a UNIX system. Moreover, I will mention C programming

---

®   Ada is a registered trademark of the U. S. Government—Ada Joint Program Office.

conventions used on UNIX systems and discuss the large variety of C programming facilities and tools available on UNIX systems.

There are many examples in this book. These examples have been drawn from a wide spectrum of application areas including interactive programming, systems programming, database applications, text processing and concurrent programming. Many of the examples have been taken from real programs. All examples have been tested.[1] Each chapter is followed by problems that complement the material presented in the chapter.

An annotated bibliography of articles and books on C, and on related topics is given at the end of the book. Most of the items in the bibliography are annotated with brief comments that highlight their main and/or interesting points. The reader is urged to read the bibliography, because it lists many interesting items, not all of which have been cited in the text.

**2.1 Notation**

I shall use the constant width (typewriter) font for C program fragments (e.g., `return;`) and the italic font for emphasis, abstract instructions and syntactic terms (e.g., *divide and conquer* strategy, *print error message* and *declarations*). Using the constant width font for C program fragments conforms with "C style" [Kernighan and Richie 1978].

## 3. Preparation of the Book

This book was prepared using the extensive document preparation tools such as *pic* (preprocessor for drawing figures), *tbl* (preprocessor for making tables), *eqn* (preprocessor for formatting equations), *mm* (collection of TROFF macros for page layout) and *troff* (formatter), which are available on the UNIX operating system.

Murray Hill, N. J.                                                        Narain Gehani
June 1984

---

1. These examples have been tested on both the AT&T UNIX Release 5.0 system [AT&T UNIX (Release 5.0) 1982] and the Berkeley UNIX system [Berkeley UNIX 81]. Most of the programs ran on both UNIX systems without any changes; however, minor changes had to be made to some programs (those with signal handlers) because of differences between the AT&T and the Berkeley UNIX systems and their C compilers. I have indicated, in appropriate places, the relevant differences between these two UNIX systems and changes that must be made to the programs.

# Acknowledgment

I am grateful to Bell Laboratories not only for giving me the opportunity to write this book, but also for the opportunity to become familiar with C. I learned C during the course of my work at Bell Labs; thinking and writing about C has enhanced my understanding of programming languages a great deal.

I must acknowledge my many friends and colleagues who have helped me, in one way or another, in writing this book. I am grateful to A. V. Aho, R. B. Allen, M. Bianchi, R. L. Drechsler, J. Farrell, J. P. Fishburn, D. Gay, B. W. Kernighan, J. P. Linderman, C. D. McLaughlin, D. A. Nowitz, W. D. Roome, L. Rosler, B. Smith-Thomas, T. G. Szymanski and C. S. Wetherell for their comments and suggestions. Bob Allen read two versions of the manuscript. Larry Rosler also provided me with information about the proposed changes to C resulting from the ANSI standardization effort.

I also appreciate the help of Fred Dalrymple, who answered questions about concurrency and of Bjarne Stroustrup, who updated me on the latest version of the data abstraction facilities in the programming language C++.

Over the last few years, John Linderman and, more recently, Bill Roome have (ungrudgingly) answered my many questions about C and helped me better understand its fine points. I am grateful for this help.

# Chapter 1

# Introduction and Basics

The C programming language was designed by Dennis Ritchie in 1972 as a systems programming language to replace assembly language programming at Bell Labs. The phenomenal success of C is shown by the fact that most programming at Bell Labs (including most of the UNIX system programming) is done in C; moreover, the use of C has spread rapidly outside Bell Labs.

## 1. A Sample C Program

The flavor of C programs is illustrated by a small program that simulates a simple calculator that can add, subtract, multiply and divide. The data appear as a list of operations in the format

$$A \theta B$$

where operator $\theta$ is one of the symbols +, -, * or /, and the operands A and B are real values. For simplicity, no embedded blanks are allowed between the operands and the operator. It is also assumed that the only mistake made by the calculator user is to type an operator symbol that is not one of the four allowed symbols.

The reader familiar with high-level languages will be able to understand the calculator program without much difficulty. The program is followed by an explanation of the concepts and facilities used in it; I will discuss them briefly in this section and reserve a detailed discussion for later sections and chapters.

1

```
/*-----------------------------------------------------*/
/* main: A Simple Calculator                           */
/*-----------------------------------------------------*/

#include <stdio.h>

#define PROMPT ':'

main()
{
   float a, b;
   char opr;
   float result;

   while(putchar(PROMPT),scanf("%f%c%f",&a,&opr,&b)!=EO

      switch (opr) {
         case '+': result = a + b; break;
         case '-': result = a - b; break;
         case '*': result = a * b; break;
         case '/': result = a / b; break;
         default:
            printf("ERROR **** illegal operator\n");
            exit(1);
      }

      printf("result is %g\n", result);
   }
   exit(0);
}

/*-----------------------------------------------------*/
```

The first three lines of the C program are comments. The character pair "/*" begins a comment while the pair "*/" ends a comment.

The next two lines in the C program are C preprocessor instructions (all preprocessor instructions begin with the character # in column 1). The first instruction

```
#include <stdio.h>
```

tells the preprocessor to replace the *include* instruction by the contents of the file `stdio.h`; this file contains appropriate declarations for the facilities provided by the standard input/output library package `stdio`. This package is contained in the standard program library `libc`—every C program is automatically compiled with the library `libc`. The angle brackets `<>` indicate that file `stdio.h` should be searched for in the "standard places" on the computer system.

File `stdio.h` also contains the declaration of the constant `EOF`; this constant is often declared as $-1$.

The second instruction

```
#define PROMPT    ':'
```

instructs the C preprocessor to associate the symbolic name `PROMPT` with the character sequence `':'` which represents the colon character; this character will be used to prompt the user for data. The C preprocessor will replace all occurrences of `PROMPT` by the right hand side used in the definition of `PROMPT`, i.e., the character sequence `':'`.

The calculator program consists of one function of the form

```
main()
{
   ...
}
```

The name of this function is `main`, the empty parentheses `()` indicate that execution of this function does not require any parameters and the curly braces `{` and `}`, enclose the body of the function. On the UNIX system, C programs start by executing the function named `main`; consequently, every complete C program must have a function named `main`.

The variable definitions

```
float a, b;
char opr;
float result;
```

specify a, b and `result` to be floating point variables and `opr` to be a character variable. Semicolons are used to terminate variable declarations and definitions, and statements.

The next statement is the *while* loop which, in this case, has the form (except for some logically irrelevant spaces separating the items)

```
while (exp != EOF) {
   statement list
}
```

The list of statements inside the *while* loop is executed repeatedly as long as *exp* does not evaluate to **EOF**. Expression *exp* is a compound expression formed from two expressions

```
putchar(PROMPT)
```

and

```
scanf("%f%c%f", &a, &opr, &b)
```

by using the comma operator. The value of an expression formed by using the comma operator is the value of its second operand; the value returned by the first operand is ignored. For example, the value of the expression

```
putchar(PROMPT), scanf("%f%c%f", &a, &opr, &b)
```

is the value returned by function `scanf`; the value returned by `putchar` is ignored.

Both functions `putchar` and `scanf` are from the standard input/output library package `stdio`. Function `scanf` corresponds to the formatted read found in languages like FORTRAN and PL/I. It takes as arguments a list of formats (e.g., `%f`, `%c` and `%d`) corresponding to the list of variables that are to be read and a list of addresses of these variables. Function `scanf` returns

EOF on encountering end of input; otherwise it returns the number of input items that were successfully matched and assigned to the corresponding variables.

All arguments in C are passed by value. Consequently, addresses of variables (e.g., &a and &opr—operator & yields the address of its variable operand) are passed to simulate the effect of passing parameters by reference. C has only functions and no pure subroutines[2] (i.e., non-value-returning functions). Each function returns a value even though this value may not be meaningful; this value is often thrown away if the function is being used like a subroutine.

It was not necessary to put the call to the function putchar in the *while* loop expression. For example, the above loop could have been alternatively written as

```
putchar ( PROMPT ) ;
while ( exp != EOF ) {
    statement list
    putchar ( PROMPT ) ;
}
```

but this would have required two instances of

```
putchar ( PROMPT ) ;
```

The *switch* statement is used when one out of several alternatives is to be selected. Execution of the *switch* statement, instead of terminating after executing the selected alternative, continues to the end of the *switch* statement. Consequently, execution of the *switch* statement must be explicitly terminated after an alternative has been executed. One way of accomplishing this is to use the *break* statement as the last statement of each alternative. In this case, execution of the *break* statement will result in the completion of the *switch* statment.

There are five alternatives in the *switch* statement used in the calculator program:

---

2. A function with the result type void is a good approximation to a pure subroutine (discussed later). The void type is a recent addition to the C language. It is not discussed in the 1978 version of the *C Reference Manual* [Kernighan and Ritchie 1978], but is discussed in the 1980 version [Ritchie 1980].

```
switch (opr) {
  case '+': result = a + b; break;
  case '-': result = a - b; break;
  case '*': result = a * b; break;
  case '/': result = a / b; break;
  default:
    printf("ERROR **** illegal operator\n");
    exit(1);
}
```

The first four alternatives deal with the cases when `opr` is one of the characters +, -, * or /, respectively. The last alternative, the *default* alternative, deals with all other values of `opr`. In this case, the library function `printf` is called with a string representing the error message. The character pair \n denotes the newline character. The backslash character \ is called an *escape* character because a backslash and the character (or up to three octal digits) following it mean something special. One use of this combination is to denote non-printable characters. The `exit` function call

```
exit(1);
```

causes termination of the program with a value of 1. By convention on the UNIX system, a non-zero value returned by a main program is used to indicate error termination, while a zero value is used to indicate normal or successful termination.

The program as written is not "user-friendly;" instead of trying to help the user correct mistakes the program terminates when the user types an incorrect operator. It can be made more user-friendly by replacing the `exit` function call

```
exit(1);
```

with the statements

```
printf("Legal operators are +, -, * and /;");
printf(" Try again\n");
continue;
```

The *continue* statement causes program execution to continue from the beginning of the *while* loop where the program prompts the user for more data.

Following the *switch* statement is the call to the function `printf`:

```
printf("result is %g\n", result);
```

The effect of this function call is to print the string

```
result is value
```

where *value* is the current value of the variable `result`; this value is printed using the g format (specified by the characters %g) in which trailing zeros are elided and a decimal point is printed only if the value is not a whole number.

Finally, after determining that the end of input has been reached, the program terminates normally by calling the function `exit` with the value 0 to signal that all is well:

```
exit(0);
```

It is not necessary to use the `exit` function to terminate a program; a program can also terminate by executing all the statements in the main function or by executing the *return* statement in the main function. However, use of the `exit` function to terminate a program allows other programs to determine success or failure of the program.

## 1.1 Compilation and Execution of the Calculator Program on the UNIX System

Once the program has been written, the programmer will want to compile and execute it.

Suppose that the source statements for the calculator program are stored in the file `calc.c`. (All C source files must have the suffix `.c` on the UNIX system. This convention, which is enforced by the C compiler, is used to advantage by tools such as `make` that are used in writing and maintaining C programs; see Appendix B for more details.)

The error checking program `lint` can be used to check the presence of some kinds of errors in C programs:

```
lint calc.c
```

After removing any program errors detected by `lint`, one uses the C compiler `cc` to compile the C program and link it with the library functions used by it:

```
cc calc.c
```

An error-free compilation produces the executable file `a.out` (default name) that can be executed directly as

```
a.out
```

The name `a.out` is not a very meaningful name for a program; the programmer can supply an appropriate name for the executable version of the program by using the `-o` option when invoking the compiler. Thus, the command

```
cc -o calc calc.c
```

Here is a sample execution of the calculator program:

```
$ calc
:59.0/4.0
result is 14.75
:39.0+44.0
result is 83
:$
```

The dollar character, i.e., **$**, is the UNIX system prompt character indicating that the UNIX system is ready to execute the next user command. The program terminated because end-of-input was indicated by the control-D character that was typed by the user (in the last line). This character is not a printable character and is therefore not shown. By convention, the control-D character is used to indicate the end-of-input or the end-of-file on UNIX systems.

Here is another sample execution of the program; this execution is eventually terminated because of an illegal operator:

```
$ calc
:2.0+37.5
result is 39.5
:5.0*4.5
result is 22.5
:5.0%4.5
ERROR **** illegal operator
$
```

## 2. Basics

### 2.1 Character Set

The *character set* of C is implementation dependent. For example, on the DEC PDP-11*, VAX-11* and AT&T 3B computers, the C character set is the ASCII character set while on the IBM 370 computers it is the EBCDIC character set. For all implementation-dependent aspects of C, I will assume, unless I state otherwise, that the C compiler is the Unix system C compiler running on a PDP-11 or VAX-11 computer. An ASCII character set is assumed for the C language in this book.

Blank, tab and newline characters, along with comments, are collectively called *white space*.

### 2.2 Identifiers

*Identifiers* are names given to program entities such as variables and functions. These names start with a letter or the underscore character "_" and may be followed by any number of letters, underscore characters and digits.[3] C is *case sensitive* [Evans, Jr. 1984]; i.e., C distinguishes between upper- and lower-case letters. As with the character set, identifier construction rules are also implementation dependent. Both upper- and lower-case characters may be used on PDP-11, VAX-11 and AT&T 3B implementations, but on some implementations only upper case is used (lower-case characters are not distinguished from upper-case characters; lower-case characters are mapped to upper case). Although identifiers may be of any length, many C compilers consider only the first 8 characters to be significant. For example, the two

---

\* PDP-11 and VAX-11 are trademarks of Digital Equipment Corporation.

3. On the UNIX system, by convention, identifiers that begin with the underscore character are reserved for system programs. To avoid conflicts, programmers should avoid giving such names to program entities.

identifiers

```
movement_detector
movement_sensor
```

are considered to be identical by some compilers because they have the same first 8 characters:

```
movement
```

Identifiers used for external program entities such as functions and external variables (discussed later) may have different restrictions depending upon the implementation.

Some identifiers are reserved words, called *keywords*, and cannot be used by the programmer for any purpose other than their intended usage. These keywords are

```
auto        break       case        char
continue    default     do          double
else        entry       enum        extern
float       for         goto        if
int         long        register    return
short       sizeof      static      struct
switch      typedef     union       unsigned
void        while
```

Keyword `entry` is not used currently, but is reserved for future use. In addition, the identifiers `fortran` and `asm` are keywords in some implementations of C.

## 2.3 Literals

A *literal*[4] is an explicit representation of a value. Literals in C can be of several types—integer, long integer, character, floating point, enumeration or string.

---

4. Literals are called constants in C terminology. The term literal is used in this book to distinguish literals from "constant identifiers" implemented by using the C preprocessor.

*2.3.1 Integer Literals:* Integer literals can be written in decimal, octal or hexadecimal. Octal literals are preceded by the digit 0, while a hexadecimal literal must be preceded by the digit 0 and the character x (or X). Letters A through F (or a through f) may be used for the hexadecimal digits 10 through 15, respectively. Some examples of integer literals are

| integer literal | explanation |
|---|---|
| 12 | decimal notation |
| 014 | octal notation for decimal 12 |
| 0xc | hexadecimal notation for decimal 12 |
| 0XC | same as above |

If the integer literals are too big to be ordinary integers, then they are treated as long integers.

*2.3.2 Long Integer Literals:* Integer literals may be specified explicitly to be long integers if they are immediately followed by the character L (or l).

*2.3.3 Character Literals:* A character literal is formed by enclosing a single character within single quotes. A character literal can be used as an integer literal whose value is the integer interpretation of the bit representation of the character literal.

Some non-graphic characters, the single quote ' and the backslash \ characters are denoted by using an *escape* sequence, as specified in the following table:[5]

---

5. The character sequence \c, where the character c is not a digit and not any of n, t, v, b, r, f, \ and ' stands for c itself.

| character | denotation |
|-----------|------------|
| newline | \n |
| horizontal tab | \t |
| vertical tab | \v |
| backspace | \b |
| carriage return | \r |
| form feed | \f |
| backslash | \\ |
| single quote | \' |

All characters can also be specified as

$$\backslash ddd$$

where ddd is one to three octal digits representing the position of the character in the ASCII character set (see Appendix D). For example, \012 denotes the newline character (also denoted as \n), \107 denotes the letter G and \0 denotes the *null* character.

Examples of character literals are

| character literal | explanation |
|-------------------|-------------|
| 'a' | character a |
| '\n' | newline character |
| '\\' | backslash character |
| '\'' | single quote character |
| '\107' | character G |

*2.3.4 Floating Point Literals:* The usual notation is used for floating point literals. Some examples are

```
24.0     2.4E1 (or 2.4e1)        240.0E-1
```

where the number following the letter E (or e) represents the exponent (base 10).

All floating point literals are assumed to be double-precision values.

*2.3.5 Enumeration Literals:* Enumeration literals are identifiers that represent values of a user-defined type (see enumeration types in Section 1.3 of Chapter 2 titled *Types and Variables*).

*2.3.6 String Literals:* String literals are formed by enclosing a sequence of zero or more characters in double quotes. Examples of strings are

```
"  "      " "      "A"

"error"        "a longer string"
```

The double quote character can be included in a string by using the *escape* character \, that is, use \" whenever the character " is to be an element of a string:

```
"\""
```

Strings may be continued over a line boundary by using the *escape* character, \, at the end of the string as in

```
"a very very very very very very very very\
long string"
```

Strings can also have non-graphic characters such as the newline and backspace characters. For example, a string with the newline character \n is

```
"first line\nsecond line"
```

Assuming that the printer is positioned at the beginning of a new line, this literal, if printed, will appear as

```
first line
second line
```

Strings are actually character arrays (see arrays and strings in Sections 2.1 and 2.6 of Chapter 2 titled *Types and Variables*). For example, the string

```
"Bell Labs"
```

is equivalent to the character array

| B | e | l | l |   | L | a | b | s | \0 |
|---|---|---|---|---|---|---|---|---|----|
| 0 | 1 | 2 | 3 | 4 | 5 | 6 | 7 | 8 | 9 |

By convention, strings in C are terminated with the *null* character \0. String processing in C is based on this convention. In case of string literals, the compiler appends the *null* character automatically. However, in case of strings that have been explicitly constructed by the programmer, e.g., by using an array of characters, the programmer must insert the null character at the end of the string to conform to this convention.

## 2.4 Comments

*Comments* start with the characters /* and are terminated by the characters */. A comment may begin on one line and end on another line. Comments cannot be nested.

## 2.5 Semicolon—The Statement Terminator

Semicolons are used as terminators for declarations and statements with one exception—a semicolon is not needed after the right curly brace } of the *compound* statement, which has the form { . . . }. This use of a semicolon as a terminator is similar to its use in PL/I and Ada, but different from its use in Pascal, where it is used as statement separator. Using the semicolon as a separator may be an elegant concept [Gries 1979], but it has been experimentally determined to be error prone in practice [Gannon 1975].

## 3. Constants

Constant definitions in C are provided by the C preprocessor (discussed in Chapter 9). Constant definitions have the form

```
#define  constant-name      literal or constant-name
#define  constant-name      (constant-expression)
```

As far as the C preprocessor is concerned, both constant definition forms are the same. They are really macro definitions of the form

```
#define identifier      replacement string
```

The effect of this definition is to cause all future occurrences of *identifier* to be textually replaced by *replacement string* (unless the definition has been changed). Therefore, when these definitions are used as C constant definitions, it is not necessary to enclose the constant expression in parentheses; however, it is prudent to enclose the constant expression in parentheses to avoid unexpected interpretations (see Chapter 9 titled *C Preprocessor* for more details).

As an example, here are some constants that were used in defining the layout of a database file and specifying the maximum size of the database:

```
#define LN        20  /* length of name + 1 for \0 */
#define LR        8   /* length of room + 1 for \0 */

#define MAX_DB   100 /* max size of data base */
```

Some examples that use the second form of the *define* statement are

```
#define EOF        (-1)
#define TOTAL_ELEM     (M*N)
                       /* M and N are constants */
```

## 4. Problems

1. Write the calculator program in the language you are most familiar with and compare it with the C version. How are non-graphic characters denoted? How are constants written? How are statements terminated?

2. What is the convention used in languages like Pascal and Ada for determining the end of a string? What are the pros and cons of terminating strings explicitly with the *null* character?

3. Why is using a semicolon as a statement separator more error prone than using it as a statement terminator?

# Chapter 2

# Types and Variables

A *type* is a set of values plus a set of operations that can be performed upon these values [Morris, Jr. 1973]. A *variable* is an entity that is used to store a value of the type associated with it. Storing a new value in a variable destroys the old value, if any, stored in the variable.

Types in C are classified into two categories—*fundamental* and *derived*. The fundamental types are character, integer, enumeration, floating point and void. Character, integer, enumeration and floating point types are also called *arithmetic* types, because they can be interpreted as numbers. Character, integer and enumeration types are also called *integral* types; *floating point* type is used to refer to both single- and double-precision floating point types. Derived types are constructed from the fundamental types; the derived types are arrays, functions, pointers, structures and unions.[6]

Before we delve into the details of the types in C, here is some additional terminology:

> An *object* is a region of storage.

> An object *declaration* is used only to specify the properties of an object; no storage is allocated for the object.

> An object *definition* is used to specify the properties of an object and to allocate storage for the object.[7]

Object declarations are used to allow references to objects that are defined later in the file containing the program or defined elsewhere in other files containing other parts of the program.

---

6. Derived types mean something very different in the Ada programming language.

7. Please remember the difference between a declaration and a definition. This difference is important not only because I shall use it often in the rest of the book, but also because many people confuse a declaration for a definition and vice versa.

While discussing types, it will sometimes be necessary to talk about variable declarations and definitions, because these are intimately related to types. Only simple forms of declarations and definitions will be used when discussing types; the general form of declarations and definitions will be discussed later.

# 1. Fundamental Types

## 1.1 Characters

Values associated with the type `char` are elements of the character set defined by an implementation, e.g., the ASCII character set. An example of a definition of character variables is

```
char c, ch;
```

which defines c and ch to be character variables.

Character values are stored as integers that correspond to the internal representation of the character. Consequently, characters can be treated as integers and vice versa.[8] This duality is exploited in programming; some functions that return character values are declared to be of type integer so that they can return an integer, such as -1 (which does not represent any character) to indicate failure or end-of-file.

Programmers must be careful in defining variables of type `char` because of the above programming convention. Variables used to store character values returned by functions should be defined to be of type `int` to take care of the integer value returned by the function in unusual or limiting cases. For example, the function `getc` (from the standard input library package `stdio`) is used to read the next character from the standard input file. However, upon encountering the end-of-file, `getc`, like many other standard functions, returns -1; consequently, `getc` is defined to return values of type `int` (and not `char`). Therefore, variables used for storing values returned by `getc` should be defined as integers!

## 1.2 Integers

Integers come in three sizes `int`, `short int` (or just `short`) and `long int` (or just `long`). Some examples of integer variable definitions are

---

8. Because characters can be treated as integers and vice versa, a compiler cannot detect potential errors such as the inadvertent addition of character and integer variables.

```
int i, n;
short int low, high;
long int max;
```

which define

- i and n to be variables of type int,

- low and high to be of type short int, and

- max to be of type long int.

An ordinary integer variable (i.e., a variable of type int) is stored in the "natural" storage unit of the underlying machine. The amount of storage allocated for variables of integer types short int and long int depends upon the implementation.[9] Using a short int instead of int may or may not lead to a saving of storage (see Appendix E on *Implementation-Dependent Characteristics*). However, using short int variables may in some cases increase program execution time because arithmetic operators convert short int values to int values prior to using them. Consequently, short int variables should be used only when it is necessary to economize on storage.

If the sign bit is not needed, then the type unsigned int (or just unsigned) may be used. Unsigned integers are used to access bits of a machine word. Unsigned integers can also be used to "squeeze an extra bit" out of a machine word whenever the sign bit is not needed [Ritchie, Johnson, Lesk and Kernighan 1978].

### 1.3 Enumeration Types

Enumeration types allow identifiers to be used as values. The use of enumeration types may improve program clarity because meaningful names may be assigned to nondescript values. For example, it is more meaningful to use the identifiers jan, feb, mar, for the months of a year instead of the integers 1, 2, 3.

The set of values associated with an enumeration type must be declared by explicitly listing the values. Enumeration type declarations[10] have the form

---

9. Note that $S(\text{short int}) \leqslant S(\text{int}) \leqslant S(\text{long int})$ where $S(x)$ is the amount of storage allocated for a variable of type $x$.

10. The type declaration mechanism typedef is discussed in detail later in Section 3.

```
typedef enum {a₀, a₁, ..., aₙ} E;
```

where $E$ is the enumeration type being declared. Enumeration literal $a_i$ is normally represented by the integer $i$.[11]

Two examples of enumeration type declarations are

```
typedef enum {mon, tue, wed, thu, fri, sat, sun} day
typedef enum {red, yellow, green} traffic_light;
```

An enumeration literal cannot be associated with two different types. For example, in presence of the declaration of `traffic_light`, the type declaration

```
typedef enum {yellow, blue, red} color;
```

would be illegal because `yellow` and `red` are already associated with the enumeration type `traffic_light`.

Variables of the enumeration types `day` and `traffic_light` may be defined as

```
day d;
traffic_light signal;
```

An example of the use of an enumeration type is

---

11. The internal representation of enumeration literals can be explicitly specified. For example, in the type declaration

```
typedef enum {a₀=v, a₁, ..., aₙ} E;
```

enumeration literal $a_i$ is represented by the integer $v+i$.

```
switch (signal) {
case red: brake; wait for traffic light to turn green; break;
case yellow: stop if possible; otherwise keep going; break;
case green: go; break;
default: error;
}
```

The instructions in italics are abstract statements. I shall use such statements when explaining or developing programs. Before a program is compiled, abstract statements must be replaced by C statements that have the same effect.

Instead of declaring enumeration types, *enumeration tags*[12] can also be declared and used to define variables. For example, day and traffic_light may be declared as enumeration tags as

```
enum day {mon, tue, wed, thu, fri, sat, sun};
enum traffic_light {red, yellow, green};
```

Enumeration tags are similar to enumeration types. For example, using the enumeration tags declared above, variables d and signal could be defined as

```
enum day d;
enum traffic_light signal;
```

Enumeration variables and constants are *currently* treated by the C language as variables and constants of type int. Consequently, erroneous use of enumeration values as integers may not be detected by C compilers. For example, the meaningless expression

```
tue + sat
```

that adds two days will not be detected as an error.

---

12. The *enumeration tag* mechanism is redundant in the presence of the more general *typedef* declaration. Both of these facilities were added to C as the language evolved.

Another limitation of C's enumeration types is that there is no mechanism to generate the elements of an enumeration type. For example, it is not possible to write a loop that executes its body once for each value of the enumeration type d ay; such a loop could be described abstractly as

```
for d in day { ... }
```

where d is the loop variable that is assigned a different element of type d for each execution of the loop body.

## 1.4 Boolean or Logical Values

C does not have boolean values; instead integers are used to substitute for boolean values. Non-zero values are interpreted as *true* and the zero is interpreted as *false*. By convention, the predefined operators and functions return the value one for *true* and zero for *false*.

For clarity, the constants TRUE and FALSE will be used in this book to denote boolean values. They will be declared as the constants one and zero, respectively:

```
#define TRUE    1
#define FALSE   0
```

## 1.5 Floating Point

There are two varieties of floating point types—float (single precision) and double (double precision). Example definitions of variables of these two types are

```
float x, y;
double eps;
```

Variables x and y are defined to be of type float and variable eps is defined to be of type double.

All floating point arithmetic in C is done in double precision. The programmer should note that the extra precision provided by double-precision arithmetic is more expensive than single-precision arithmetic because of the following reasons: because of the extra precision, double-precision arithmetic generally takes longer than single-precision arithmetic. In addition, there is the conversion cost—all variables of type float must be converted to double precision prior to a floating point operation and double-precision results must be converted back to single-precision before being stored in `float` variables.[13]

## 1.6 Void

Type `void` represents an empty set of values. It is used

- to specify the type of functions that do not return any values, i.e., functions used as subroutines, and

- to indicate that the value of an expression is not going to be used, but that the expression is being evaluated only for its side effects (see Section 5.3 titled *Explicit Type Conversion—Casting*).

The use of `void` is optional; the value of an expression is discarded if it is not used. However, its use will stop the program checker `lint` and the better C compilers from giving warning messages indicating that the value of an expression is being discarded.

# 2. Derived Types

## 2.1 Arrays

An array is a composite object consisting of component objects (called elements), all of which have the same type. Simple array definitions have the form

$$data\text{-}type \quad \mathbf{x}[n_1] \quad [n_2] \quad \ldots \quad [n_k]$$

where `x` is an identifier that is being defined as the name of the array and $n_i$ is the size of the $i^{th}$ dimension of the array. Array `x` is said to be a *k-dimensional* array with elements of type *data-type*. The elements of the $i^{th}$ dimension of `x` are indexed from 0 to $n_i - 1$.

The array element type can be one of the fundamental types, another array type, a pointer type, a structure type or a union type, but not a function type. Although array elements cannot be functions, they can be pointers to functions (pointers are discussed in Section 2.5).

Some examples of array definitions are

---

13. These conversions are not necessary in implementations that treat `float` and `double` values identically.

```
int page[10]; /* one-dimensional array with 10 */
              /* elements numbered from 0 to 9 */
char line[81];
float big[10][10], sales[REGION][MONTHS][ITEMS];
```

In the last definition, two arrays are defined together: `big` is defined as a two-dimensional array and `sales` is defined as a three-dimensional array (`REGION`, `MONTHS` and `ITEMS` are constants that must have been declared previously by using the *#define* instruction).

Elements of a k-dimensional array **x** are referenced using the notation

$$x[i_1] \ [i_2] \ \ldots \ [i_k]$$

where the subscripts $i_j$ are integer expressions and $0 \leqslant i_j \leqslant n_j-1$, $n_j$ being the size of the $j^{th}$ dimension of **x**. Some examples are

```
page[5]
line[i+j-1]
big[i][j]
```

A p-dimensional subarray of a k-dimensional array $(p \leqslant k)$ can be referenced by giving only the first p subscripts, e.g.,

| element | refers to |
|---------|-----------|
| `sales[i]` | 2-dimensional subarray of `sales` |
| `sales[i][j]` | 1-dimensional subarray of `sales` |
| `sales[i][j][k]` | 0-dimensional subarray, i.e., a simple element of `sales` |

The general form of array definitions will be discussed in Section 4 titled *Definitions and Declarations*. There is a intimate relationship between arrays and pointers; it will be discussed in Section 2.4 titled *Pointers*.

## 2.2 Structures

A *structure* (record in Pascal/Ada terminology) is a composite object that consists of components of any type except functions. A structure may be a *heterogeneous* object while an array must be a *homogeneous* object.

Structure types have the form

```
struct {
    list of declarations
}
```

There must be at least one component in a structure. Structure types are used to define structures. Structure definitions have the form

*data-type declarators*;

where *data-type* specifies the structure type of objects that are being defined in the *declarators*. In their simplest form, *declarators* are ordinary variable names, array names, pointer names and function names. (Definitions will be explained in detail in Section 4; for the moment I will continue to illustrate them by means of examples.)

The definition

```
struct {
    double x, y;
} a, b, c[9];
```

defines a and b to be structures, each with two components **x** and **y**. Variable c is defined to be an array of 9 such structures.

The definition

```
struct {
    int year;
    short int month, day;
} date1, date2;
```

defines two variables date1 and date2, each with three components: year, month and day.

Names can be associated with a structure type by using a type declaration of the form

```
typedef struct {
    list of declarations
} structure-type-name;
```

These names can then be used to define structures. (The general form of the *typedef* declaration is discussed in detail later.)

An example of a structure type is employee, whose declaration is

```
typedef struct {
    char name[30];
    int id;
    dept d;
    family f;
} employee;
```

where dept and family are types, actually structure types, that were previously declared by the user. Structure type employee can be used to define variables; e.g., the definition

```
employee chairperson, president, e1, e2;
```

declares the variables chairperson, president, e1 and e2 to be structures of type employee.

There is another mechanism for associating names with structure types; names associated with structure types using this mechanism are called *structure tags*. Structure tags are similar to *enumeration tags*. A structure tag is declared as

```
struct tag {
    list of declarations
};
```

where *tag* is an identifier. For example,

```
struct student {
  char name[25];
  int id, age;
  char sex;
};
```

declares student to be a structure tag.  Structure tags are used to define structures by using a definition of the form

struct *tag identifier-list*;

An example definition is

struct student s1, s2;

The use of structure tags is necessary for declaring recursive structures—the *typedef* mechanism is not sufficient by itself.  An example of a recursive structure tag declaration is

```
struct node {
  int data;
  struct node *next;
};
```

Structure tag node is recursive because it is used in its own declaration, i.e., in declaring next.  (Because of the presence of the character *, next is declared to be a pointer to objects of type node; I will be discussing pointers soon.)

Structures cannot be directly recursive; a structure of type S cannot contain a component that is a structure of type S.  However, a structure of type S can contain a component that *points* to a structure of type S.

*2.2.1 Accessing Components of a Structure:*  Components of a structure are accessed using the *selected component* notation.  The general form of this notation is

*s*.*c*

where *s* is a structure variable or a structure value with component *c*; *s* can be an expression that evaluates to a structure; e.g., *s* might be a function call that yields a structure as its value. Components of the structure variable `date1` defined above may be accessed as

```
date1.year
date1.month
date1.day
```

*2.2.2  Bit Fields:* Structures can also be used to access bits of a word. Use of bit fields is necessary only in a few cases, such as programs in which it is important to economize on storage and in systems programs that interact directly with the hardware; when writing device drivers, it may be necessary to access specific bits of the device register.[14]

Components of a structure may be packed into words by specifying the position and the number of bits occupied by each component. Such components are called *fields*. Although the C language allows fields to be of any type, C implementations are required to support only integer fields; *The C Reference Manual* [Ritchie 1980] suggests the use of `unsigned` fields because `int` fields may be treated differently on different machines. *The C Reference Manual* also warns the user that implementations may place severe restrictions on how fields may be used; e.g., in all implementations arrays of fields cannot be declared and the *address of* operator may not be applied to fields.

In general, a *field structure* (a structure whose components are fields) type has the form

_____

14. On computers with memory mapped I/O, such as the VAX-11, a device register is a location in memory; I/O is controlled via memory locations.

```
struct {
    [unsigned identifier₁]:  field—width₁;
    [unsigned identifier₂]:  field—width₂;

    .
    .
    .

    [unsigned identifierₙ]:  field—widthₙ;
}
```

where $field-width_i$ is a constant integer expression specifying the number of bits occupied by the bit field $identifier_i$. A field width of zero specifies alignment with the next word boundary.

Fields are allocated contiguously; they are allocated right-to-left (i.e., from the least significant bit to the most significant bit) on some machines (e.g., the PDP-11 and the VAX-11) and left-to-right on other machines. Unnamed fields (fields for which only the width is specified) are used to specify those bits of a word that will not be accessed. Fields cannot be wider than the word of the underlying machine; a field that is wider than the number of bits left in the current word is allocated in the next word.

As an example, consider the field structure `save_211` specified according to the format for the command and status register of the RX211 disk used on the VAX-11 computer:

```
struct {

    unsigned error: 1; /* bit 15; on the VAX-11  */
                       /* computer, bits are     */
                       /* assigned right to left */
    unsigned initialize : 1;     /* bit 14 */
    unsigned unibus_addr: 2;     /* bits 13-12 */
    unsigned rx02       : 1;     /* bit 11 */
    unsigned            : 2;     /* field is not  */
                                 /* named because */
                                 /* bits 10-09    */
                                 /* are not used  */
    unsigned density     : 1;    /* bit 08 */
    unsigned trans_req   : 1;    /* bit 07 */
    unsigned int_enable  : 1;    /* bit 06 */
    unsigned done        : 1;    /* bit 05 */
    unsigned unit_select : 1;    /* bit 04 */
    unsigned function    : 3;    /* bits 03-01 */
    unsigned go          : 1;    /* bit 00 */

} save_211; /* RX211 Disk command and status */
            /* register format */
```

Field structures can also contain ordinary components (e.g., a char component). Such components are allocated automatically at appropriate word boundaries—some bits may be left unused.

Bit fields are referenced the same way as components of ordinary structures are referenced.

### 2.3 Unions

A *union* is similar to a structure except that only one of its components is in use, i.e., active, at any given time. Union types have the form

```
union {
    declaration of component₁ ;
    declaration of component₂ ;
    ·
    ·
    declaration of componentₙ ;
}
```

All these components are allocated the same storage in memory, i.e., they are overlaid. Although this memory can be accessed using any one of the components, it should be accessed using only components that lead to a meaningful result.

As mentioned earlier, unions are similar to structures. Components of a union are accessed the same way as the components of a structure. *Union tags* can be declared just as structure tags are declared.

Unions are used

- to minimize use of storage when it is known that only one object out of many will be active at any given time.

- to interpret the underlying representation of an object of one type as if it were associated with some other type.

The role of unions is similar to the role of the *equivalence* declarations in FORTRAN. Components a and b of a union object have the same relationship to each other as two objects that are *equivalenced* to each other in FORTRAN.

As an example of a definition of a *union* object, consider the union geom_fig defined as

```
union {
    float radius;      /* circle */
    float a[2];        /* rectangle */
    int b[3];          /* triangle */
    position p;        /* point */
                       /* "position" is a user */
                       /* declared type */
} geom_fig;
```

In this example, it is meaningful to access only the active component, i.e., the component last assigned a value. For example, after assigning component radius a value, it does not make sense to access b[0].

## 2.4 Variant Structures

Programs often contain objects that are conceptually very similar to each other, differing only in some minor details. For example, consider the representation of geometric figures. Common information might include items such as area and perimeter. However, applicable information about their dimensions may be different and may depend upon their shape.

Languages like Ada and Pascal provide a type called the *variant record* whose objects have a set of common components plus some components that are not common to all the other objects. In C, a type similar to a variant record, called a *variant structure* can be implemented by using a combination of a structure and a union. As an example, consider the structure fig:

```
typedef struct {
   float area, perimeter; /* common components  */

   int type;      /* active component tag keeps  */
                  /* track of the figure         */

   union {        /* variant component */
     float radius; /* circle    */
     float a[2];   /* rectangle */
     float b[3];   /* triangle  */
     position p;   /* point     */
   } geom_fig;
 } figure;
```

Each object of type figure will have the three components area, perimeter and type, in common. Component type is called the *active component tag* because it is used to indicate which one of the components of the union geom_fig (i.e., radius, a, b or p) is currently active. Such a structure is called a *variant structure* because its components vary with the value of the active component tag.

Assume that the following constant definitions have been given:

```
#define CIRCLE 1
#define RECT 2
#define TRIANGLE 3
#define POINT 4
```

and that variable fig has been defined as

```
   figure fig;
```

Then, by convention, before assigning a value to one of the components in the union, an appropriate value would also be assigned to fig.type to indicate the active component, e.g.,

```
fig.type = CIRCLE;
fig.geom_fig.radius = 5.0;
```

Similarly, before accessing a component in the union, a check should be made to ensure that the component is active, e.g.,

```
switch (fig.type) {
case CIRCLE: do processing for a circle; break;
case RECT: do processing for a rectangle; break;
case TRIANGLE: do processing for a triangle; break;
case POINT: do processing for a point; break;
default: error;
}
```

An enumeration type could have been used instead of the constant definition mechanism to define CIRCLE, RECT, TRIANGLE and POINT, e.g.,

```
typedef enum {CIRCLE, RECT, TRIANGLE,
                        POINT} figure_class;
```

Component type of figure would then have been declared as a variable of type figure_class. Use of the enumeration type figure_class will allow the C compiler to warn the programmer of potentially erroneous assignments such as

```
fig.type = 44;
```

Variant structures will in general consist of three parts—a set of common components, the active component tag and the variant component part. The general form of variant structures is

```
struct {
  common components ;
  active component tag ;
  union {
    declaration of component₁ ;
    declaration of component₂ ;
    ⋮
    declaration of componentₙ ;
  } identifier ;
}
```

Another example of a variant structure is `health_record` defined as

```
struct {
  /* common information */
    char name[25];
    int age;
    char sex;

  /* active component tag */
    marital_status ms;

  /* variant part */
    union {
      /* single */
        /* no components */

      /* married */
        struct {
          char marriage_date[8];
          char spouse_name[25];
          int  no_children;
        } marriage_info;

      /* divorced */
        char date_divorced[8];
    } marital_info;
} health_record;
```

where `marital_status`, the type of the active component tag `ms`, is declared as

```
typedef enum {SINGLE, MARRIED, DIVORCED}
                            marital_status;
```

Some examples of referring to components of a variant structure are

```
health_record.name
health_record.ms
health_record.marriage_info.marriage_date
```

## 2.5 Pointers

A *pointer* is a typed entity that refers to some region of storage.  A pointer definition is of the form

$$data\text{-}type \;\; *id_1, \;\; *id_2, \;\; \ldots, \;\; *id_n \;;$$

Variables $id_1$, $id_2$, ..., $id_n$ are defined to be of type *pointers to data-type* (denoted as *data-type* $*$); these variables refer to objects of type *data-type*, which is called the *base* type of the pointer variables.

Some examples of pointer definitions are

```
int *pi, *qi; /* pointers to integer objects */

struct { int x, y; } *p;
            /* pointer to a structure with */
            /* components x and y */

complex *x;  /* pointer to an object of a  */
            /* user-declared type complex */
```

*2.5.1 Dynamic Objects:* Pointers are used in the creation and manipulation of dynamic objects.  Defined objects are created by specifying them in a definition.[15]  Dynamic objects, on the other hand, are created dynamically and

---

15. *Defined* objects are also called *static* objects. I will not use the adjective *static* because I want to avoid any possible ambiguity with the storage class static in C.

explicitly during program execution. The storage allocators `malloc` and `calloc` are used to create dynamic objects. The number of dynamic objects, unlike the number of defined objects, is not fixed by the program text— dynamic objects are created or destroyed as desired, during program execution. Dynamic objects, unlike defined objects, do not have explicit names and must be referred to by means of pointers.

The pointer value 0 is associated with all pointer types. The pointer value 0 indicates that no object is being referred to by the pointer. Using this value to refer to a dynamic object results in an error. By convention, the constant `NULL` is used to represent 0. It is declared as

```
#define NULL     0
```

in the standard input/output package declarations file `stdio.h`.[16]

*2.5.2 Creation of Dynamic Objects:* The storage allocators `malloc` and `calloc` have the specifications[17]

```
char *malloc(size)
unsigned size;
     /* amount of storage to be allocated */


char *calloc(nelem, elsize)
unsigned nelem;
     /* number of elements to be allocated */
unsigned elsize;
     /* storage to be allocated for each */
     /* element */
```

Both `malloc` and `calloc` return a character pointer that points to the allocated storage.

---

16. Note that the `NULL` value is different from the *null* character `\0`.

17. By convention, a *function specification* includes the first line of the function definition and declarations of the function parameters. (See Chapter 5 titled *Functions and Complete Programs* for more details).

The `sizeof` operator may be used in determining the amount of storage that needs to be allocated:[18]

| **form** | **meaning** |
|---|---|
| `sizeof`(*expression*) | amount of storage required for storing *expression* |
| `sizeof`(*T*) | amount of storage required for values of type *T* |

The storage allocators `malloc` and `calloc` return a pointer to the dynamic object created. Actually, the storage allocators return character pointers and these must be explicitly converted to the appropriate pointer types (for more discussion on type conversions see Section 5.3 titled *Explicit Type Conversion—Casting*). The values returned by the storage allocators are used to refer to the dynamic objects. For example, the statement

```
pi = (int *) malloc(sizeof(int));
```

causes allocation of storage for one integer value. The address of this storage is assigned to `pi` after it has been converted from the type `char *` (pointer to character), which is the type of value returned by `malloc` to the type `int *` (pointer to integer), which is the type of the variable `pi`. Pictorially, the dynamic object pointed to by `pi` may be depicted as

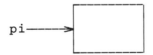

where the empty box is a placeholder for an integer.

*2.5.3 Accessing Dynamic Objects:* A value is assigned to the object pointed to by `pi` by using its name `*pi`, e.g.,

---

18. Parentheses are not required in the first form of the `sizeof` operator; however, I have used parentheses so that both forms of the `sizeof` operator look the same.

```
*pi = 55;
```

Pictorially, the effect of this assignment may be depicted as

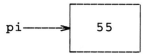

The same pointer value may be assigned to more than one pointer variable. Thus, a dynamic object may be referred to using one or more pointers. An object that can be referred to via two or more pointer objects is said to have *aliases*. For example, as a result of the assignment

```
qi = pi;
```

both `qi` and `pi` point to the same object, i.e., they are aliases. Pictorially, the effect of this assignment may be depicted as

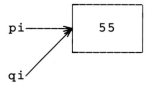

Uncontrolled use of aliases can be detrimental to program readability, because the same object can be accessed and modified using the various aliases and this may not be obvious from a local analysis of the program.

*2.5.4 Lifetime of a Dynamic Object:* Dynamic objects must be deallocated explicitly if the space occupied by them has to be used for other purposes. Otherwise, this storage will be lost; i.e., it may not be possible to reuse it. Explicit deallocation is done using the function `free`, which has the specification

```
free(ptr)
char *ptr;
```

Care must be taken to avoid errors resulting from the *dangling reference* problem [Horowitz 1983]; that is, one must avoid referencing objects that have been deallocated.

Storage occupied by inaccessible objects can be automatically reclaimed if the implementation provides a *garbage collector*. Unlike Lisp and Snobol, C does not provide a garbage collector.

*2.5.5 Pointing to Defined Objects:* Pointers can point to defined objects. The address of a defined object can be determined by using the *address of* operator &. For example, consider the variables i and pi defined as

```
int i, *pi;
```

The assignment

```
pi = &i;
```

allows the object with name i to also be referred to via the pointer pi by using the notation *pi. The names i and *pi are aliases. The use of the *address of* operator can also lead to the dangling reference problem. It is also the standard means of simulating *passing parameters by reference* (see Chapter 5 titled *Functions and Complete Programs*).

*2.5.6 Pointing to Arbitrary Locations in Memory:* Pointers can be made to point to arbitrary locations in memory by means of explicit conversions. For example, suppose pt is a pointer of type T *; it can be made to point to location 0777000 in memory as follows:

```
pt = (T *) 0777000;
```

Referencing specific memory locations is often necessary in programs that interact with the hardware. For example, in device drivers it is necessary to access specific locations in memory, such as those associated with the device's buffer and status registers, to control the device. Although this facility is useful and even necessary for some applications, it must be used with care. (Most operating systems prevent arbitrary users from referencing some absolute memory addresses to preserve the integrity of the system facilities and to protect other users.)

*2.5.7 Relationship Between Pointers and Arrays:* Arrays and pointers are intimately related in C; in fact, arrays may be considered to be syntactic sugar for pointers. Every array name is treated as a pointer to the first element of the array. The array element a[i] is the element pointed to by a+i, i.e., *(a+i), where the value of a is the address of the first element of the a which is a[0]. Expression a+i is an example of pointer arithmetic—integer i is being added to a pointer, the address of the first element of the array a. The value of this expression is a plus the amount of storage occupied by i elements of a. See Chapter 3 on *Operators and Expressions* for more details of pointer arithmetic.

Suppose that x is an 2-dimensional array. Then a reference to the subarray x[i] is a reference to row i of x; x[i] yields the address of the first element of this row, i.e., *(x+i). Elements of each row are stored contiguously because arrays are stored in *row major* order; i.e., the last subscript varies the fastest when laying out the elements in storage.

Similarly, a reference to y[i], where y is a n-dimensional (n > 1) array, is a reference to the (n−1)-dimensional subarray whose elements are y[i, $j_2, j_3, \cdots j_n$] where $j_k$ have values consistent with the definition of y; y[i] yields the address of the first element of this subarray, i.e., *(y+i). All elements of this (n−1)-dimensional subarray are stored contiguously.

*2.5.8 Strings—More on the Intimate Relationship Between Pointers and Arrays:* Strings are arrays of characters. By convention, the last character must be the null character \0. Because an array name is really a pointer to the first element of an array, string variables can also be considered to be of type char *. For example, the second variable string_array in the following definition

```
char *string_pointer, string_array[81];
```

can also be treated as a character pointer. Storage must be allocated explicitly for the string represented by the first variable string_pointer; on the other hand, storage has been allocated for the array string_array and the variable string_array points to it. Note that storage must also be allocated or reserved for the string terminator \0.

Not only is the interpretation of string variables (i.e., character arrays) as pointers quite common, but strings are often treated in a dual fashion—both as arrays and as pointers—in the same program! This is especially important when strings are passed as arguments to a function. The calling program may treat the string as a character array while the called function may treat it as a character pointer.

Using character pointers for strings can be advantageous when the string length is variable. Although variable-length strings can also be implemented using arrays, this implementation is wasteful of storage and puts an upper bound on the length of the string. For example, an array of character pointers can be made to hold strings of different lengths; however, the alternate implementation using a two-dimensional character array will in general waste storage because it would require that the number of columns be equal to the size of the largest possible string.

*2.5.9 Pointers and Structures:* Consider the structure tag student that was declared earlier as

```
struct student {
  char name[25];
  int id, age;
  char sex;
};
```

and the pointer new_student that is defined as

```
struct student *new_student;
```

Suppose that storage has been allocated to make new_student point to a student object. Then components of this object are referenced as

```
(*new_student).name
(*new_student).id
(*new_student).age
(*new_student).sex
```

Because pointers are commonly used to point to structures, C provides the *right arrow* selection operator especially for referencing components of such structures. For example, the above components can also be referenced using the *right arrow* operator -> as

```
new_student->name
new_student->id
new_student->age
new_student->sex
```

As another example illustrating the relationship between structures and pointers, consider the type stat_reg declared as

```
typedef struct {

    unsigned error: 1; /* bit 15; on the VAX-11   */
                       /* computer, bits are      */
                       /* assigned right to left */
    unsigned initialize : 1;     /* bit 14 */
    unsigned unibus_addr: 2;     /* bits 13-12 */
    unsigned rx02        : 1;     /* bit 11 */
    unsigned             : 2;     /* field is not   */
                                  /* named because  */
                                  /* bits 10-9 are  */
                                  /* not used */
    unsigned density     : 1;     /* bit 8 */
    unsigned trans_req   : 1;     /* bit 7 */
    unsigned int_enable  : 1;     /* bit 6 */
    unsigned done        : 1;     /* bit 5 */
    unsigned unit_select: 1;      /* bit 4 */
    unsigned function    : 3;     /* bits 3-1 */
    unsigned go          : 1;     /* bit 0 */

} stat_reg; /* RX211 disk command and status */
            /* register format */
```

Type stat_reg is used to define the pointer variable ptr_rx_sr:

```
stat_reg *ptr_rx_sr;
```

Pointer ptr_rx_sr is made to refer to the RX211 disk command and status register located at address 0777170 by the assignment

```
ptr_rx_sr = (stat_reg *) 0777170;
```

Components of the RX211 register can now accessed as

```
ptr_rx_sr->error
ptr_rx_sr->density
ptr_rx_sr->int_enable
```

and so on.

## 3. Type Declarations

Type declarations are used to collect the common properties of objects in one place and give them a name. This *type name* can then be used in subsequent declarations of these objects. Type declarations have the form

typedef *type-specifier declarators* ;

where *type-specifier* is a fundamental or a derived type, or a type that has been declared earlier by the programmer. Names of the types being declared are represented by the identifiers in the declarators.

Some examples of type declarations are

```
typedef float miles, speed;
          /* declares "miles" and "speed" as */
          /* synonyms for "float"            */

typedef float a[5], *pf;
       /* declares type "a" as an array of 5  */
       /* floating point components; type "pf" */
       /* is declared as a pointer to "float"  */
       /* objects                             */

typedef  struct { float x, y; } point;

/* structure type "emp" declares layout of  */
/* records of a database file; the constants */
/* used here were declared earlier          */

     typedef struct {
       char name[LN];
       char room[LR];
       char ext[LE];      /* extension */
       char desig[LD];    /* designation */
       char compid[LC];   /* company id */
       char sig[LS];      /* electronic signature */
       char logid[LL];    /* login id */
       char maild[LM];    /* directory where mail */
                          /* is received */
     } emp;
```

These types can be used to define objects, just as types `float` and `int` are used to define objects.  For example, the definition

```
point s1, s2, *p;
```

defines `s1` and `s2` to be structures of type `point` and `p` to be a pointer to a structure of type `point`.

Type declarations in C do not introduce new types; instead, they introduce synonyms for existing types or types that can be derived from existing types. For example, the types `miles` and `speed` declared above are synonyms of each other and the predefined type `float`; they are all equivalent.

## 4. Definitions and Declarations

A *variable* consists of two components: an object and the name of the object. Names can be identifiers or expressions. For example, the expression

```
*p
```

is the name of the object pointed to by the pointer p.

Identifiers are defined and declared using definitions and declarations of the form

    *storage-class data-type declarators*;

where the *storage-class* or *data-type* may be omitted. The *storage-class* and *data-type* apply to each declarator, each of which specifies one identifier. Each declarator may be followed by an *initializer*, which specifies the initial value associated with the identifier in the declarator.

### 4.1 Storage Classes

The lifetime and the scope of an identifier are determined by the *storage class* associated with it. There are four kinds of storage classes:

| storage class | implication |
|---|---|
| auto | local identifiers that are allocated at block (i.e., compound statement) entry and deallocated at block exit (auto is short for automatic). |
| static | local identifiers that exist across block executions. Unlike auto identifiers, static identifiers are allocated only once—at the beginning of program execution and they exist for the duration of the program. |
| extern | permanent identifiers, called *external identifiers*, that are used for communication between functions, including independently compiled functions (which reside in different files). The storage associated with these identifiers is permanent, but the contents of the storage can change. These identifiers are declared outside functions. |

`register`      identifiers similar to `auto` identifiers that should be stored, if possible, in machine registers for fast access.

If the storage class of a identifier is not specified explicitly, then its storage class is determined by the textual location of its definition; if the identifier is defined inside a function, then it has the storage class `auto`; otherwise, it has the storage class `extern`.

Let us now consider a C program whose source text is distributed over many files. Functions in these files use `extern` identifiers to share data (for communication). If a function references an `extern` identifier, then the file containing it must have a declaration or a definition of this identifier. Explicit specification of the `extern` storage class implies that the identifier has been defined in another file and that no storage is to be allocated here—the declaration is being given only for type checking and code generation purposes.[19] Storage is allocated for an `extern` identifier only when the storage class is not specified explicitly[20] Although there may be many files containing a declaration of an external identifer, there must be exactly one file containing the definition of the `extern` identifier.

As implied in the above discussion, the scope of external identifiers is not restricted to the file containing their definitions, but also includes files that contain the corresponding declarations (with the `extern` storage class). However, qualifying definitions of external identifiers by `static` restricts their scope to the file containing them.

As an example, consider the definitions and declaration outside functions of variables x and i in two files a.c and b.c. File a.c contains the definitions

```
int x;
static int i;
.
.
.
```

and file b.c contains the declaration and definition

---

19. When declaring external arrays, the size of the first dimension need not be specified—it will be determined from the corresponding definition—a user convenience.

20. Explicit specification of the storage class `extern` differentiates an external declaration from an external definition.

```
extern int x;
static int i;
  .
  .
  .
```

Variable x is shared between the two files; storage for it is allocated by the definition in file a.c and this variable may be used for communication between functions in the two files. On the other hand, each file has its own local variable i; storage is allocated for each of the two definitions of i. Each variable i can be accessed only by functions in the file containing its definition.

Because most computers have only a few registers available, only the first few variables can be stored in registers. The register declaration will help improve program execution speed only in the case of C compilers that do not optimize programs at all or optimize very little. In some cases, register declarations may actually slow down a program.[21] Certain restrictions apply to the use of register variables; e.g., it is not possible to determine the address of a variable allocated in a register (by using the *address of* operator &); moreover, only simple types such as int and char, and pointer values can be stored in registers.

### 4.2 Data Types

The data type specified in a declaration or a definition can be one of the *type specifiers*

---

21. Suppose a programmer designates the storage class of a lightly used variable to be register. Allocation of a register for such a variable will slow program execution if this prevents better use of the register. Note that some C compilers do not heed register declarations.

```
char
int
short int (or just short)
long int (or just long)
unsigned int (or just unsigned)
unsigned char
float
double (or long float)
void
struct tag
union tag
enum tag
typedef-name
```

where the *tags* and the *typedef-name* must have been previously declared.

By default, if a data type is not given in a declaration or a definition, then it is assumed to be int.

### 4.3 The Declarators

Each declarator contains exactly one identifier which is the name being given to the object being declared or defined by the declarator. Declarators must be separated by commas:

*declarator, declarator, ..., declarator*

The form and semantics of the declarators are explained in the table given below. Assume that T is the data type specified in the object definition:

| declarator | meaning |
|---|---|
| *identifier* | *identifier* of type $T$ is being defined |
| (*declarator*) | same as *declarator* |
| *declarator* | same as *declarator* in an object definition with the data type *pointer to T* |
| *declarator*( ) | same as *declarator* in an object definition with the data type *function returning a value of type T* |
| *declarator*[ N ] | same as *declarator* in an object definition with the data type *array with* N elements of type $T$; N is a constant expression and the elements are numbered from 0 to N-1 |

There are some restrictions on the declarators allowed. Functions cannot return arrays or functions as values (they can return pointers to arrays or pointers to functions). Also, arrays of functions cannot be declared or defined nor can functions be components of a structure or a union.

The dereferencing (indirection) operator * has a lower precedence than the other two operators, i.e., "[ ]" (for specifying arrays) and "( )" (for specifying functions), used in declarations and definitions.

### 4.4 Examples of Object Definitions and Declarations

The definition[22]

```
int i, *ip, f( ), *fip( ), (*pfi)( );
```

which contains the declarators i, *ip, f( ), *fip( ) and (*pfi)( ), leads to the identifiers in the declarators to be defined or declared[23] as follows:

---

22. The semantics of definitions and declarations depend upon whether they have been given inside or outside a function. In the examples, I will use the convention that definitions and declarations are given inside functions unless it is clear from the context or it has been explicitly specified that they have been given outside functions.

23. Definitions and declarations can be intermingled as illustrated by the hybrid definition-declaration

```
int i, *ip, f( ), *fip( ), (*pfi)( );
```

| i | an integer variable |
|---|---|
| ip | pointer to an integer variable |
| f | function returning an integer |
| fip | function returning a pointer to an integer |
| pfi | pointer to a function that returns an integer |

All the variables in this definition are, by default, defined to be of type auto.
In the definition

```
static emp *db[MAX_DB];
```

db is defined to be an array of pointers to elements of type emp. Elements of
db are numbered from 0 to MAX_DB-1.

The definition

```
static int size, cur = 0;
```

defines size and cur to be static variables of type int. Variable cur is
initialized to 0.

*4.4.1 Syntactic Difference Between Object Declarations and Definitions:* An
object declaration can be syntactically distinguished from an object definition
by observing the following points:

1.  The presence the keyword extern specifies that the objects are being
    declared and not defined.

2.  The absence of the function parameters and the associated body indicates
    that a function is being declared and not defined.

3.  Function parameters are declared and not defined.

Here are some more example declarations and definitions:

---

I shall generally call such a hybrid a definition. In this definition, identifiers i, ip and pfi
are defined while identifiers f and fip are declared. Identifiers f and fip refer to functions
for which no storage is allocated here; these functions are defined elsewhere.

```
/* declarations */

  char *strcat(), *index(), *strcpy();
  extern int max(), no_of_processes;
  extern float a[];

/* definitions */

  struct node *head;    /* structure definition  */
                        /* using tag "node" */

  point x, y;           /* structure definitions */
                        /* using type "point" */
  static union {
    automobile a;
    bus b;
    truck t;
  } vehicle;

  day d;
  emp list_of_emp[100];
```

## 4.5 Initializers

Initializers are used for specifying initial values of variables in their definitions. They have the following forms:

= *value*

= { *list of values* }

where each value is a constant expression and the values are separated by commas. A value can be an *aggregate value*, i.e., a list of values enclosed in curly braces. Static and external variables are initialized by default to 0 while automatic variables are not initialized by default.[24] Moreover, automatic

---

24. I shall always explicitly initialize variables before using them; this tends to make programs clearer.

aggregates cannot be initialized.

Some examples of variable initialization are

```
static float eps = 0.0001;

int i = 0, j=0;

int year[12] = {31, 28, 31, 30, 31, 30, 31,
                           31, 30, 31, 30, 31};

char greetings[21] = "Welcome to Bell Labs";
   /* the length of the string is 21--one  */
   /* element must be reserved for the end */
   /* of string character in this variable */

char error[] = "Buffer length exceeded";
   /* the size of an array need not be      */
   /* specified because the C compiler can  */
   /* deduce it from the initialization     */

/* example of a nested initialization */

float matrix[5][3] = { {1.0, 1.0, 1.0},
                       {2.0, 2.0, 2.0},
                       {3.0, 3.0, 3.0},
                       {4.0, 4.0, 4.0},
                       {5.0, 5.0, 5.0}
                     };
         /* elements of row i are assigned */
         /* the value i */

point p = {0.0, 0.0};
         /* structure type "point" was */
         /* declared earlier */
```

## 4.6  Comments on Declaration/Definition Syntax

The syntax for declarations and definitions in C is similar to the syntax used for accessing values of these objects; that is, it is similar to the syntax used to represent object values in expressions. This is an important difference between C and languages like ALGOL 68, Pascal and Ada, where the syntax used for declaring object types reflects the structure of the type. Declarations and definitions in C are sometimes hard to read and understand, particularly if they involve compound-type expressions that contain the pointer dereferencing operator *. The primary reason for this difficulty is that the dereferencing operator is a prefix operator, while all the other operators used in declarations and definitions are postfix operators. The reader unaccustomed to programming in C may at first find it hard to understand definitions and declarations such as

```
int *(*(*x)[6])();
char (*(*(y())[])();    /* taken from ANDE80 */
```

where

1.  x is defined to be a pointer to an array of 6 elements each of which is a pointer to a function returning a pointer to an integer object.

2.  y is declared as a function that returns a pointer to an array of pointers to functions that return character values.

The reader will find it easier to understand C declarations and definitions if he/she keeps in perspective that an object declaration or definition looks very much like the way the object will be referenced in an expression.

Anderson [Anderson 1980] suggests the use of the following approximate equivalences with ALGOL-like or Pascal-like declarations and definitions to help understand and write C declarations and definitions (intermediate forms of declarations and definitions are used to help determine the equivalences):

| C syntax | | intermediate form | | Pascal-like syntax |
|---|---|---|---|---|
| `int x` | | | ≡ | `x: int` |
| `int *x` | ≡ | `*x: int` | ≡ | `x: pointer to int` |
| `int x[]` | ≡ | `x[]: int` | ≡ | `x: array[] of int` |
| `int x()` | ≡ | `x(): int` | ≡ | `x: function()` |
| | | | | `   returning int` |

where the character : should be interpreted as *is of type*.

Type `int` is used only for illustration. Similar equivalences also apply to other types.

When converting a Pascal-like declaration or definition to a C declaration or definition, or vice versa, remember that the pointer dereferencing operator * has a lower precedence than the operators [ ] and ( ) used to declare or define arrays and functions, respectively. For example, the declaration

```
char *a[];
```

parses as

```
char *(a[]);
```

which declares a as an array of pointers to characters and not as

```
char (*a)[];
```

which declares a as a pointer to an array of characters. Parentheses may be used freely to override the precedence rules or for clarity.

### 4.7 Examples Illustrating the Use of Equivalences

The equivalences suggested by Anderson will now be used to illustrate how C declarations and definitions may be easily understood and constructed.

The definition

```
int *(*(*x)[6])();
```

given earlier may be easier to understand if an equivalent Pascal-like definition is constructed as follows:

```
*(*(*x)[6])(): int;

≡ (*(*x)[6])(): pointer to int;

≡ (*(*x)[6]): function returning
                            pointer to int;

≡ *(*x)[6]: function returning pointer to int;

≡ (*x)[6]: pointer to function returning
                            pointer to int;

≡ (*x): array[0..5] of pointer to function
                    returning pointer to int;

≡ *x: array[0..5] of pointer to function
                    returning pointer to int;

≡ x: pointer to array[0..5] of pointer to
            function returning pointer to int;
```

In the next example, y is declared as a function that returns a pointer to an array of pointers to functions that return character values. The C declaration will be constructed using the equivalences given earlier:

```
y: function returning pointer to array of
                pointer to function returning char;
≡ y(): pointer to array of pointer to function
                            returning char;
≡ *y(): array of pointer to function
                            returning char;
≡ (*y()): array of pointer to function
                            returning char;
≡ (*y())[]: pointer to function
                            returning char;
≡ *(*y())[]: function returning char;
≡ (*(*y())[]): function returning char;
≡ (*(*y())[])(): char;
≡ char (*(*y())[])();
```

## 4.8 Using *typedef* to Simplify the Understanding of Declarations and Definitions

Zahn [Zahn 1979] suggests that a series of type declarations can be used to simplify the writing of complex type declarations. For example, variable **x**, which is defined as

```
x: pointer to array[0..5] of pointer to function
                            returning pointer to int
```

can be defined to be of type **PA6PFPI**, which is constructed gradually by using the following series of type declarations:

```
typedef int *PI;      /* PI pointer to int */

typedef PI FPI();
        /* FPI: function returning pointer */
        /* to int                          */

typedef FPI *PFPI;
        /* PFPI: pointer to function */
        /* returning pointer to int  */

typedef PFPI A6PFPI[6];
        /* A6PFPI: array of pointer */
        /* to function returning    */
        /* pointer to int           */

typedef A6PFPI *PA6PFPI;
        /* PA6PFPI: pointer to array */
        /* of pointer to function    */
        /* returning pointer to int  */
```

Variable x can now be defined as

```
PA6PFPI x;
```

Although *typedef* declarations solve, to some degree, the readability problem with C's cryptic declarations, their use may still not always result in clear and concise declarations.

### 4.9 Concluding Comments on C Declarations and Definitions

Fortunately, complicated declarations do not often turn up in real programs. Most programmers will rarely encounter declarations as complicated as those given in the examples.

Now for some differences between C and Pascal-like definitions and declarations. All objects in a Pascal-like definition or declaration have exactly the same type; e.g., in the definition

```
a, b: array[0..5] of integer;
```

both a and b are defined as integer arrays and this information is factored out. (All common type information is factored out in Pascal definitions.) On the other hand, in C definitions and declarations, only some common type information can be factored out. For example, in the definition

```
int a[6], b[6];
```

only the element type `int` could be factored out; it was not possible to factor out the array size even though both a and b are arrays of the same size. (If it is desirable to factor all the common type information, then an appropriate type should be declared using the `typedef` mechanism and this type should then be used to define objects.)

In contrast C allows variables of different types to be defined or declared together; e.g., in the definition

```
int a[6], *c;
```

a is defined as an `int` array, while c is defined as a pointer to an `int` object. It is just not possible to write such definitions using Pascal-like definitions.

### 4.10 Type Equivalence

When do two objects have equivalent types? There are several schemes for determining whether or not two objects have equivalent types. Two common schemes are *structural type equivalence* and *name type equivalence*. According to structural type equivalence, two objects have the same type only if they have the same type of components; according to name type equivalence, two objects have the same type only if they were defined using the same type name.

Most C implementations use the structural type equivalence scheme. However, *The C Reference Manual* [Ritchie 1980] ignores the issue of type equivalence and an implementation is free to choose its own scheme for determining type equivalence. Consequently, it is possible that a program may run correctly on one C compiler, but not on another compiler.

## 5. Type Conversions

Values may be converted from one type to another. This type conversion can occur implicitly or can be done explicitly by the programmer. In this book, explicit type conversions will be used whenever necessary for program clarity, even in places where an explicit conversion might not be necessary because an implicit conversion would have produced the same effect.

### 5.1 Implicit Type Conversion

Implicit type conversions are performed primarily to make operator and function arguments comform (if possible) to the type of values expected by these operators and functions. Implicit type conversions that may be used in the examples given in this book are listed in the following table. No other implicit conversions will be used.[25]

| type | implicitly convertible to |
|------|---------------------------|
| `char` | • `int, short int, long int` (conversion of a character to a longer value may or may not involve sign extension—this is implementation dependent; elements of the character set are guaranteed to be coerced to non-negative integers) |
| `int` | • `char, short int, long int` (conversion to a longer integer will involve sign extension; conversion to a shorter integer causes truncation of the excess high-order bits) |
| | • `float, double` |
| | • `unsigned int` (unsigned integer interpretation of |

---

25. Several allowable implicit conversions have not been listed here because their use may be detrimental to program clarity and error detection. For example, implicit pointer conversions have been left out; pointer conversions should be done explicitly.

the bit pattern)

short int • similar to `int`

long int • similar to `int`

float • `double`

• `int`, `short int`, `long int` (machine dependent; result is undefined if the value being converted is too large)

double • `float` (rounding followed by truncation)

• `int`, `short int`, `long int` (see `float`)

## 5.2 Arithmetic Conversions

C arithmetic operators automatically convert their operands to some desired types if they are not of these types to start with. The conversion scheme used by these operators is called the *usual arithmetic conversions*; this scheme can be described by the following rules:

1. Convert `char` and `short int` operands to `int`; convert `float` operands to `double`.

2. If either operand is of type `double`, then the other operand is converted to `double` (assuming it is not `double`) and the result type will be `double`.

3. If either operand is of type `long`, then the other operand is converted to `long` (assuming it is not `long`) and the result type will be `long`.

4. If either operand is of type `unsigned`, then the other operand is converted to `unsigned` (assuming it is not `unsigned`) and the result type will be `unsigned`.

5. Finally, if cases 2 through 4 do not apply, then both operands must be of type `int` and the result type will also be `int`.

These conversion rules are illustrated by the following figure [Feuer 1982].

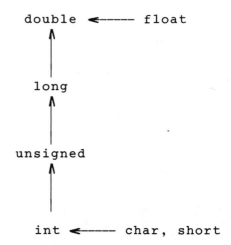

Horizontal conversions are always performed.
Vertical conversions are performed only when necessary.

Arithmetic Conversion Rules

### 5.3 Explicit Type Conversion—Casting

Expressions can be explicitly converted from one type to another; i.e., an expression of one type can be *cast* to another type. An expression *E* is cast to a type *type-name* by writing it as

    ( *type-name* )  *E*

where *type-name* is of the form

  *type-specifier abstract-declarator*

Abstract declarators are similar to declarators except that they do not contain an identifier that is to be defined or declared. The meaning of a *type-name* of the form

  T *abstract-declarator*

where T is a type specifier, can be determined from the following table:

| form of *abstract declarator* | meaning of `` T *abstract declarator* '' |
|---|---|
| *empty* | *type* T |
| *( abstract-declarator )* | *type* T *abstract-declarator* |
| *∗abstract-declarator* | *pointer to type* T |
| *abstract-declarator ( )* | *function returning value of type* T |
| *abstract-declarator [ n ]* | *array with n elements of of type* T |
| | *n is a constant expression* |

Some examples of type names are

```
char
char[8]
char *
char( )
char *( )
char (*)( )
```

Suppose the following definitions and declaration have been given:

```
int i;
char *pc, *name;
char *calloc( ), *strcpy( );
```

Then some examples of casts are

```
(char) i /* convert an "int" value to a "char" */
         /* value */

pc = (char *) 0777
               /* converts octal literal 0777 to  */
               /* a character pointer value so     */
               /* that it can be assigned to "pc"  */

(emp *) calloc(1,sizeof(emp))
               /* converts the "char" pointer      */
               /* value returned by "calloc" to    */
               /* an "emp" pointer value           */

(void) strcpy(name, "gehani");
               /* discard the value returned by    */
               /* "strcpy"                         */
```

All types can be cast to the void type; however, the void type cannot be cast to any other type. Structure and union casts are not implemented [Ritchie 1980].

## 6. Problems

1. Why does C not allow the same enumeration literal to be a member of two different enumeration types?

2. Write a variant structure type that allows structures to hold data about different types of vehicles—trucks, buses, cars and motorcycles. All vehicles have some common type of information—owner, make and model. Each one of the different kinds of vehicle has some specialized information:

   | | |
   |---|---|
   | trucks | number of axles, weight |
   | buses | seating capacity |
   | cars | number of doors (2 or 4) |
   | motorcycle | engine type (2-stroke or 4-stroke) |

3. Explain how the *address of* operator & can lead to the dangling reference problem.

4. Consider the program

```
#include <stdio.h>
main ()
{
  char *test[5];
  int i;

  for (i=0; i<=4; i++)
    test[i] = "0123456789";
  test[1][3]='*';
  for (i=0; i<=4; i++)
    printf("%s\n", test[i]);
}
```

What will be the output of this program?[26] Will the assignment

```
test[1][3]='*';
```

affect just the string pointed to by `test[1]` or all the elements of `test`? What is the reason for this? Run the program on your C compiler to see the result.

How can elements of `test` be made to point to different strings with the same value?

5. What is the type of `k` in the following declaration?

```
int *(*k())()[]
```

6. Why is the following function declaration illegal?

---

26. The *for* loop statement

```
for (i=0; i<=4; i++)
  S
```

causes statement $S$ to be executed five times. Variable i has the value 0 for the first execution of $S$; this value is increased by 1 for each successive execution of $S$.

```
int ((*F()) ())[];
```

7.  Define variable **x** as an array of pointers to functions that return pointers to an array of pointers to integers. Use equivalences to Pascal-like notation in arriving at the definition.

8.  Use a series of *typedef*s to define the variable **x** in problem 7.

9.  C arithmetic operators convert `float` operands to `double` prior to operating upon them. What are the ramifications of this automatic conversion? Examine this issue from the viewpoints of precision and program execution speed.

# Chapter 3

# Operators and Expressions

## 1.  Operators

C has a rich variety of operators.  In this section, I will discuss the semantics of these operators.  Associated with each operator are two characteristics: its *precedence level* and its *associativity*.  If in an expression all the operators have the same precedence level, then the expression is evaluated left to right or right to left as specified by operator associativity (all operators of the same precedence level have the same associativity).  However, if an expression has operators with different precedence levels, then the highest precedence level operators are evaluated first, followed by operators of the next precedence level are evaluated, and so on.  As before, operators of each precedence level are evaluated in the order specified by their associativity.

Groups of operators will be presented in order of decreasing precedence; operators with the same precedence will be grouped together.  The precedences of the operators are summarized later in Section 1.16.

### 1.1  Function Call, Subscript and Selection Operators

The parentheses in a function call, the square brackets used for subscripting arrays, and the dot and the right arrow used for selecting components of a structure or union are all treated as operators in C.

### Function Call and Selection Operators

Precedence Level 1, Associativity Left to Right

| operator | description | comments |
|----------|-------------|----------|
| ( ) | function call | e.g., `sqrt(x)`, `puts(s)`, `printf("result is %f\n", result)` |
| [ ] | array subscript | e.g., `sales[i]`, `sales[i][j]` |
| . | structure selector | e.g., `fig.type`, `(*new_student).name` |
| -> | structure selector (via a pointer) | e.g., `new_student->name` where `new_student` is a pointer to a structure |

65

### 1.2 Unary Operators

Unary operators take only one operand; these operators are either prefix or both prefix and postfix. The `sizeof` operator has two forms: prefix operator and a unary function.

## Unary Operators

Precedence Level 2, Associativity Right to Left; Prefix Unless Otherwise Stated

| operator | description | operand type | result type | comments |
|---|---|---|---|---|
| * | derefer-encing or indirection | pointer to any type T excluding `void` | T | |
| & | address of | variable of any type T excluding `void` | pointer to T | |
| – | negation | arithmetic | `int`, `unsigned`, `long`, `double` | usual arithmetic conversions performed |
| ! | logical negation | arithmetic or pointer type | `int` | result is 1 if operand is 0; otherwise it is 0 |
| ~ | one's complement | integral type | `int`, `long`, `unsigned` | usual arithmetic conversions performed |
| ++ | increment | arithmetic or pointer type | `int`, `unsigned`, `long`, `double`, pointer | usual arithmetic conversions per-formed; operand is incremented and the value returned is the new operand value. A pointer is incremented by the size of the object it points to; other operands are incremented by one. |

(More unary operators on next page)

## Unary Operators (continued)

| operator | description | operand type | result type | comments |
|---|---|---|---|---|
| `++` *(postfix)* | increment | arithmetic or pointer type | `int`, `unsigned`, `long`, `double`, pointer | usual arithmetic conversions performed; operand is incremented and the value returned is the old operand value. Pointers are incremented by the size of the objects pointed to by them; other operands are incremented by one. |
| `--` | decrement | same as `++` | same as `++` | same as `++`, but operand is decremented |
| `--` *(postfix)* | decrement | same as `++` *(postfix)* | same as `++` *(postfix)* | same as `++` *(postfix)*, but operand is decremented |
| `sizeof` | storage required in bytes | value of any type or a type name | `unsigned` | it is used as `sizeof`(*expression*) or `sizeof`(*type-name*) |

## 1.3 Multiplicative Operators

Usual arithmetic conversions are performed when necessary.

# Multiplicative Operators

Precedence Level 3, Associativity Left to Right

| operator | description | operand types | result type | comments |
|----------|-------------|---------------|-------------|----------|
| * | multiplication | arithmetic | `int,`<br>`unsigned,`<br>`long,`<br>`double` | |
| / | division | arithmetic | `int,`<br>`unsigned,`<br>`long,`<br>`double` | when positive integers are divided, truncation is towards 0; if either operand is negative, then the truncation is machine dependent |
| % | remainder | integral | `int,`<br>`unsigned,`<br>`long` | sign of remainder is machine-dependent |

Integer division and the remainder operations are related by the following equivalence:

$$(a/b)*b \ + \ a\%b \ \equiv \ a \ (b \neq 0)$$

## 1.4  Additive Operators

Usual arithmetic conversions are performed when necessary.

### Additive Operators

Precedence Level 4, Associativity Left to Right

| operator | description | operand types | result type | comments |
|----------|-------------|---------------|-------------|----------|
| + | addition | arithmetic types | `int`, `unsigned`, `long`, `double` | |
| | | one pointer and one integral type (both operands cannot be pointers) | pointer | prior to the addition, the integer operand is multiplied by the size of the pointer's base type |
| − | subtraction | arithmetic types | `int`, `unsigned`, `long`, `double` | |
| | | one pointer and one integral type | pointer | prior to the subtraction, the integer operand is multiplied by the size of the pointer's base type |
| | | pointer operands of the same type | `int` | number of objects separating the two pointers |

*1.4.1  Pointer Arithmetic:*  Pointer arithmetic is different from ordinary integer arithmetic and is defined as follows. Suppose that i is an integer expression, and pointers p and q point to elements of type T. Adding (subtracting) i to (from) p is equivalent to adding (subtracting) the number of locations (in bytes) occupied by i elements of type T. Similarly, the result of subtracting two pointers of type *T is not the difference in the values of the two pointers, but the number of elements of type T that can be fitted in between the locations referred to by these pointers.

No other pointer arithmetic is allowed. Pointer subtraction is meaningful only when the pointers refer to elements of the same array because addresses of array elements differ by an integer multiple of the element size. In other cases, even when pointers are of the same type, pointers may not differ by an integer multiple of the element size.

Pointer arithmetic can be more formally defined as

```
p + i  ≡  (T *) ((long) p + (long) sizeof(T) * i)
i + p  ≡  (T *) ((long) p + (long) sizeof(T) * i)
p - i  ≡  (T *) ((long) p - (long) sizeof(T) * i)
p - q  ≡  ((long) p - (long) q) / ((long) sizeof(T))
```

(On some implementations, `unsigned` should be used instead of `long` in the above equivalences.)

**1.5 Shift Operators**

Usual arithmetic conversions are performed when necessary.

## Shift Operators

Precedence Level 5, Associativity Left to Right

| operator | description | operand types | result type | comments |
|---|---|---|---|---|
| << | left shift | integral | same as left operand | right operand is converted to `int`; left operand is shifted by the value of the right operand; vacated bits are 0-filled |
| >> | right shift | integral | same as left operand | right operand is converted to `int`; left operand is shifted by the value of the right operand; right shift is guaranteed to be a logical shift (0-fill) if left operand is `unsigned` |

### 1.6 Relational Operators

Usual arithmetic conversions are performed when necessary.

## Relational Operators

Precedence Level 6, Associativity Left to Right

| operator | description | operand types | result type |
|----------|-------------|---------------|-------------|
| < | less than | arithmetic or pointer types | `int` |
| > | greater than | arithmetic or pointer types | `int` |
| <= | less than or equal to | arithmetic or pointer types | `int` |
| >= | greater than or equal to | arithmetic or pointer types | `int` |

Pointer comparison is portable only when the pointers refer to elements in the same array.

### 1.7 Equality/Inequality Operators

Usual arithmetic conversions are performed when necessary.

## Equality/Inequality Operators

Precedence Level 7, Associativity Left to Right

| operator | description | operand types | result type |
|----------|-------------|---------------|-------------|
| == | equality | arithmetic or pointer types | `int` |
| != | inequality | arithmetic or pointer types | `int` |

The only integer that pointers can be compared with is 0.

### 1.8  Bitwise *and* operator

Usual arithmetic conversions are performed.

## Bitwise *and* operator

Precedence Level 8, Associativity Left to Right

| operator | description | operand types | result type |
|----------|-------------|---------------|-------------|
| &        | bitwise *and* | integral     | int, long, unsigned |

### 1.9  Bitwise *exclusive or* Operator

Usual arithmetic conversions are performed.

## Bitwise *exclusive or* Operator

Precedence Level 9, Associativity Left to Right

| operator | description | operand types | result type |
|----------|-------------|---------------|-------------|
| ^        | bitwise *exclusive or* | integral | int, long, unsigned |

### 1.10  Bitwise *inclusive or* Operator

Usual arithmetic conversions are performed.

## Bitwise *inclusive or* Operator

Precedence Level 10, Associativity Left to Right

| operator | description | operand types | result type |
|----------|-------------|---------------|-------------|
| ¦        | bitwise *inclusive or* | integral | int, long, unsigned |

## 1.11 Logical (Conditional) *and* Operator

# Logical (Conditional) *and* Operator

Precedence Level 11, Associativity Left to Right

| operator | description | operand types | result type | comments |
|---|---|---|---|---|
| && | logical *and* | arithmetic or pointer types | int | result is 0 if first operand is zero; otherwise, the result will be 1 if the second operand is non-zero and 0 if the second operand is zero (the second operand is not evaluated if the first one is false) |

## 1.12  Logical (Conditional) *or* Operator

# Logical (Conditional) *or* Operator

Precedence Level 12, Associativity Left to Right

| operator | description | operand types | result type | comments |
|----------|-------------|---------------|-------------|----------|
| ¦ ¦ | logical *or* | arithmetic or pointer types | int | result is 1 if first operand is non-zero; otherwise the result will be 1 if the second operand is non-zero and 0 if the second operand is zero (the second operand is not evaluated if the first one is true) |

## 1.13  Conditional Operator

Usual arithmetic conversions are performed.

# Conditional Operator

Precedence Level 13, Associativity Right to Left

| operator | description | operand types | result type | comments |
|----------|-------------|---------------|-------------|----------|
| ? : | conditional operator | arithmetic types; second and third operands can be of pointer, structure or union types | int, long, unsigned, double, pointer, structure or union types | the second and third operands are converted to a common type |

The conditional operator is the only operator that requires three operands; it is used as

$a \ ? \ b \ : \ c$

where $a$, $b$ and $c$ are expressions. If $a$ is non-zero, then the result of the expression $a \ ? \ b \ : \ c$ is $b$; otherwise, the result is $c$. Only one of the second or third operands is evaluated. An example of the use of a conditional expression is the expression

```
max = (x>y) ? x : y
```

whose result is the maximum of x and y. In most languages, the above computation would have to be written as (using Pascal syntax)

**if** x > y
  **then** max := x
  **else** max := y

which requires the programmer to make an explicit assignment to a variable (possibly a temporary variable).

## 1.14 Assignment Operators

## Assignment Operators

Precedence Level 14, Associativity Right to Left

| operator | description | operand types | result type | comments |
|---|---|---|---|---|
| = | simple assignment | arithmetic, pointer, union or structure | if both operands have arithmetic types, then right operand value is converted to left operand type | |
| $\theta$ = | compound assignment | see discussion below | see discussion below | $\theta$ is one of +, -, *, /, %, >>, <<, &, ^ or ¦ (see discussion below for semantics) |

The assignment expression

$$v = e$$

where *v* is a variable and *e* is an expression, results in the value of *e* becoming the new value of *v*.

The assignment expression

$$v\ \theta = e$$

is roughly equivalent to the assignment expression

$$v = v\ \theta\ e$$

The operand and result types of the compound assignment operator can be determined by using this equivalence.

The equivalence for the compound assignment operator given above is not quite correct—operand *v* is evaluated only once in

$$v\ \theta = e$$

while it is evaluated twice in

$$v = v\ \theta\ e$$

This makes a difference only when the evaluation of *v* results in a side effect, e.g., when the value of a variable is changed.  For example, in the assignment expression

```
a[i++] *= n
```

evaluation of left hand operand a[i++] has the side effect of incrementing i. Consequently, this assignment is not equivalent to the assignment

```
a[i++] = a[i++] * n
```

The first assignment is equivalent to

```
a[i] = a[i] * n
i = i + 1
```

while the second assignment is equivalent to either

```
a[i] = a[i+1] * n
i = i + 2
```

or

```
a[i+1] = a[i] * n
i = i + 2
```

depending upon whether the right hand side of the assignment operator is evaluated before the left hand side or vice versa; the order of evaluation is not defined.

**1.15  Comma Operator**

## Comma Operator

Precedence Level 15, Associativity Left to Right

| operator | description | result type | comments |
|----------|-------------|-------------|----------|
| , | comma | same as type of right operand | combines two expressions into one; the value of the compound expression is the value of the right operand; value of the left operand is discarded; the left operand is evaluated only for side effects. |

Expressions involving the comma operator must be enclosed in parentheses in contexts where the comma is used for other purposes such as separating function arguments.

### 1.16 Operator Precedence Summary

Operator precedence is summarized by the following table, the operators being listed vertically in order of decreasing precedence:

## Operator Precedence and Associativity Summary

| precedence | operators | symbols | associativity |
|:---:|:---|:---|:---|
| 1 | Function Call/Selection | ( )   [ ]   .   -> | left to right |
| 2 | Unary | *  &  -  !  ~<br>++  --  sizeof | right to left |
| 3 | Multiplicative | *  /  % | left to right |
| 4 | Additive | +  - | left to right |
| 5 | Shift | <<  >> | left to right |
| 6 | Relational | <  >  <=  >= | left to right |
| 7 | Equality/Inequality | ==  != | left to right |
| 8 | Bitwise *and* | & | left to right |
| 9 | Bitwise *exclusive or* | ^ | left to right |
| 10 | Bitwise *inclusive or* | ¦ | left to right |
| 11 | Logical *and* | && | left to right |
| 12 | Logical *or* | ¦¦ | left to right |
| 13 | Conditional | ? : | right to left |
| 14 | Assignment | =  $\theta$ = | right to left |
| 15 | Comma | , | left to right |

## 2. Expressions

Expressions are entities constructed using operators, literals, constants, variables (including array, structure and union components) and function calls. The order of expression evaluation is defined *only* to the extent that it is consistent with operator semantics and that operator precedence rules and associativity rules will be obeyed. Subject to these constraints, a compiler is free to evaluate the expression in any desired order even if evaluation of subexpressions may cause side effects.

Unlike most languages, parentheses cannot be used to force a specific order of expression evaluation because a C compiler is free to rearrange expressions involving associative and commutative operators (*, +, &, ¦, ^) arbitrarily, even if parentheses have been used. Multiple assignments, using temporary variables if necessary, must be used to force the evaluation of an expression in some desired order.

Expressions with side effects should be used with care because the effect of evaluating them may not be immediately obvious and the evaluation may be implementation-dependent. For example, as a result of the assignment statements

```
j = 3;
i = (k = j + 1) + (j = 5);
```

the value of i will be 9 or 11 depending upon which subexpression of the second statement is evaluated first. Thus, the results may be different on different C compilers.

## 2.1 Constant Expressions

*Constant expressions* are expressions formed by using integer, char, and enum constants, sizeof operator, the unary operators - and ~, the binary operators

$$+ \ - \ * \ / \ \% \ \& \ | \ \char`\^ \ << \ >> \ == \ != \ < \ > \ <= \ \text{and} \ >=,$$

and the ternary operator ? :.

Constant expressions are used in the *switch* statement (after the case), in array bounds initializers and in the preprocessor *#if* statement (see Chapter 9 titled *The C Preprocessor*). In initializers, the *address of* operator & can also be used (with some restrictions). The sizeof operator and enumeration constants are not allowed in the preprocessor *#if* statement.

# 3. Problems

1. The logical *or* and *and* operators (|| and &&) are conditional logical operators—the second operand is evaluated only if it is necessary. Logical operators in other languages such as Pascal and FORTRAN always evaluate both operands even if the result can be determined by evaluating one operand. What are the pros and cons of conditional and unconditional logical operators?

2. Unlike FORTRAN, C does not itself provide an exponentiation operator; however, an exponentiation function exp is provided in the math library (see Appendix A titled *Some Library Functions*). Give one reason for not providing an exponentiation operator. What are the disadvantages from a user's viewpoint assuming the user does not have access to the math library?

   Suppose that $x^y$ is to be computed (for some nonnegative integer y). The obvious, but inefficient, way of implementing exponentiation to an integer value is to use repeated multiplication. A better algorithm is

```
a = x; b = y; z = 1;   /* za^b≡x^y  initially  */
                       /* at the end of the */
                       /* algorithm z≡x^y      */

while ( b != 0) {
  if (odd(b)) {
    z = z * a;
    b--;
  }
    else {
      a = a * a;
      b = b / 2;
    {
}
/* value of "z" is the result */
```

Operation $odd(x)$ returns 1 if $x$ is an odd number and 0 if $x$ is an even number. How will you implement operation $odd$?

Are you convinced that this algorithm works? An argument to show that it works can be based on the fact that the program tries to preserve the equivalence relationship $za^b \equiv x^y$ while moving b towards 0. At the end of the algorithm, b will be 0 at which the equivalence relationship becomes $z \equiv x^y$.

# Chapter 4

# Control Flow

C has the usual kind of control flow statements found in languages like Pascal and Ada. These statements, in the spirit of structured programming philosophy advocated by Dijkstra (in *Structured Programming* [Dahl, Dijkstra and Hoare 1972]), are primarily *one-entrance, one-exit* constructs. Although C provides the *goto* statement, which has been considered detrimental to program readability and understandability [Dijkstra 1968], it also provides the *break* and *continue* statements for controlled jumps. The *break* or *continue* statement should be used instead of the *goto* statement whenever possible. In contrast, languages like FORTRAN and Pascal do not provide mechanisms for controlled jumps.

## 1. Expressions and Statements

Any expression can be converted to a statement by appending a semicolon to it:

*expression*;

is a statement. The value of *expression* is discarded. The effects of such a statement are the side effects produced by the evaluation of *expression*.

The following two statements, each of which is formed by appending a semicolon to an expression, are special and will be discussed separately:

- the assignment statement and
- the *function-call* statement used for *non-value-returning* functions.

## 2. *Null* Statement

The *null* statement is denoted by a semicolon:

;

Its use is necessary in cases where the presence of a statement is required by the syntax, but no action is logically needed. For example, a *null* statement is used as the body of the following *while* loop

81

```
while ((c = getchar()) == BLANK)
    ;
```

which skips to the first non-blank character (where BLANK is a user-defined constant).

## 3. *Compound* or *Block* **Statement**

The *compound* or *block* statement is used

- to group many statements into one logical statement,
- as the body of a function and
- to restrict the visibility of definitions to a part of the program, i.e., to localize the effect of declarations.

The *compound* statement has the form

```
{
    definitions and declarations
    statements
}
```

Variables defined inside the *compound* statement override (hide) definitions of variables with the same name for the scope of the *compound* statement. These variables are only visible (accessible) inside the *compound* statement. Global variables are visible inside the *compound* statement provided their definitions have not been overridden by local definitions.

## 4. *Assignment* **Statement**

The *assignment* statement has the form

```
variable = expression;
```

where *variable* is an expression that refers to an object in storage. Some examples are

```
i = i + 1;
*pc = 'c';
```

The *assignment* statement is the expression

   *variable*  =  *expression*

converted to a statement by appending a semicolon to it. The value of this expression is the value assigned to the variable. Consequently, multiple variables can be assigned values by using a series of assignment operators in one statement, that is, by means of *multiple* assignments. For example, the *multiple assignment* statement

```
i = j = k = 0;
```

causes i, j and k to be assigned the value 0.

An *assignment* statement can also be constructed from the compound-assignment operators. Such an assignment statement has the form

   *variable*  $\theta$= *expression*;

where $\theta$ is one of

   +  -  *  /  %  >>  <<  &  ^  |

(as discussed in Section 1.14 titled *Assignment Operators* of Chapter 3 titled *Operators and Expressions*).

## 5.  *If* Statement

The *if* statement has two forms:

```
if  (expression)  statement₁;
```

and

```
if  (expression)
   statement₁;
else
   statement₂;
```

If *expression* evaluates to true (non-zero), then *statement*₁ is executed in both forms of the *if* statement. If *expression* evaluates to false (zero), then execution of the first form of the *if* statement is complete, while in case of the second form, *statement*$_2$ is executed.[27]

Intermixing the two forms of the *if* statement results in an ambiguity called the *dangling else* problem. For example, the nested *if* statement

```
if (e₁) if (e₂) sₐ ; else s_b ;
```

could be interpreted[28] as

```
if (e₁)
   if (e₂)
      sₐ ;
   else
      s_b ;
```

or as

```
if (e₁)
   if (e₂) sₐ ;
else
   s_b ;
```

This ambiguity is resolved in C by using the rule that an *else* part is always associated with the syntactically rightmost (ignoring any indentation) *if* statement without an *else* part. Consequently, the first interpretation is the interpretation used in C.

A simple way of avoiding this ambiguity is to avoid mixing the two kinds of *if* statements when nesting *if* statements. A *null* statement may be used when necessary. For example, the second interpretation given above may be written as

---

27. Syntactically, *statement*$_1$ and *statement*$_2$ must be single statements. Consequently, if more than one statement needs to be executed in their place, then these statements must be combined into one logical statement by enclosing them in curly braces (i.e., by using a *compound* statement).

28. The two interpretations are shown by indenting them appropriately. Unlike human readers, the C compiler is not influenced by indentation.

```
if (e₁)
   if (e₂)
      sₐ ;
   else
      ;       /* a semicolon by itself denotes */
              /* the null statement */
else
   s_b ;
```

Alternatively, curly braces may be used to specify the programmer's intent explicitly. For example, the two above interpretations may be written explicitly as

```
if (e₁) {
   if (e₂)
      sₐ ;
   else
      s_b ;
}
```

and

```
if (e₁) {
   if (e₂) sₐ ;
}
else
   s_b ;
```

## 6. *Switch* **Statement**

The *switch* statement is used for multiway branching. It has the form:

```
switch (e) {
case ce₁: s₁; break;
case ce₂: s₂; break;
  ⋮
case ceₖ: sₖ ; break;
default: sₖ₊₁ ;
}
```

where

1.  $e$ is an integer expression (or an expression that is convertible to an integer expression),

2.  $ce_i$ are constant integer expressions (or expressions that are convertible to constant integer expressions) and

3.  $s_i$ represents zero or more statements.

The *case* labels $ce_i$, which identify the alternatives, must be unique; no two labels can be identical. Only one alternative may be given the prefix *default*.

Execution of the *switch* statement results in the selection of the alternative with a label $ce_i$ that is equal to the value of the *switch* expression $e$; the associated statements $s_i$ are then executed. If the value of the *switch* expression is not equal to any one of the *case* expressions, then the *default* statements $s_{k+1}$ are executed; if there is no *default* alternative, then none of the alternatives in the *switch* statement is executed.

An example of a *switch* statement is a program segment from a simple Polish notation interpreter:

```
switch (c) {
case '+': add; break;
case '-': subtract; break;
case '*': multiply; break;
case '/': divide; break;
default: put on stack;
}
```

If actions in two or more alternatives are identical, then these alternatives can be combined by using multiple *case* prefixes for an alternative statement $s_i$:

```
switch (e) {
case ce₁₁: case ce₁₂:   ... : case ce₁ₙ₁: s₁; break;
case ce₂₁: case ce₂₂:   ... : case ce₂ₙ₂: s₂; break;
 :
 :
case ceₖ₁: case ceₖ₂: ... : case ceₖₙₖ: sₖ ; break;
default: sₖ₊₁ ;
}
```

In the two forms of the *switch* statement illustrated, the alternative actions $s_i$ are mutually exclusive because of the *break* statement that follows these actions. The *break* statement is not required by C; its absence will allow execution to go on from one alternative to the next. However, its use is strongly recommended in the interest of program readability, reliability and modifiability [Feuer and Gehani 82]. The *default* alternative is also not required by C. Again, in the interest of program readability, the use of the *default* alternative is recommended even if the action to be performed is just the *null* statement, which would be the effect if it were omitted.

## 7. Loops

There are three kinds of loops: the *while*, the *for* and the *do* loops.

### 7.1 *While* Loop

The *while* loop statement has the form

```
while (e) s;
```

Statement $s$ is executed as long as expression $e$ is true; $e$ is evaluated prior to each execution of $s$.

### 7.2 *For* Loop

The *for* loop statement

```
for (e₁; e₂; e₃) s;
```

is a convenient abbreviation of the following paradigm using the *while* loop:

```
e₁ ;
while (e₂) {
    s ;
    e₃ ;
}
```

Expression $e_1$ represents the loop initialization, expression $e_2$ represents the loop test and expression $e_3$ represents the loop reinitialization. Any one of the expressions $e_1$, $e_2$ and $e_3$ can be left out. If $e_1$ and $e_3$ are omitted, then the *for* loop will not have initialization and reinitialization parts, respectively. Omission of $e_2$ results in a default value of TRUE being substituted for it.

For example, the *for* loop with the expressions $e_1$ and $e_3$ missing

```
for ( ; e₂; ) s;
```

is equivalent to

```
while (e₂) s;
```

The *for* loop with all the expressions missing

```
for ( ; ; ) s;
```

is equivalent to

```
while (TRUE) s;
```

This loop is an infinite loop; such a loop can be terminated only by explicitly exiting from it using a *break*, *goto* or *return* statement contained in body of the loop *s*.

Although it looks similar, the *for* loop of C is not the semantic counterpart of the iterative *for* loops of Pascal and Ada, or the iterative *do* loops of FORTRAN and PL/I. C's *for* loop is more general than the *for* and *do* loops of the other languages; however, unlike these other loops, the number of iterations of C's *for* loop cannot, in general, be determined prior to the execution of the loop.

The *for* loop and its alternate *while* loop form have almost equivalent semantics; however, their semantics are not identical, as indicated in the *C Reference Manual* [Ritchie 1980]. For example, consider the case when statement *s* is the *continue* statement or a *compound* statement containing the *continue* statement. The effect of the *continue* statement is to skip to the end of the loop. This has different effects in the *for* loop and its equivalent *while* loop form. In the case of the *for* loop, the reinitialization expression $e_3$ is executed prior to evaluating $e_2$, while in the case of the equivalent *while* loop, the reinitialization expression $e_3$ is skipped.

### 7.3 *Do* Loop

The loop

```
do statement while (e);
```

is executed as long as *e* is true. Unlike the *while* loop where the loop test occurs prior to the execution of the loop body, the loop test in the *do* loop occurs after the execution of the loop body. Consequently, the body of the *do* loop will be executed at least once, even if *e* is false to start with. The *do* loop is the counterpart of the *repeat* loop in Pascal with one difference. The *repeat* loop is executed until some terminating condition becomes true while the *do* loop, as mentioned earlier, is executed as long as some condition is true.

## 8. *Break* Statement

The *break* statement is used to exit from the immediately enclosing *while*, *do*, *for* or *switch* statement. Control passes on to the statement following the exited statement. The *break* statement has the form

```
break;
```

## 9. *Continue* Statement

The *continue* statement is used to skip the remaining portion of the current iteration of the immediately enclosing loop. The next iteration is then initiated provided it is allowed by the loop conditions; otherwise, the loop is terminated. The *continue* statement has the form

```
continue;
```

The effect of a *continue* statement in the bodies of following loops is equivalent to a *goto* (see Section 12) to the label next.[29]

```
while ( ... ) {
  ...
  next: ;
}


do {
  ...
  next: ;
} while ( ... );


for ( ... ) {
  ...
  next: ;
}
```

## 10. *Function Call* Statement

A *function call* statement has the form

*function-name ( actual parameter list ) ;*

This statement is used to call non-value-returning functions[30] or functions whose result is to be discarded. Functions are discussed in more detail in Chapter 5 titled *Functions and Complete Programs*.

---

29. I am assuming that the *continue* statement is not inside a nested loop.

30. Non-value returning functions are called subroutines in FORTRAN and procedures in Pascal and Ada.

   The expression

   *function-name ( actual parameter list )*

   is used to call value-returning functions; this expression can be a part of any larger expression.

## 11. *Return* **Statement**

The *return* statement is used in a function to return the function result to the calling program and terminate the execution of the function. The *return* statement has two forms

```
return e;
```

where *e* is an expression that represents the function result, and

```
return;
```

A function can have zero or more *return* statements. The first form of the *return* statement should only be used in value-returning functions; the second form should only be used in non-value-returning functions. The *return* statement is also discussed in more detail Chapter 5 titled *Functions and Complete Programs*.

## 12. *Goto* **Statement**

The *goto* statement is used to unconditionally transfer control to the statement with the specified label. It has the form

```
goto label;
```

The unrestricted use of the *goto* statement is considered to be harmful because it hampers program understandability [Dijkstra 1968]. Consequently, a programmer should justify every use of a *goto* statement.

## 13. **Statement Labels**

Any statement in a C program can be prefixed by a label:

*label*: *statement*

where *label* is an identifier. Statements are labeled so that they can be referenced in *goto* statements.

## 14. **Problems**

1.  What is the result of executing the program segment

```
int i, test[2];

i = 0;
test[i] = i = i + 1;
    /* multiple assignment with side effects */
```

Confirm your result experimentally by running a test program on your C compiler.

2. Write a nested *if* statement equivalent to the general form of the *switch* statement shown in the text. Is the nested *if* statement more powerful than the *switch* statement?

   The *switch* statement does not require the use of the *break* statement at the end of each alternative. If some or all of these *break* statements were omitted, then can this version of the *switch* statement be simulated easily using *if* statements?

3. Suggest an alternative syntax for the *if* statement that will avoid the ambiguity problem arising from nesting the two forms of *if* statements.

4. Why are constant integer expressions required in *case* labels of the *switch* statement? What would be the impact of allowing general integer expressions instead of constant integer expressions? Examine both user convenience and implementation aspects.

5. The *for* loops in FORTRAN, Pascal and Ada always terminate; the *for* loop in C is more general and it may or may not terminate. What restrictions can be imposed upon the form of the *for* loop in C so that it will always terminate?

# Chapter 5

# Functions and Complete Programs

## 1. Functions

Control abstraction is provided in C by means of functions. All functions can be recursive. C does not have subroutines (procedures); however, a function need not return a value. Consequently, functions may be partitioned into two categories—value-returning functions and non-value-returning functions (subroutines).[31]

Definitions of value-returning functions have the format[32]

> [static] *result-type function-name* (*formal parameters* )
> *formal parameter declarations*
> {
>   *function body*
> }

where *function-name* is a declarator (see Chapter 2 titled *Types and Variables*) and *function body* is of the form

> *definitions and declarations*
> *statements*

---

31. This partitioning of functions into two categories is not suggested in the *C Reference Manual* [Ritchie 1980]; however, using different forms for these two categories of functions can enhance program clarity and readability.

32. Specification of the *result-type* of a function is optional in C. If the result type is not specified, then it is assumed to be int. Because specification of a function type leads to better program clarity, program readability, and better error checking, the function type should always be specified explicitly.

A function cannot return an array or a function, although a function can return a pointer to an array or a pointer to a function. A value-returning function should terminate by executing a *return* statement of the form

```
return e;
```

which causes the function to yield the result *e*. A value-returning function may contain more than one such *return* statement.

Definitions of non-value-returning functions have the format[33]

```
[ static ] void function-name(formal parameters)
formal parameter declarations
{
    function body
}
```

A non-value-returning function terminates by completing the execution of its body or by executing a *return* statement of the form

```
return;
```

A non-value-returning function may contain more than one such *return* statement.

The optional storage class `static` limits the visibility of a function and other external definitions. A function with the storage class `static` is not visible outside the file containing it (see Section 1.2 in this chapter).

As a simple example, the following function computes the maximum of its two parameters:

---

33. As mentioned earlier, the `void` type is a recent addition to the C language. On compilers not supporting the `void` type, the programmer can define `void` as

```
#define void        int
```

and use it for defining non-value-returning functions.

It is recommended that this convention be adopted for enhancing program clarity. However, in such cases the compiler will not be able to detect incorrect uses of these non-value-returning functions to return values because they are really functions that return values of type `int`.

```
int max(a, b)
int a, b;
{
   return (a>b) ? a:b;
}
```

A function declaration should be given if a function is referred to before its definition is encountered. Function declarations are of the form

[static | extern] *result-type function-name* ( ) ;
[static | extern] void *function-name* ( ) ;

If the storage class is left out, then by default it is assumed to be extern.

Some examples are

```
int max();
extern char *strcpy();
char *malloc();
```

### 1.1 Parameter Declarations

Parameter declarations are similar to definitions of ordinary variables except that the only storage class that can be specified is register. When declaring array formal parameters, the size of the first dimension may be omitted, e.g.,

```
int a[], b[4], d[][4], e[2][4];
        /* legal array parameter declarations */
```

The parameter declaration

```
int c[][];      /* invalid array parameter */
                /* declaration */
```

is illegal because the size of the second dimension of c has not been specified.

### 1.2 Controlling Function Visibility

Functions cannot be nested. Consequently, it is not possible to define functions that are local to a function; that is, it is not possible to define functions that are not visible outside the function containing them. This restriction on function nesting is not a handicap in most practical situations because function visibility can be controlled by using the `static` attribute. For example, suppose it is necessary to ensure that function a is accessed only from function b. Then these two functions can be defined in a separate file with a having the attribute `static`:

```
static int a(...)
{
   .
   .
   .
}

int b(...)
{
   .
   .
   .
}
```

Function a can be called from function b, but no other function (physically located in another file) will be able to call a.

### 1.3 Calling Functions

Value-returning function calls have the form

*function-name( actual parameter list )*

where the actual parameters[34] can be expressions. Some examples are

---

34. The parameters specified in a function header are called *formal parameters*. The parameters specified in a function call are called *actual parameters*. Both formal parameters and actual parameters will be called parameters; the adjectives formal and actual will be used only when it is not clear from the context what is meant.

Some programming languages, e.g., FORTRAN, use a different terminology; actual parameters are called *arguments* and formal parameters are called *parameters*.

```
a = max( a, 5 );
max( max( a, 5 ), e )
getchar( )
fs = fopen( argv[ 1 ], "r" );
```

Non-value-returning function calls are similar, but are converted into statements:

*function-name ( actual parameter list ) ;*

Some examples are

```
delay( 0.5 );
least_square( x, y, n, &a, &b );
partition( a, 1, u, &i, &j );
quicksort( a, 1, j );
```

Two common ways of passing parameters are *passing by value* and *passing by reference*. C provides only one way of passing parameters—*all parameters are passed by value*. When parameters are passed by value, the values of the actual parameters are copied into the formal parameters prior to the execution of the function. When parameters are passed by reference, the formal parameters effectively become synonyms for the actual parameters. If the actual parameter is an expression, then the corresponding formal parameter becomes a synonym for the temporary variable containing the value of this expression.

Passing parameters by value is fine when a function returns a value without changing its actual parameters. However, if a function is to change the value of its actual parameters, then another parameter mechanism, such as passing parameters by reference, must be used. Passing parameters by value can also be inefficient if it causes much copying; in this case, passing parameters by reference would be more appropriate. The effect of passing parameters by reference can be achieved in C by passing a pointer to the object in question. Although passing pointers to the objects is by itself not much of an inconvenience, then in the called function these objects must be treated differently from the objects that are passed by value.

There is one exception to the rule that all parameters are passed by value—the treatment of an array name as a pointer to the array effectively results in an array being passed by reference.

## 1.4 Referring to Functions Before Their Definitions

A function can be called or passed as a parameter before its definition is encountered in the program text, provided a declaration for the function has been encountered.[35] A function declaration just specifies the type of the function result and, optionally, its storage class. This requirement is necessary for code generation and limited error checking.

An example illustrating the use of a function before its definition has been encountered is

_____

35. Of course, the definition of a function may be in a different file (see Chapter 6 titled *Independent Compilation and Data Abstraction*).

```
void add();
int in_table();
 .
 .
 .
main ()
{
   ...
   if (!in_table(a))
     add(a, it);
   ...
}
 .
 .
 .
void add(x, it)   /* add to item "a" which has    */
                  /* the type "it" to the symbol  */
                  /* table                        */
char *x;
item_type it;
{
   ...
}

int in_table(x)
char *x;
{
   ...
}
```

Calls to functions `add` and `in_table` precede their definitions in the
program text; of course, declarations of these functions

```
   void add();
   int in_table();
```

precede the calls.

## 1.5  Passing Parameters—An Illustrative Example

The difference between passing parameters by value and by reference will be
illustrated now.  Consider the function `swap` that is supposed to exchange the

values of its parameters:

```
/* initial version of "swap" */
void swap(a, b)
int a, b;
{
   int temp;

   temp = a;
   a = b;
   b = temp;
}
```

Calling this function has no effect on the actual parameters; i.e., the call

```
swap(x, y);
```

has no effect on the values of x and y (which are int variables). Values of x and y are copied into the formal parameters a and b, respectively; it is the values of the formal parameters that are then exchanged. The original values of x and y are left unchanged.

Function swap must be modified if it is to exchange the values of its actual parameters. This version of swap will expect to receive the addresses, instead of the values, of the variables whose values are to be exchanged:

```
/* correct version of "swap" */
void swap(a, b)
int *a, *b;
{
   int temp;

   temp = *a;
   *a = *b;
   *b = temp;
}
```

The call to the function swap must be changed so that it passes the addresses, not the values, of the variables whose values are to be exchanged. The *address of* operator & is used to determine addresses x and y as illustrated in the following function call:

```
swap(&x, &y);
```

Note the difference in the two versions of swap—when addresses are passed as
actual parameters, the dereferencing operator * must be used. In languages
that allow parameters to be passed by reference, there is no need to use the
dereferencing operator when parameters are passed by reference.

### 1.6 Automatic Conversions of Actual Parameters

The following type conversions occur during parameter passage:

### Type Conversions During Parameter Passing

| actual parameter type | conversion |
|---|---|
| float | All float actual parameters are converted to double before being passed to a function. Consequently, all float formal parameters have their type changed to double. |
| char and short int | All char and short int actual parameters are converted to int. Consequently, all char and short int formal parameters have their type changed to int. |
| arrays | An array name is really a pointer to the first element of the array. Consequently, when an array name is used as an actual parameter, it is the array address that is passed. Declarations of all array formal parameters are altered to make them pointers.[36] |

---

36. One consequence of this alteration is that array formal parameters are variables and their
values can be changed by the programmer. On the other hand, local or external array names
are constants whose values cannot be changed by the programmer.

### 1.7  Passing Functions as Parameters

Functions can be passed as parameters. Like arrays, the value actually passed in the case of functions is the address of the function. As an example, consider a function cmp that compares two elements of the structure type employee and yields TRUE or FALSE depending upon the values of the elements:

```
int cmp();
```

Function cmp is passed as a parameter to a function sort that sorts arrays with elements of type employee; function sort is called as

```
sort(emp, n, cmp);
```

where emp is the array to be sorted, n is the size of the array and cmp is the ordering function discussed above.

The definition of sort may look like

```
void sort(a, n, fp)
employee a[];
int n;
int (*fp)();   /* "fp" points to the comparison */
               /* function */
{
    .
    .
    .
    if ((*fp)(a[i], a[j]) > 0)
                /* illustrates use of "fp" */
    .
    .
    .
}
```

The ability to pass functions as parameters can be very useful. For example, suppose that the call

```
sort(emp, n, greater);
```

leads to the array emp being sorted in increasing order, where greater(x, y) returns TRUE if x is greater than y according to some ordering rule; otherwise it returns FALSE. Now consider the function smaller(x, y) that returns TRUE if x is smaller than y according to the same ordering rule used by greater; otherwise it returns FALSE. The call

```
sort(emp, n, smaller);
```

will sort the array emp in decreasing order.

By parameterizing sort with the comparison function, we can sort the actual parameter array according to any desired ordering rule. This allows us to write a *generic* sort function, i.e., a sort function that represents a family of sort functions.

### 1.8 Function Specifications

The user-interface information of a function, called a *function specification*, by convention, consists of three parts:

1. A list of *include* statements specifying the files to be included. These files usually contain declarations necessary for using the function.

2. The function declaration.

3. Declarations of the function parameters.

Every function specification has at least the function declaration. If the function has parameters, then the function specification also contains the parameter declarations.

An example of a function specification is

```
#include <stdio.h>

int putc(c, stream)
char c;
FILE *stream;
```

The purpose of a function specification is to provide the user with sufficient information to

1. include all files necessary for using the function;

2. declare variables that will be used as actual parameters or as components of actual parameters;

3.  declare variables that will be used to store the function result;

4.  use a function in an expression in a manner consistent with its type;

5.  write syntactically correct function calls so that the C compiler or the type checker `lint` does not complain about incorrect function usage.

A function specification does not supply any semantic information about what the function does other than that implied by the function name and type, and parameter names and types.

## 2. Lexical Scope of Identifiers

The *lexical scope* of an identifier is the region of a program where its declaration or definition is in effect. The lexical scope of

- an external identifier ranges from its declaration or definition to the end of the file containing it.

- a formal parameter of a function is the function itself.

- an identifier defined in a block is the block.

- a label is the function in which it is declared.

Defining an identifier in a block hides any definition of the same identifier that is given outside the block; a local definition hides a global definition.

As an example illustrating the lexical scope of identifiers, consider a file named `scope.c` that contains the following program:

```
extern float lower, upper;
static float accuracy;
float f();
double fabs();

float integrate(fp, a, b, eps)
float (*fp)(), a, b, eps;
{
   float sum;

   ... fabs(...) ...
}

main()
{
   ... integrate(f, lower, upper, accuracy) ...
}

float f(a)
float a;
{
   float accuracy;

   ...
}
```

The scope of identifiers lower, upper, accuracy (the one defined outside function f), f, fabs, integrate and main ranges from their declarations or definitions (whichever is encountered first) to the end of file scope.c. However, because function f contains a local identifier accuracy, the first definition of accuracy is hidden in the body of function f; the second definition of accuracy is the effective one in function f.

Because the scope of a function parameter is the corresponding function body, there is no conflict due to the fact that both functions integrate and f have a parameter with the same name, i.e., a.

Notice that it was necessary to declare functions f and fabs because they are referenced in file scope.c before their definitions are encountered. The definition of fabs is not contained in file scope.c and must be contained in some other file for successful execution of the complete program. The declaration of function f would not have been necessary had its definition been encountered before all references to it; this is exactly what happens in the case of function `integrate`.

## 3. Input/Output

A program will not be complete, useful or interesting unless it produces some output and, possibly, consumes some input. Technically, the C programming language does not provide any facilities for input and output. However, input and output facilities are provided by means of numerous library functions. The use of these functions is so widespread that they are considered to be part of the standard C environment. In fact, the ANSI standard version of C is likely to define these facilities as being part of C itself.

A *file descriptor* on the UNIX system is a non-negative integer that describes a file. Integers 0, 1 and 2 are the file descriptors normally associated with the standard input file, the standard output file and the standard error file. These file descriptors are made available to every C program automatically. File descriptors are used to manipulate the files associated with them. They must be specified when using low-level input and output functions such as `read` and `write`.

Most programs read input from and write output to a *stream* instead of a file. A *stream* is a file that has been associated with a buffer to allow for efficient user-level input/output.[37] Stream buffers are generally not accessed directly to read input from or write output to a stream; instead, *stream pointers* are used to manipulate streams. A stream pointer refers to a structure that contains information about the corresponding file. Normally three streams, called the *standard streams*, are opened automatically for every program. These streams can be referred to by using the constant pointers, `stdin`, `stdout` and `stderr`, which are predefined in the standard input/output package

-------------

37. Input from and output to a file is most efficient when done in blocks of *pbs* characters, where *pbs* is the *physical block* size associated with the peripheral device on which the file is stored.

If a program reads input from and writes output to a file using low-level input/output functions such as `read` and `write`, then for efficient program execution input and output should be done in blocks of size *pbs*. If the program does input/output using other block sizes, then input and output must be buffered explicitly by the programmer for efficient program execution. Prior to the first program input request, *pbs* characters are read into an array; the program then reads its input from this array, instead of the file. The next read is done only when the array becomes empty. Similarly, program output is collected in an array; the contents of this array are written to the file only when it gets filled or upon program completion.

On the other hand, if the programmer uses streams for program input and output, then all this buffering is done automatically for the programmer. Using streams for input and output is appropriate in most cases. Low-level input/output functions should be used only in cases where the programmer desires finer control over input/output than available with streams.

definitions file `stdio.h`:

| stream pointer | associated file |
|---|---|
| stdin | standard input file |
| stdout | standard output file |
| stderr | standard error file |

Streams are defined using the predefined type FILE (on the UNIX system, the declaration of FILE is given in the file `stdio.h`). The standard streams are defined as

```
FILE *stdin, *stdout, *stderr;
```

A file can be opened as a stream, i.e., a buffer can be associated with a file, by using the function fopen.[38]

The standard input/output package `stdio` (part of the library `libc` that is loaded automatically with every program by the C compiler) contains many functions and macros for reading from and writing to streams. I will briefly describe them here; additional details about these functions and macros are given in Appendix A titled *Some Library Functions*.

Functions and macros used for input are summarized in the following table:

---

38. Alternately, a file can be first opened, e.g., by using the function open, and then converted into a stream by using the function fdopen.

| input functions and macros | explanation |
|---|---|
| getc | get the next character from the specified stream (macro) |
| getchar | get the next character from stdin |
| fgetc | same as getc, but fgetc is a genuine function |
| getw | get the next word from the specified stream |
| scanf | read different types of variables from stdin as specified in the format string |
| fscanf | read different types of variables from the specified stream as specified in the format string |
| gets | get a string from stdin |
| fgets | get a string from the specified stream |

Functions and macros used for output are summarized in the following table:

| output functions and macros | explanation |
|---|---|
| putc | write a character to the specified stream (macro) |
| putchar | write a character to stdout |
| fputc | same as putc, but putc is a genuine function |
| putw | write a word to the specified stream |
| printf | write the list of values specified on stdout as specified in the format string |
| fprintf | write a list of values specified on the specified stream as specified in the format string |
| puts | write a string to stdout |
| fputs | write a string to the specified stream |

Most of these functions and macros take a stream pointer as one of their arguments. However, some of the commonly used input and output functions and macros implicitly use `stdin` and `stdout`. Some examples illustrating the use of these functions and macros are

```
putchar(PROMPT);

printf("acopy: cannot open file %s\n", src);

printf("%f\n", sine(x * 3.1416/180.0, eps));
              /* sine is a user-defined function */

fprintf(stderr, "Error-No free storage");

scanf("%f%c%f",&a,&opr,&b);

while ((c = fgetc(fs)) != EOF) ...;
```

Now for some miscellaneous functions. Function `ungetc` is used to push a character back to the input stream. Functions `fseek` and `rewind` are used to reposition the *file pointer* associated with a stream; the file pointer marks the position of the next input or output on a stream. Function `sprintf` is used to place the output on a string; function `sscanf` is used to read its input from a string. These two functions may be used for converting internally a data item from one format to another.

### 3.1 Using Streams Other Than The Standard Streams

A file is opened for reading or writing by calling `fopen` with an appropriate argument; `fopen` returns a pointer to the stream associated with the file. Data can be read from the file by using the function `fscanf` and data can be written to a file using the function `fprintf`. After the file has been processed, it must be closed using the function `fclose`. All files are closed automatically upon program termination.

The following program segment illustrates the use of a stream other than the standard streams:

```
FILE *fopen(), *fp;
  .
  .
  .
/* "db_file": character pointer that points to */
/* a string which is the name of a file        */
   if ((fp = fopen(db_file,"r")) == NULL) {
       printf("ERROR: cannot open %s\n", db_file);
       exit(1);
   }
  .
  .
  .
while(fscanf(fp,"%s%s%s%s%s%s%s%s", db[i]->name,
    db[i]->room, db[i]->ext, db[i]->desig,
    db[i]->compid, db[i]->sig, db[i]->logid,
    db[i]->maild) != EOF)
{
  .
  .
  .
}
  .
  .
  .
fclose(fp);
  .
  .
  .
```

## 4. Redirection of Input and Output (on UNIX systems)

Suppose a C program, which is stored in a file enhance.c, reads its input from stdin and writes its output to stdout. This program is compiled and its executable version is put in the file enhance:

```
cc -o enhance enhance.c
```

Program enhance expects its input directly from the terminal[39] because it reads from the file `stdin`. It writes the output directly to the terminal because it writes to the file `stdout`. This is the mode of operation when `enhance` is executed as

```
enhance
```

By default, all output written to the error stream `stderr` is sent to the terminal.

Input for `enhance` can be *redirected* so that it is taken from a specified file instead of the terminal by using the UNIX command level input redirection operator `<`. For example, in the command

```
enhance <data
```

`enhance` takes its input from the file `data`. (Program `enhance.c` has not been changed!) Output is still sent directly to the terminal.

The output produced by `enhance` can also be *redirected* so that it goes to a specified file instead of the terminal by using the UNIX command level output redirection operator `>`. For example, in the command

```
enhance >result
```

`enhance` sends its output to the file `result`. Output written to the standard error stream `stderr` is still sent to the terminal. The error output can also be redirected by using the operator `2>` as in

```
enhance >result 2>error
```

Input and output can both be redirected simultaneously, e.g.,

---

39. End of input on the UNIX system is indicated by a typing a line with the control-D character
   `^D`.

```
enhance <data >result
```

## 5. Main Programs

A typical C program has the form

>*preprocessor statements —constant and macro definitions, file inclusions*
>*external variables*
>```
>main( )
>{
>```
>   *definitions and declarations*
>   *statements*
>```
>}
>```
>*functions*

where all of the above text will be contained in one file. A C program can also be split across many files. For example, some of the functions may be placed in another file permitting independent compilation. A function declaration should be given if a function is referred to before its definition is encountered or if its definition is contained in another file.

The function with the name `main` is executed first.[40] The form given for C main programs is an informal guideline and does not cover all cases. For example,

- C preprocessor statements can be given anywhere in the file and are not restricted to the top portion of a program; the only restriction is that preprocessor definitions should precede use of the identifiers defined by them.

- Other function definitions can precede the definition of function `main`.

To allow the writing of commands that can be called with parameters, C allows parameters to be passed to a main program;[41] the format for declaring and accessing the command line parameters is illustrated by the following program

---

40. This is the convention used by the UNIX system and most other operating systems.

41. To be precise, the special significance of the function `main` and the arguments that can be passed to it are UNIX features rather than C features. C is so closely associated with the UNIX system that often what is considered to be part of C is really a facility provided by the UNIX system or its command language.

segment:

```
main(argc, argv)
int argc;       /* number of arguments */
char *argv[];   /* "argv" array contains     */
                /* pointers to the arguments */
                /* given at the UNIX system  */
                /* command level */
{
    .
    .
    .
}
```

Suppose a complete program cmd.c is compiled, named cmd and is executed as the command

cmd $a_1$ $a_2$ ... $a_n$

Inside the main program in cmd.c, argc is $n+1$, where $n$ is the number of command line arguments (argc is $n+1$ because the command name is implicitly passed as one of the arguments). The array argv contains the name of the program (cmd in the above example) and the names of the arguments. Element argv[0] is the name of the compiled program; elements argv[1], argv[2], ..., argv[argc-1] are the arguments to the command argv[0]. Each of these arguments is a string of characters terminated by the null character \0. Finally, argv[argc] is 0, i.e., the null pointer.

As an example, consider the command echo, which just prints out its command line arguments:

```
/*---------------------------------------------*/
/* echo: print out the command level arguments  */
/*---------------------------------------------*/

#include <stdio.h>

main(argc, argv)
int argc;
char *argv[];
{
   int i;

   for (i = 1; i != argc; i++)
     printf("%s ", argv[i]);
   printf("\n");

   exit(0);
}

/*---------------------------------------------*/
```

## 6. Examples

I will now give several examples to illustrate the versatility of C in writing a variety of programs. The first example illustrates the use of C for a simple text processing application. The second example, taken from a prototype electronic form system, produces a two-dimensional display from a tabular description of the display. The third example underlines text that is be displayed on a Hewlett-Packard 2621 CRT terminal (HP2621). To produce an underlined display, control characters need to be sent to the terminal telling it when to start underlining and when to stop the underlining. The fourth and fifth examples, computation of the *sine* function and curve fitting, illustrate the use of C for scientific programming. The sixth example, the *quicksort* sorting algorithm, illustrates the use of recursion. The seventh example illustrates the use of C to write a simple device driver. The eighth example, on integration, illustrates the passing of functions as parameters. The final example, which is about linearly searching an array, illustrates a simple use of pointer arithmetic and a type declaration that uses both the *typedef* and the structure tag mechanisms.

## 6.1 Stripping Formatting Characters Sequences From Ada Program Text

When I was writing Ada programs for publication in a book [Gehani 1983b], I had to insert font control characters, macros and escape characters in the program text. To test the programs directly from their machine readable form, the font control characters, macros and escape characters had to be stripped off and replaced by appropriate equivalent characters where necessary.

The problem is to write a program that performs the following actions on the font control characters, macros and escape characters:

| character sequence | explanation | action |
|---|---|---|
| \fI | change to italic font | remove |
| \fR | change to roman font | remove |
| \fP | change to previous font | remove |
| \fB | change to bold font | remove |
| \- | minus sign | replace by  - |
| $-$ | minus sign | replace by  - |
| $dd$ | macro | replace by  -- |
| $*$ | macro | replace by  * |
| $star$ | macro | replace by  * |
| $app$ | macro | replace by  ' |

The backslash and dollar characters are used in an Ada program text only as described above; they are not used for any other purpose.

As an example, consider the following Ada routine

```
procedure SWAP(X, Y: in out FLOAT) is
  T: FLOAT;   --temporary variable
begin
  T := X;
  X := Y;
  Y := T;
end SWAP;
```

which was produced by the using the following text:

```
\fBprocedure\fR  SWAP(X, Y: \fBin out\fR FLOAT) \fBis
   T: FLOAT;      $dd$temporary variable
\fBbegin\fR
   T := X;
   X := Y;
   Y := T;
\fBend\fR SWAP;
```

The above text must be stripped of the formatting characters before it can be compiled and executed as an Ada program:

```
procedure SWAP(X, Y: in out FLOAT) is
   T: FLOAT;      --temporary variable
begin
   T := X;
   X := Y;
   Y := T;
end SWAP;
```

The program that removes the formatting character sequences is based on the following abstract algorithm, which is described using a mixture of C and English:

```
while ((c = getchar()) != EOF) {
  if (c == '$') {
    c = getchar();
    switch (c) {
    case '-': replace $-$ by minus sign;  break;
    case 'd': replace $dd$ by 2 minus signs;  break;
    case 's': replace $star$ by *;  break;
    case '*': replace $*$ by *;  break;
    case 'a': replace $app$ by ';  break;
    default: print error message;
    }
  }
  else if (c == '\\') {
    c = getchar();
    switch (c) {
    case '-': replace \- by minus sign;  break;
    case 'f': remove \fx where x is B, I, R or P ;  break;
    default: print error message;
    }
  }
  else
    putchar(c);
}
```

```
/*---------------------------------------------------*/
/* clean: strips font control characters, etc.,      */
/*         from an Ada program                        */
/*---------------------------------------------------*/

#include <stdio.h>

main()
{
  int c;
  void replace();

  while ((c = getchar()) != EOF) {
    if (c == '$') {
      c = getchar();
      switch (c) {
      case '-':
        replace("$", "-");
        break;
      case 'd':
        replace("d$", "--");
        break;
      case 's':
        replace("tar$", "*");
        break;
      case '*':
        replace("$", "*");
        break;
      case 'a':
        replace("pp$", "'");
        break;
      default:
        fprintf(stderr, "clean: misuse of $\n");
        exit(1);
      }
    }
    else if (c == '\\') {
      c = getchar();
      switch (c) {
      case '-':
        putchar('-');
        break;
      case 'f':
```

```
              if ((c = getchar()) != 'B' && c != 'I' &&
                                  c != 'R' && c != 'P') {
                 fprintf(stderr, "clean: Error, B, I,");
                 fprintf(stderr, " R or P expected\n");
                 exit(1);
              }
              break;
           default:
              fprintf(stderr, "clean: misuse of \\ \n");
              exit(1);
           }
      }
      else
         putchar(c);
  }
}
/*------------------------------------------------*/

/*------------------------------------------------*/
/* replace(in, out): replaces string "in" by      */
/*                   string "out"                  */
/*------------------------------------------------*/

void replace(in, out)
char in[], out[];
{
   int i;

   for (i = 0; in[i] != NULL; i++) {
      if (getchar() != in[i]) {
         fprintf(stderr, "clean: Error, expected %c\n"
                                         , in[i]);
         exit(1);
      }
   }
   printf("%s", out);
}
/*------------------------------------------------*/
```

## 6.2 Producing the Form Display From a Table

The problem is to write a program that takes tabular input describing the display part of a two-dimensional electronic form and produces a two-dimensional version of the form. The form uses a two-dimensional display with

79 columns and 23 rows. It has border lines in columns 0 and 78 (using the character ¦), and in rows 0 and 22 (using the character -).

The tabular input describing the form gives the rectangular coordinates of the items to be displayed. The position of each item is described by a data line; each such line has the format

*RowNumber ColumnNumber DisplayText*

where $1 \leqslant RowNumber \leqslant 21$ and $1 \leqslant ColumnNumber \leqslant 77$. For example, the input

```
1  20 Tuition Reimbursement Application
1  60 Form#:
3  5 Last Name, Initials:
3  50 Company Id#:
4  5 Room#:
4  30 Extension:
6  5 School Name:
7  5 Address:
9  7 Course#
9  20 Title
9  35 Credits
9  50 Tuition
10 3 1.
11 3 2.
12 3 3.
13 40 Total Cost
15 5 Working for Diploma? Yes or No:
16 10 Diploma Title:
17 10 Credits Required:
17 35 Credits Finished:
19 5 Signature:
19 30 Date:
20 7 Supervisor Signature:
20 50 Date:
21 7 Department Head Signature:
21 50 Date:
```

should lead to the production of the following two-dimensional image (shown in reduced size characters)

```
!---------------------------------------------------------------------!
!                 Tuition Reimbursement Application      Form#:       !
!                                                                     !
!   Last Name, Initials:                      Company Id#:            !
!   Room#:                     Extension:                             !
!                                                                     !
!   School Name:                                                      !
!   Address:                                                          !
!                                                                     !
!      Course#       Title          Credits        Tuition           !
! 1.                                                                  !
! 2.                                                                  !
! 3.                                                                  !
!                                 Total Cost                          !
!                                                                     !
!   Working for Diploma? Yes or No:                                   !
!         Diploma Title:                                              !
!         Credits Required:       Credits Finished:                   !
!                                                                     !
!   Signature:             Date:                                      !
!     Supervisor Signature:                    Date:                  !
!     Department Head Signature:               Date:                  !
!---------------------------------------------------------------------!
```

The following program converts the tabular input of a form into a two-dimensional image:

```
/*----------------------------------------------------*/
/* main: Convert a tabular description of a form */
/*        into a two-dimensional display            */
/*----------------------------------------------------*/

#include <stdio.h>

#define NUMB_ROWS    23
#define NUMB_COLS    79

#define MAX_ROW (NUMB_ROWS-1)
#define MAX_COL (NUMB_COLS-1)

main( )
{
  int i,j; /* i is the row and j is the col */
  char c;
  char display[NUMB_ROWS][NUMB_COLS];

  /* initialize display with blanks and the */
  /* border */
    for(i = 0; i <= MAX_ROW; i++)
      for (j = 0; j <= MAX_COL; j++)
        if (j == 0 || j == MAX_COL)
          display[i][j] = '|';
        else if (i == 0 || i == MAX_ROW)
          display[i][j] = '-';
        else
          display[i][j] = ' ';

  /* read the tabular description from standard */
  /* input and construct the form */
    while(scanf("%d%d%c", &i, &j, &c) != EOF)
        /* "c" is used to read the extra blank */
        /* after col#--discard */
      while ((c = getchar()) != '\n')
        display[i][j++] = c;

  /* put the display mask on standard output */
    for(i = 0; i <= MAX_ROW; i++) {
      for(j = 0; j <= MAX_COL; j++)
      putchar(display[i][j]);
      putchar('\n');
```

```
        }

    exit( 0 );
}
/*------------------------------------------------------*/
```

### 6.3  Enhancing Form Display on an HP2621 Terminal

This example illustrates how a user program can be used to control the display format of a terminal. Although the example is specific to a HP2621 terminal, programs to control the display format of other terminals will be similar to the program developed here.

When providing electronic versions of paper forms it is important to distinguish the *display text* of a form from the information filled by the user. On terminals, such as bitmap terminals, where different fonts can be used for individual characters, one font can be used for the display text and another for the text filled in by the user.

The HP2621 terminal, on which the form is to be displayed and filled out by the user, does not have different fonts. However, underlining can be used to distinguish different texts.

The underline function of the HP2621 terminal is turned on and off by means of the following character sequences:

| Code | Description |
|---|---|
| ESC & d A | Enable the underline function; subsequent characters sent to the terminal will be underlined on the display screen |
| ESC & d @ | Disable the underline function |

where ESC is the escape character that has the ASCII code 27.

The problem is to write a program that takes a text file and produces a new file with appropriate insertions of the HP2621 escape sequences to underline the letters and digits when the modified file is displayed on a HP2621 terminal.

The algorithm to generate a file with the above sequences can be described as the abstract program

```
   while ((c = getchar() != = EOF)
     if (c is an alphanumeric character ) {
       enable the underline function
       putchar(c);
       print all characters up to the first non-alphanumeric character
       disable the underline function
       if (c != EOF) putchar(c);
     }
     else putchar(c);
```

The corresponding C program for enhancing files is

```
/*-----------------------------------------------------*/
/* main: HP2621 Display Enhancer                       */
/*-----------------------------------------------------*/

#include <stdio.h>
#include <ctype.h>       /* contains definition for */
                         /* function "isalnum";     */
                         /* isalnum(c) returns true */
                         /* (non zero) if c is       */
                         /* alphanumeric and false  */
                         /* (0) otherwise            */

#define START_UNDERLINE "\33&dA"
         /* 33 is decimal 27; \33 represents */
         /* the escape character ESC         */
#define STOP_UNDERLINE "\33&d@"

main()       /* program to enhance the display */
             /* form of a file only letters and */
             /* digits are enhanced standard    */
             /* input and output files are used */

{
  int c;

  while ((c = getchar()) != EOF)
    if (isalnum(c)) {
      /* enable the underline function */
        fputs(START_UNDERLINE, stdout);
      putchar(c);
```

```
       /* print all characters up to the first */
       /* non-alphanumeric character */
         while (c = getchar( ), isalnum(c))
           putchar(c);
       /* disable the underline function */
         fputs(STOP_UNDERLINE, stdout);
       if (c != EOF)
         putchar(c);
    }
    else
       putchar(c);
  exit(0);
}

/*------------------------------------------------*/
```

Note that a program like this one that interacts with the hardware by means of escape sequences cannot be written in standard Pascal because control characters such as ESC are not legal elements of the predefined character type in Pascal.

### 6.4 The Sine Function [Wirth 1973]

The following example illustrates the implementation of the *sine* function in which the accuracy of the result is specified by the user (within the bounds of the accuracy that can be achieved using double precision arithmetic). Of course, for normal use it will be more convenient to use the sine function $sin$ provided in the mathematical library $libm$ (see Appendix A titled *Some Library Functions*).

The *sine* of a value $x$ (in radians) is given by the series

$$\text{sine}(x) = x - \frac{x^3}{3!} + \frac{x^5}{5!} - \cdots + (-1)^{i-1} * \frac{x^{2i-1}}{(2i-1)!} + \cdots$$

Computation of the sine should be terminated when the value of the last term is less than or equal to the sum of the earlier terms multiplied by *eps*, an arbitrary small value.

The above series consists of the recursive terms

$$k_j = k_{j-1} + 2$$

$$t_j = -t_{j-1} * \frac{x^2}{k_j * (k_j - 1)}$$

where $k_1 = 1$ and $t_1 = x$.

The sine function is implemented by the function `sine` defined as

```
/*---------------------------------------------------*/
/* sine(x, eps): the sine of "x" computed to an      */
/*               accuracy of "eps"                   */
/*---------------------------------------------------*/

#include <math.h>    /* contains the absolute */
                     /* function "fabs"        */

double sine(x, eps)
double x, eps;
{
   double sum, term;
   int k;

   term = x;  k = 1;  sum = term;
   while (fabs(term) > eps * fabs(sum))
   {
     k += 2;
     term *= (x * x) / (k * (k - 1));
     sum += term;
   }
   return sum;
}

/*---------------------------------------------------*/
```

## 6.5  The Least-Squares Method of Curve Fitting [Hamming 1973]

Suppose we have $n$ measured values that are Cartesian coordinates of the form $(x_i, y_i)$ to which we would like to fit a straight line of the form

$$y(x) = a + b x$$

where coefficients $a$ and $b$ are parameters. The values of these parameters are to be determined by the *least-squares method* that minimizes the sum of the squares of the difference between the computed values and the measured values; i.e., it minimizes the function

$$\sum_{i=1}^{n}[y(x_i)-y_i]^2$$

with respect to the coefficients $a$ and $b$. Differentiating this function with respect to these parameters and rearranging the resulting equations leads to the two equations

$$a\,n + b \sum_{i=1}^{n} x_i = \sum_{i=1}^{n} y_i$$

$$a \sum_{i=1}^{n} x_i + b \sum_{i=1}^{n} x_i^2 = \sum_{i=1}^{n} x_i y_i$$

From these equations the values of *a* and *b* are determined to be

$$b = \frac{\sum_{i=1}^{n} x_i \sum_{i=1}^{n} y_i - n \sum_{i=1}^{n} x_i y_i}{(\sum_{i=1}^{n} x_i)^2 - n \sum_{i=1}^{n} x_i^2}$$

$$a = \frac{\sum_{i=1}^{n} y_i - b \sum_{i=1}^{n} x_i}{n}$$

where $n \geqslant 2$ (which is reasonable because at least two points are needed to determine a straight line).

The problem is to write a program that reads in the measured values and computes the coefficients *a* and *b* using the above equations.

```
/*--------------------------------------------------*/
/* main: Least Squares Curve Fitting                */
/*--------------------------------------------------*/

#include <stdio.h>

#define MAX        500

main()
{
  float x[MAX], y[MAX];    /* the measured values */
  float a, b;      /* the coefficients of the      */
                   /* equation "y(x) = a + bx"      */
                   /* which are to be computed      */
  int n;     /* number of elements */
  float p, q;    /* temporary variables */

  void least_square();

  n = 0;
  while (scanf("%f%f", &p, &q) != EOF) {
    if (n >= MAX) {
      printf("Sorry, room for only %d samples\n", MAX);
      exit(1);
    }
    else {
      x[n] = p;
      y[n] = q;
      n++;
    }
  }

  if (n <= 1) {
    printf("Error: Less than 2 input coordinates\n");
    exit(1);
  }

  least_square(x, y, n, &a, &b);

  printf("coefficients a = %g and b = %g\n", a, b);

  exit(0);
}
```

```
/*----------------------------------------------*/

/*----------------------------------------------*/
/* least_square: determine the values of the    */
/*               parameters                      */
/*----------------------------------------------*/

void least_square(x, y, n, pa, pb)
float x[], y[];
int n;
float *pa, *pb;
{
   int i;
   float sum_x = 0.0, sum_y = 0.0,
         sum_xy = 0.0, sum_x2 = 0.0;

   for (i = 0; i < n; i++) {
     sum_x += x[i];
     sum_y += y[i];
     sum_xy += x[i] * y[i];
     sum_x2 += x[i] * x[i];
   }

   *pb = (sum_x * sum_y - n * sum_xy) /
                   (sum_x * sum_x - n * sum_x2);
   *pa = (sum_y - *pb * sum_x) / n;
}

/*----------------------------------------------*/
```

### 6.6 Quicksort

The problem is to write a function to sort an array with elements of type float using the quicksort technique [Hoare 1962]. Quicksort uses the *divide and conquer* strategy to sort. First, the array is divided (i.e., partitioned) into two parts, a left part and a right part, such that all the elements of the left part are less than or equal to all the elements of the right part. Then quicksort recursively sorts the two parts to produce a sorted array.

The quicksort algorithm can be described in more detail as the following abstract algorithm:

```
void quicksort(a, 1, u);
float a[];      /* array to be sorted  */
int 1, u;       /* bounds of the array */
{
   if (a  has 0 or 1 elements)
      do nothing;
   else if (a  has 2 elements)
      order them (swap if necessary);
   else {
      divide a into two partitions such that
         the left partition has elements ≤ r,
         and the right partition has elements ≥ r
         (where r is an arbitrary element of the array a)

      quicksort  the left partition;
      quicksort  the right partition;
   }
}
```

To ensure that the recursion terminates, it is necessary for each partition to have at least one element less than the original array.

Dividing the array into two parts as specified above can be described abstractly as follows:[42]

---

42. The notation a[i..j] is used to refer to the subarray of a with elements from a[i] to a[j]. If i is less than j, then the subarray in question is the null array, that is, an array with no elements.

*Let* r *be the middle element of* a

```
i = 1; j = u;
    /* the left partition a[1..i-1] will always  */
    /* contain elements <= r; to start with it    */
    /* is empty; similarly, the right  partition */
    /* a[j+1..u] will always contain elements      */
    /* >= r                                        */

while (i <= j) {
```
*Extend left partition* a[1..i-1] *as far as possible by increasing* i
*Extend right partition* a[j+1..u] *as far as possible by decreasing* j
*Exchange elements* a[i] *and* a[j] *so that extending of*
*partitions can continue; update the values of* i *and* j
```
}
```

With this algorithm, it is possible that the two partitions overlap by one element whose value is equal to r.

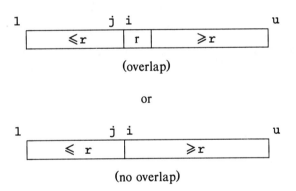

(overlap)

or

(no overlap)

The overlapping element need not be sorted because it is already in position — the elements to its left are ≤ r and the elements to its right are ≥ r. Upon termination of the loop, there will be an overlap if i = j + 2 and no overlap if i = j + 1. Sorting of the overlapping element can be avoided by taking a[1..j] to be the left partition and a[i..u] to be the right partition.

Based on the algorithm described above, function partition is defined as

```
/*----------------------------------------------------*/
/* partition: rearrange the elements of a float  */
/*            array so that the elements in the  */
/*            left partition will  be <=         */
/*            elements in right  partition        */
/*----------------------------------------------------*/
void partition(a, l, u, ri, rj)
float a[];    /* array to be partitioned */
int l, u;     /* bounds of the array */
int *ri, *rj;  /* partition points to be */
              /* returned */
{
  float r, temp;
  int i, j;

  r = a[(l+u)/2];     /* middle element */
  i = l; j = u;

  while (i <= j) {
    /* extend the left partition;      */
    /* upon loop termination a[i] >= r */
      while (a[i] < r)
        i++;

    /* extend the right partition;     */
    /* upon loop termination a[j] <= r */
      while (a[j] > r)
        j--;

    /* exchange the elements and update i and j */
      if (i <= j) {
        temp = a[i]; a[i] = a[j]; a[j] = temp;
        i++;
        j--;
      }
  }

  /* return the partitioning positions */
    *ri = i;
    *rj = j;
}
```

```
/*----------------------------------------------------*/
```

Function `quicksort` can now be defined as

```
/*----------------------------------------------------*/
/* quicksort: a fast sorting technique          */
/*            (This program sorts only "float"  */
/*            arrays)                           */
/*----------------------------------------------------*/

void quicksort(a, l, u)
float a[];
int l, u;
{
   int i, j;
   float temp;
   void partition();

   if (u-l <= 0)
     ;
   else if (u-l == 1) {
     if (a[u] < a[l]) {
       /* swap a[l] and a[u] */
         temp = a[l]; a[l] = a[u]; a[u] = temp;
     }
   }
   else {
     partition(a, l, u, &i, &j);
     quicksort(a, l, j);
     quicksort(a, i, u);
   }
}

/*----------------------------------------------------*/
```

### 6.7  Automobile Cruise Controller

The problem is to write a program to monitor and maintain an automobile at a constant speed, i.e., an *automobile cruise controller*. The cruise controller program will be executed by a dedicated microprocessor. The cruise controller is activated when memory location 020 of the microprocessor becomes non-zero and deactivated when it becomes zero. The current speed of the automobile, an integer value, can be accessed from memory location 024. The speed of the automobile can be increased or decreased by some value by writing this value to memory location 0 2 6. The automobile takes about half a second to respond to the change in speed. The externally defined function delay may be used to suspend program execution until the automobile speed has changed as instructed.

The cruise controller should accept only speeds between 25 and 55 miles per hour as valid cruising speeds; if the driver attempts to set a cruising speed outside these limits, an alarm signal is sent by writing a non-zero value to memory location 0 2 2. An alarm signal is also sent if the controller is unable to maintain the automobile within 2 miles of the desired cruising speed. In both cases, the controlling mechanism should deactivate automatically.

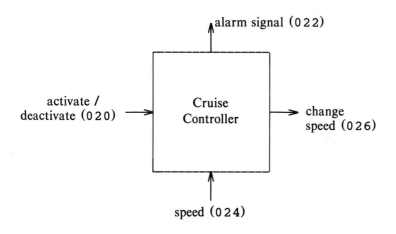

Automatic Speed Controller

The program for the cruise controller is

```
/*-------------------------------------------------*/
/* Main: An Automobile Cruise Controller           */
/*-------------------------------------------------*/

#define ABS(x)                ((((x)>0)?(x):-(x))

#define ON_OFF_ADDR           020
#define ALARM_ADDR            022
#define SPEED_ADDR            024
#define CHANGE_SPEED_ADDR     026

#define VARIATION             2
#define RESPONSE_TIME         0.5
#define LOW_LIMIT             25
#define HIGH_LIMIT            55
#define TRUE                  1

main ()
{
  /* external connections */
    int *on = (int *) ON_OFF_ADDR;
    int *alarm = (int *) ALARM_ADDR;
    int *speed = (int *) SPEED_ADDR;
    int *change_speed = (int *) CHANGE_SPEED_ADDR;

  int current_speed, cruising_speed;
  void delay();

  for (;;) {     /* infinite loop */

    while (*on == 0)    /* busy wait */
      ;

    cruising_speed = *speed;

    if (cruising_speed < LOW_LIMIT ||
                    cruising_speed > HIGH_LIMIT) {
      *alarm = TRUE; *on = 0;
    }
    else {
      while (*on != 0) {
        current_speed = *speed;
        if (ABS(cruising_speed - current_speed)
```

```
                                        > VARIATION)  {
        *alarm = TRUE;
        *on = 0;
        break;
      }
      else
        *change_speed =
            cruising_speed - current_speed;

        delay(RESPONSE_TIME);
      }
    }
  }

}

/*----------------------------------------------------*/
```

Note that this program must be loaded with the function `delay`.

The cruise controller program *busy waits* until the cruise mechanism is activated. A program is said to *poll* if it actively and repeatedly checks for the occurrence of an event that originates outside the program. A program *busy waits* if in between polling it does nothing useful (as is the case of checking for the activation of the cruise controller). Polling and busy waiting are acceptable only in some situations; e.g., in a program that executes on a dedicated processor. It is usually undesirable on computers that are shared by many different programs because it wastes system resources.

The cruise control microprocessor is likely to be a very small microprocessor with limited capabilities. High-level programs for such microprocessors are often compiled on a bigger computer[43] and the translated version is then transferred to the microprocessor. Often such programs are first tested under simulated conditions on the computer where the program is compiled. The program given was tested only under simulated conditions.

*6.7.1 Implementation of the* `delay` *Function:* Implementation of the `delay` function on the microprocessor will require access to a real-time clock so a delay interval can be computed. Alternately, if such a facility is not available, a process can be delayed by making it execute a large number of

---

43. Compiling a program on one machine for use on another machine is called *cross compilation*.

instructions, such as the following nested loop:

```
for (i=0; i<=M; i++)
   for (j=0; j<=N; j++)
      ;
```

The time required to execute such a loop can be determined analytically by examining the code produced by a C compiler and using the execution times of these instructions on the microprocessor or experimentally by running the program on the microprocessor. Parameters M and N can be tuned to achieve the desired delay.

### 6.8 Passing Functions as Parameters—Integration

Write a function integrate that finds the definite integral of a function f

$$f\colon \text{real} \rightarrow \text{real}$$

between the limits a and b

$$I = \int_{i=a}^{i=b} f(x)\ dx$$

using the trapezoidal rule. It should be possible to integrate different functions by passing them as actual parameters to integrate.

The trapezoidal rule approximates the integral of a function between the two limits a and b by the area of the trapezoid with base b-a and heights f(a) and f(b).

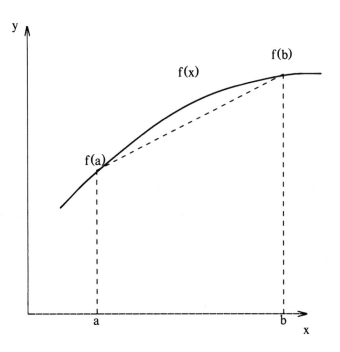

Approximating the integral of function f using one interval

This approximation can be improved by dividing a and b into two equal subintervals, taking the area of the two resulting trapezoids and adding them up.  Each of these subintervals can be further divided into two more equal subintervals and the process repeated.

The approximate integral $I_n$ of a function f between the limits a and b using n subintervals

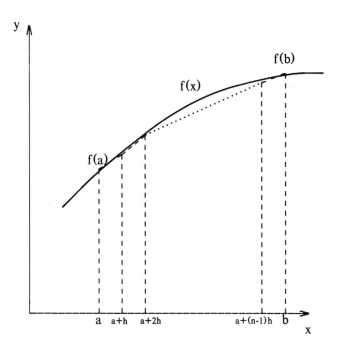

Approximating the integral of function f using n intervals

is given by the equation

$$I_n = h\left(\frac{f(a)}{2}+f(a+h)+f(a+2h)+ \cdots +f(a+(n-1)h)+\frac{f(b)}{2}\right)$$

where h, the width of the interval, is given by

$$h = \frac{(b-a)}{n}$$

The subdividing process is repeated until two successive approximations of the integral of the function f as calculated by the trapezoidal rule differ in absolute value by less than eps (eps > 0), the desired stopping tolerance.

The trapezoidal integration algorithm can be described abstractly as

```
new_approx = 0;
do {
  previous_approx = new_approx;
  Calculate new_approx;
  Divide each subinterval into two equal subintervals;
} (abs(new_approx - previous_approx) >= eps);
```

Based on this integration algorithm, function `integrate` is defined as

```
/*----------------------------------------------*/
/* integrate: uses the trapezoidal rule to      */
/*            integrate a "float" function using */
/*            limits and accuracy specified by   */
/*            the user                           */
/*----------------------------------------------*/

#include <math.h>    /* math library definitions   */
                     /* for the absolute function  */
                     /* "fabs"                     */

float integrate(fp, a, b, eps)
float (*fp)(), a, b, eps;
          /* "fp": pointer to the function that is */
          /* to be integrated; "a" and "b"         */
          /* represent the integration interval    */
          /* boundaries; "eps" is the required     */
          /* accuracy                              */
{
  float new_approx = 0.0;     /* initial value */
  float previous_approx;
  int n = 1;        /* number of intervals */
  double h;         /* interval size */
  double sum;       /* temporary variable */
  int i;            /* loop variable */

  h = (b - a);      /* initial interval size */
  do {
    previous_approx = new_approx;
    /* calculate new_approx */
      sum = (*fp)(a) / 2.0;
      for (i = 1; i < n; i++)
        sum += (*fp)(a + i * h);
```

```
      sum += (*fp)(b) / 2.0;
      new_approx = sum * h;
   n *= 2;      /* number of intervals for next */
                /* approximation */
   h /= 2.0;    /* size of interval for next */
                /* approximation */
 } while (fabs(new_approx-previous_approx) >= eps);
 return new_approx;
}
/*--------------------------------------------------*/
```

As an alternative to using the math library function `fabs`, the user could have defined a private absolute value function or macro. For example, here is the macro `ABS` that was used earlier in the *Automobile Cruise Controller* example:

```
#define ABS(x)   (((x)>0)?(x):-(x))
```

Function `integrate` does not work correctly if the first approximation of the integral of `f` is within `eps` of 0.0, the initial value assigned to `new_approx`. This problem can be solved by forcing the computation of at least two approximations.

Calling function `integrate` is straightforward. For example, if a function `cube`, which is declared as

```
    float cube();
        /* returns the cube of its argument */
```

is to be integrated between two limits `l` and `u`, with an accuracy of `small`, then `integrate` is called as

```
    integrate(cube, l, u, small)
```

Function `integrate` also illustrates the use of the various compound assignment operators.

### 6.9 Searching an Array

Process table `pt` is an array whose elements are structures of type `pcb`:

```
typedef struct pcb
   {
      long pid;
      proc_states state;
      long delay;
      int fp;
      struct pcb *parent;
   } pcb;
```

Notice the combination of a `typedef` and a structure tag. Identifier `pcb` is declared both as a type and a structure tag. It was necessary to declare `pcb` as a structure tag because the declaration of `pcb` is recursive; on the other hand, although it was not necessary to declare `pcb` as a type name by using *typedef*, such a declaration does allows `pcb` to be used like the predefined types (i.e., it is not necessary to use the keyword `struct` when declaring or defining structures of type `pcb`).

The enumeration type `proc_states` used in `pcb` is declared as

```
typedef enum
   {
      ready,
      service,
      select,
      transaction,
      completed
   } proc_states;        /* process states */
```

These type declarations and the following constant and variable declarations are contained in file `proc.h`:

```
#define NULL            0
#define NULL_PID        (-1)

extern pcb pt[];        /* the process table */
extern pcb *pt_last;    /* last element of   */
                        /* process table     */
```

The external variables are defined and initialized in another file. The address of the first element of `pt` is denoted by `pt` itself (or `&pt[0]`) and the address of the last element of `pt` is given by the pointer variable `pt_last`.

The problem is to write a function `next_ready` that returns the address (not the index) of an element of `pt` such that its component `pid` has a value that is not equal to `NULL_PID` and its component `state` has the value `ready`. If there is no such element, then `next_ready` returns `NULL`.

```
/*-------------------------------------------------------*/
/* next_ready: finds the address of the process  */
/*             table element that is ready       */
/*-------------------------------------------------------*/

#include "proc.h"

pcb *next_ready()
{
   pcb *p;

   /* search process table for a ready process */
     for (p = &pt[0]; p < pt_last; p++) {
        if (p->pid != NULL_PID && p->state == ready)
           return p;
     }
   return NULL;
}

/*-------------------------------------------------------*/
```

The effect of the pointer expression `p++` is to increment `p` by `sizeof(pcb)` rather than just one.

## 7. Problems

1. Write a function `sqrt` that computes the square root of a floating point value `x` using Newton's method. According to this method, the $k+1$[th] approximation of the square root of a value `x` is given by the formula

   $$a_{k+1} = 0.5 \, (a_k + \frac{x}{a_k})$$

   The iteration is stopped when the absolute difference between two successive approximations is less than the user-supplied stopping value `eps`.

2. The *least squares curve fitting* program expects to read an even number of input values. The result is meaningless if the user supplies an odd number of input values; however, the program does not indicate an error

in such a case. Modify the program so that it prints an error message if the user does not supply an even number of input values. (*Hint:* function `scanf` returns the number of items successfully matched except when the input ends before the first item is read, in which case it returns `EOF`.)

3. Write a function `merge` that merges two sorted arrays a and b to produce a third sorted array c:

```
void merge(a, b, c)
```

4. Write a function `mergesort` that sorts an array using a divide-and-conquer strategy similar to the one used in `quicksort`. The basic idea is to divide the array into two parts, sort each part and then to merge the two sorted parts (using function `merge` of the previous problem) to produce the sorted array. The `mergesort` algorithm may be described abstractly as (adapted from [McGettrick and Smith 1983])

```
void mergesort(a, l, u);
float a[];     /* array to be sorted  */
int l, u;      /* bounds of the array */
{
   if ( a has 2 or more elements )  {
      Divide a into two non-empty partitions p and q;
      mergesort the partition p;
      mergesort the partition q;
      merge(p, q, a);
   }
}
```

5. The series for computing the *sine* of a value *x*, given earlier, converges quickly only for small values of *x* satisfying

$$0 \leqslant \text{abs}(x) \leqslant \frac{\pi}{4}$$

For larger values of *x*, the following equivalences should be used [Wirth 1973]:

|   | equivalence | condition |
|---|---|---|
|   | $sine(x) \equiv sine(x-2\pi n)$ | $2\pi n \leqslant abs(x) < 2\pi(n+1)$ |
|   | $sine(x) \equiv -sine(x-\pi)$ | $\pi \leqslant abs(x) < 2\pi$ |
|   | $sine(x) \equiv sine(\pi-x)$ | $\dfrac{\pi}{2} \leqslant abs(x) < \pi$ |
|   | $sine(x) \equiv cosine(\dfrac{\pi}{2}-x)$ | $\dfrac{\pi}{4} < abs(x) < \dfrac{\pi}{2}$ |
|   | $sine(x) \equiv -sine(-x)$ | $x < 0$ |

where *cosine(x)* is given by the series

$$cosine(x) = 1 - \frac{x^2}{2!} + \frac{x^4}{4!} - \cdots$$

Modify function s i n e to incorporate these equivalences.

6. In the *least-squares* curve fitting example, the program for fitting a curve is not *robust* in that it does not check to make sure that the user supplies an even number of coordinates. Modify the program to make it robust.

7. On the UNIX system, characters ^H (backspace) and @ are often used as special characters that erase the last character typed and delete the current line, respectively. Write a program that reads text input containing these characters and produces, as output, a version of the input edited by these characters. For example, the program should transform the input[44]

```
Their^H^Hre was an Old Pear^H^Hrson of K^HCromer,
Who frequented the top of a tree@
Who stood on one leg to read homer^H^H^H^H^HHomer;
When he found he grew still^H^Hff, he jumped over
  the cliff,
Who was sadly annoyed by a flea@
Which concluded the person of c^HCromer.
```

to

---

44. This text was taken from *The Nonsense Books of Edward Lear* [Lear 1964].

```
There was an Old Person of Cromer,
Who stood on one leg to read Homer;
When he found he grew stiff, he jumped over
  the cliff,
Which concluded the person of Cromer.
```

8. Modify the `echo` program given in this chapter so that if the first argument is -N, then it prints its arguments on new lines. For example,

```
echo a b c
```

prints

```
a b c
```

while

```
echo -N a b c
```

prints

```
a
b
c
```

A command line argument of the form *-letter* (such as -N) is called a command option or a flag in UNIX terminology.

# Chapter 6

# Independent Compilation and Data Abstraction

The text of a C program can reside on one file[45] or, alternately, it may be distributed over several files. Files containing components of a C program (functions, declarations and definitions) can be compiled independently. Independently compiled program components, along with precompiled library functions, can be joined together to produce a complete program.

Because C files can be compiled independently, it is convenient and advantageous to partition large C programs into smaller and more manageable parts. Programs may be partitioned to group together logically related entities such as constants, variables, types and functions. Partitioning programs into smaller pieces helps in building, understanding and maintaining large systems [Horning 1979]. Independent compilation allows files containing C program components to be checked separately for syntactic and semantic errors and even tested for run-time errors. Moreover, when a program is modified, only the components affected need to be recompiled (program `make` is often used to automate this process; for details, see Appendix B titled *Some C Tools*). Complete recompilation of a large program for every change made to the program is undesirable because it may take considerable time and is wasteful of resources.

Files can also be used as an information hiding and data encapsulation mechanism. Only external objects with the storage class `extern` can be referenced in other files; objects declared to have the storage class `static` cannot be referenced from other files. Files can therefore be used to control the visibility of objects. For example, a programmer may allow only certain functions defined in a file to be referenced from other files. Implementation details of these functions, such as the data structures used and shared by them, may be hidden from the users of the functions. This hiding will prevent users from exploiting knowledge about the implementation details in their programs. Consequently, files can be used to prevent a programmer from making a program dependent on specific implementation details. Once specification of

---

45. A *file* is an entity, supported by the operating system controlling the computer, that is used to hold text or data permanently.

147

the visible components of a file has been agreed upon, the implementor of these components is free to implement, or change the implementation of, these components in any way consistent with the agreed-upon specifications.

A C file can contain constant definitions, object definitions and declarations, and function definitions; a suggested format for C files is

> *constant definitions*
> *external definitions and declarations*
> *function definitions*

The syntax of external definitions and declarations is the same as that of the definitions and declarations given inside functions with one difference—function bodies can be given only in external definitions (functions cannot be nested).

## 1. Scope of External Definitions and Declarations

There are two kinds of scope associated with external identifiers: *lexical scope* and *external scope* (or visibility). Lexical scope of an identifier was defined earlier as the region of a program where its declaration or definition is in effect.

External scope is defined as the part of the program where all references to the same external identifier refer to the same object. External objects and functions can have the storage class `extern` (which is also the default storage class) or `static`. The scope of an external declaration or a definition with the storage class `static` is restricted to the file containing the definitions and declarations. The scope of other external definitions and declarations (those whose storage class is `extern`) includes all other files comprising the program.

As mentioned earlier, the appearance of the keyword `extern` indicates that the storage associated with the identifier being declared will be allocated in another file. The treatment of functions is slightly different. All external function declarations, with or without the keyword `extern`, are equivalent; e.g., the two declarations

```
extern void sort( );
void sort( );
```

are equivalent. A function definition differs from a function declaration in that it lists the formal parameters and their declarations, and specifies the function body. Of course, there must be only one external function definition (i.e., a definition without the keyword `static`) of each function in a program.

## 2. Independent Compilation

A complete C program (one containing a `main` function on UNIX systems) that has been partitioned into many files, say $file_1$ . c, $file_2$ . c, ..., $file_n$ . c can be compiled into one executable program, say `final`, as follows:[46]


```
cc -o final file₁.c   file₂.c   ...   fileₙ.c
```


Alternately, each file can be independently compiled; after all the files have been compiled, their translated versions can be combined to produce the final version of the complete program. For example, suppose each file $file_i$ . c is independently compiled using the command


```
cc -c fileᵢ.c
```


which results in the production of the *object*[47] file $file_i$ . o.[48] After all the component files $file_1$ . c, $file_2$ . c, ..., $file_n$ . c have been compiled, the corresponding object files can be *linked* i.e., joined together, to produce an executable version of the program by using the command


```
cc -o final file₁.o   file₂.o   ...   fileₙ.o
```


## 3. Abstract Data Types and Information Hiding

Files can be used to implement *data abstraction* in much the same way that subprograms are used to implement control abstraction and information hiding. An *abstract data object* is an object that can be manipulated using *only* the operations supplied by the definer of the object. The user cannot directly manipulate the underlying implementation of an abstract data object. Details of how an abstract data object is implemented are hidden from the user. Hiding the details prevents the user from

---

46. The UNIX C compiler expects files containing C programs to have the suffix . c. This convention is also followed by other tools used in conjunction with C programs, e.g., the type checker `lint` and the program group maintainer `make`.

47. An *object file* is the machine language translation (i.e., a file produced by a compiler) of a program in a high-level language.

48. By convention, object files produced by the UNIX C compiler have the suffix . o.

1. making programs dependent on the representation. The representation of an abstract data type can be changed without affecting the rest of the program. For example, the abstract data type *set* may be initially implemented as an array, but this representation may be changed to an ordered list later on for storage efficiency.

2. accidentally or maliciously violating the integrity of an abstract data type object. Integrity of abstract data type objects is preserved by forcing the user to manipulate these objects using only the operations provided by the designer of the abstract data type.

Some examples of abstract data objects are queues, sets, databases and binary trees.

### 3.1 An Example—The Stack

Consider an abstract data object that is to be manipulated using only the following operations:

| | |
|---|---|
| `push(i)` | add integer element `i` to the abstract data object |
| `pop()` | remove the top element from the abstract data object |
| `top()` | yield the value of the top element of (element most recently added to) the abstract data object |
| `empty()` | yield `TRUE` if the abstract data object is empty; otherwise yield `FALSE` |
| `full()` | yield `TRUE` if the abstract data object is full; otherwise yield `FALSE` |
| `clear()` | empty the abstract data object |

A data object that can be manipulated in this manner is called a *stack*.

The definitions and declarations given below implement a stack of integer elements. All these definitions and declarations must be contained in one file. The stack is implemented by using an integer array `s` to store the values put on the stack. Variable `next` is used to point to the next free element in the array `s`. These implementation details are hidden from the stack users by restricting the visibility of array `s` and variable `next` to the file containing them; storage class `static` is used to restrict the visibility.

```
/*----------------------------------------------------*/
/* push, pop, top, empty, full, clear: Stack        */
/*                                       routines   */
/*----------------------------------------------------*/

#define MAX_SIZE        200

static int s[MAX_SIZE];
static int next = 0;
     /* points to first free element on stack */

/*----------------------------------------------------*/

void push(i)    /* add element "i" to the stack   */
int i;
{
  if (next == MAX_SIZE) {
    printf("push: Stack Full Error\n");
    exit(1);    /* terminate the program */
  }
  s[next++] = i;
}

/*----------------------------------------------------*/

void pop()    /* remove the top element from the */
              /* stack */
{
  if (next == 0) {
    printf("pop: Stack Empty Error\n");
    exit(1);
  }
  next--;
}

/*----------------------------------------------------*/

int top()    /* return value of the top stack   */
             /* element*/
{
  if (next == 0) {
    printf("top: Stack Empty Error\n");
    exit(1);
```

```
  }
  return s[next-1];
}

/*-----------------------------------------------*/

int empty()      /* return TRUE if the stack is   */
                 /* empty and FALSE otherwise     */
{
  return next == 0;
}

/*-----------------------------------------------*/

int full()       /* return TRUE if the stack is   */
                 /* full and FALSE otherwise      */
{
  return next == MAX_SIZE;
}

/*-----------------------------------------------*/

void clear()     /* empty the stack */
{
  next = 0;
}

/*-----------------------------------------------*/
```

Only the functions can be referenced from other files because they have the storage class `extern` (by default).

Attempts to insert an element when the stack is full, or attempts to delete an element or determine the value of the top element when the stack is empty, will result in program termination.

### 3.2 Limitations of Files as a Data Abstraction Facility

A file is not a true data abstraction facility, because it only partially supports data abstraction. For example, it is not possible to define an array of files or to define a pointer to a file. Specifically, in the case of the stack example, it is not possible to define directly an array of stacks or pass a stack as a parameter.

Files were not designed as a mechanism for information hiding and data abstraction! They were provided as a facility to support program partitioning and independent compilation.

## 4. Classes

To enhance C's data structuring facilities, B. Stroustrup has proposed the addition of the *class* facility [Stroustrup 1983, 1984a and 1984b]. This class facility is based on a similar facility in Simula 67.

At present, classes are not considered part of standard C [Ritchie 1980] and are therefore not supported by the standard C compilers; they are supported only by a compiler for C++, which is a superset of C.[49] However, it is likely that they will be incorporated into standard C sometime in the future.

Classes are discussed here for several reasons:

- to familiarize the reader with a data abstraction facility.

- to illustrate the additional capabilities offered by classes compared to the *typedef* mechanism.

- to illustrate the evolution of C.

As defined earlier, a type is a set of values plus operations on these values. The class mechanism allows the declaration of full-fledged user-defined types. The *typedef* mechanism is not really a type declaration facility because it does not provide a mechanism for declaring operations. It only allows the declaration of a set of values. The operations associated with the type cannot be defined.

A class declaration consists of two parts: a class specification and the definitions of the functions declared in the class declaration. Class specifications are similar to structure declarations. They have the form

---

49. C++ [Stroustrup 1984b] is standard C [Ritchie 1980] plus facilities such as classes, operator and function overloading, in-line functions, a new function declaration syntax and function argument checking.

```
class  class-name
{
```

*private declarations*

```
public:
```

*public declarations*

```
};
```

The public and private declarations consist of data and function declarations. Function declarations differ slightly from the standard C function declarations—the types of the formal parameters may also be specified in the interest of better type checking and program readability.

The user of a class has access only to those objects declared in the public part of a class declaration. Objects declared in the private part of a class declaration are not accessible by the user. They can be accessed only in the definitions of the functions declared in the class declaration.

The public part of a class is the user interface of the abstract data type implemented by the class; the private part of the class contains implementation details that do not concern the user. Access to a class is controlled by putting appropriate objects that are used to build the class in the public and private parts of the class. This control is used to ensure that programs using a class do not become dependent on the class representation and that they do not violate the integrity of a class object.

The notation used to access components of a class object is similar to that used for accessing elements of a structure, i.e., *class-object . class-element*. Function definitions are given separately. For example, a function *f* declared in the specification of class *c* must be defined separately as

*type c . f ( parameter declarations )*
```
{
  .
  .
  .
}
```

The syntax of a class function is slightly different from that of an ordinary function. The class function name must include the name of the class as a prefix and the declarations of the formal parameters must be given in the function header itself.

Consider the declaration of a class stack to implement integer stacks. Its specification is

```
#define MAX_SIZE        200

class stack {
   int s[MAX_SIZE];
   int next;
public:
   void push(int);     /* note the specification    */
                       /* of the formal parameter   */
                       /* type                       */
   void pop();
   int top();
   int empty();
   int full();
   void clear();
};
```

The functions declared in the class are now defined:

```
/*--------------------------------------------------*/

void stack.push(int i)      /* note how formal */
                            /* parameters are  */
                            /* declared */
{
  if (next == MAX_SIZE) {
    printf("push: Stack Full Error\n");
    exit(1);
  }
  s[next++] = i;
}

/*--------------------------------------------------*/

void stack.pop()
{
  if (next == 0) {
    printf("pop: Stack Empty Error\n");
    exit(1);
  }
  next--;
}

/*--------------------------------------------------*/

int stack.top()
{
  if (next == 0) {
    printf("top: Stack Empty Error\n");
    exit(1);
  }
  return s[next - 1];
}

/*--------------------------------------------------*/

int stack.empty()
{
  return next == 0;
}

/*--------------------------------------------------*/
```

```
int stack.full()
{
  return next == MAX_SIZE;
}

/*--------------------------------------------------*/

void stack.clear()
{
  next = 0;
}

/*--------------------------------------------------*/
```

The class specification and the class functions are usually placed in different source files.

Classes can be used like other types in object declarations, e.g.,

```
stack s[5], sa, sb, *ps;
```

Variable s represents an array of stacks, variables sa and sb are individual stacks and ps is a pointer to a stack. These stacks must be manipulated by using the functions declared in class stack:

```
s[3].clear();    /* initialize stack "s[3]" to */
                 /* empty */
sa.push(i+14);   /* add element "i+14" to the  */
                 /* stack "sa" */
```

Class objects can be explicitly allocated and deallocated using the predefined operators new and delete:

```
ps = new stack;
delete ps;
```

An important advantage of using classes is that the representation of the class, the private declarations, can be changed without affecting the user of the class. For example, the implementation of class stack can be changed so that a list is used instead of an array without affecting a user of the class stack.

An important difference between the use of files and classes to implement data abstraction is that classes are full-fledged types while files are not. For example, using the class version of a stack, it is possible to define an array of stacks or a pointer to a stack; however, it is not possible to do this using the file version of a stack.

## 4.1 Constructors, Destructors and Operator/Function Overloading in C++

I will now briefly mention some other facilities in the C++ language that are related to the class facility.

*4.1.1 Constructors:* One of the constructor functions associated with a class type is executed automatically when a class object is defined; such a function can be used to initialize a class object. For example, a constructor function may be used to initialize `stack` objects to empty when these objects are defined.

*4.1.2 Destructors:* A destructor function associated with a class type is executed automatically when a class object goes out of scope. Such functions may be used to clean up prior to the destruction of an object; e.g., they may be used to explicitly deallocate storage used by objects so that the storage can be reused.

*4.1.3 Operator/Function Overloading:* Operators and functions can be *overloaded*; i.e., the same operator symbol or function identifier may be associated with more than one operation or function. Such a facility is particularly helpful when using classes. For example,

1.  overloading allows the user to extend the usual arithmetic operators for complex arithmetic (to be used in conjunction with a user-defined class type `complex`), thus providing the user with a natural notation for complex arithmetic.

2.  the assignment operator can be overloaded to allow the assignment of class objects (overloading the assignment operator implicitly allows class objects to be passed as parameters).

## 4.2 Final Remarks on Classes

The incorporation of classes into C will significantly enhance its program structuring facilities. I have discussed only the simplest uses of classes here; for example, I have not illustrated how new classes can be derived from existing classes or how existing classes can be used in the construction of new classes [Stroustrup 1983]. The reader interested in finding out more about C classes (and C++) is referred to the literature [Stroustrup 1983, 1984a and 1984b].

# 5. Examples

There are three examples in this section. The first two examples illustrate the use of files to implement data abstraction while the third example illustrates the use of the class mechanism to implement data abstraction.

## 5.1 Symbol Table Manager Example

The problem is to write a set of functions implementing a symbol table. A file containing a set of declarations for the benefit of symbol table users must also be provided. The symbol table functions perform the following actions:

1. Insert an item and associated information into the symbol table (the items are strings).

2. Retrieve the information associated with an item from the symbol table.

3. Determine whether or not the symbol table is full.

4. Check to see if an item is in the symbol table.

5. Reinitialize (reset) the symbol table.

An item is inserted into the symbol table only if the symbol table is not full. The symbol table should be able to hold at least 200 items. The information associated with an item indicates whether the item is a variable identifier, a function or procedure name, a keyword, or a label name. This example is a simplified version of a real symbol table.

The type declarations used by the symbol table functions and their users are given in the file `symtab.h`:

```
/*---------------------------------------------------*/
/* symtab.h: Symbol Table Declarations File          */
/*---------------------------------------------------*/

typedef enum {var, fun, proc, key_word,
                                label} item_type;

typedef struct {
  char *id;
  item_type t;
} item_info;

void add(), clear();
int in_table(), full();
item_type get();

/*---------------------------------------------------*/
```

The various symbol table functions are now defined:

```
/*---------------------------------------------------*/
/* add, in_table, full, get, clear: Symbol table */
/*                                      routines  */
/*---------------------------------------------------*/

#include "symtab.h"        /* insert the contents */
                           /* of "symtab.h" here  */

#define N   200
#define TRUE    1
#define FALSE   0

int strcmp();    /* string comparison function    */
                 /* from the standard library     */
char *strcpy();  /* string copy function from     */
                 /* the standard library          */

static item_info st[N]; /* the symbol table */
static int next = 0;    /* symbol table entries */
                        /* are in st[0..next-1] */

/*---------------------------------------------------*/
```

```
void add(x, it)
char *x;
item_type it;
{
   char *malloc();    /* storage allocator from the */
                      /* standard library "libc"    */
                      /* that is automatically      */
                      /* loaded                     */
   int strlen();      /* string length function     */
                      /* from the standard library  */

   if (next == N) {
     printf("add: Error--Symbol table overflow\n");
     exit(1);
   }

   /* allocate storage for item "x" in symbol      */
   /* table and then copy "x"                       */
     st[next].id = malloc((unsigned) strlen(x) + 1);
     strcpy(st[next].id, x);
   st[next].t = it;
   next++;
}

/*---------------------------------------------------*/

int in_table(x)
char *x;
{
   int i;

   for(i = 0; i < next; i++)
     if (strcmp(x, st[i].id) == 0)
       return TRUE;
   return FALSE;
}

/*---------------------------------------------------*/

item_type get(x)    /* "get" should be called only */
                    /* after ensuring that item    */
                    /* "x" is in the symbol table   */
char *x;
{
```

```
    int i;

    for(i = 0; i < next;  i++)
      if (strcmp(x, st[i].id) == 0)
        return st[i].t;
    printf("get: %s item not in symbol table\n", x);
    exit(1);
}
```

```
/*-----------------------------------------------------*/
```

```
int full()
{
    return next == N;
}
```

```
/*-----------------------------------------------------*/
```

```
void clear()
{
    next = 0;
}
```

```
/*-----------------------------------------------------*/
```

The storage allocator `malloc` returns the null pointer value `NULL` (0) when there is no more memory available for allocation. Referring to the null memory location leads to an illegal-memory-location error with an unintelligible error message such as

```
Bus error - core dumped
```

A better error message can be given to the user by adding the code fragment

```
    if (st[last].id == NULL) {
      printf("add: Error--no more free storage\n");
      exit(1);
    }
```

after the call to the storage allocator

```
st[last].id = malloc((unsigned) strlen(x)+1);
```

Alternatively, the call to the storage allocator and the code fragment that prints the error message can be written together as

```
if ((st[last].id=malloc((unsigned) strlen(x)+1))
                                    == NULL) {
    printf("add: Error--no more free storage\n");
    exit(1);
}
```

The simple representation of the symbol table used in this example is not an efficient representation when the number of searches performed is large. In such a situation, a more complex representation, such as a hashed table or an ordered binary tree representation, will be more appropriate.

### 5.2 List Manipulation Functions

The problem is to write a set of functions to manipulate lists. These functions may be informally described as

| | |
|---|---|
| `add(head, i)` | add the integer i to the list pointed to by head |
| `delete(head, i)` | delete the integer i from the list pointed to by head |
| `in_list(head, i)` | return TRUE if the integer i is in the list pointed to by head and FALSE otherwise. |
| `empty(head)` | return TRUE if the list pointed to by head is empty and FALSE otherwise. |

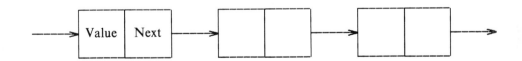

A List

Unlike the symbol table functions that operate only with one symbol table, the list manipulation functions can operate on different lists because the head of the list being manipulated is supplied explicitly as a parameter. The list heads must be declared in the user program as pointers to list elements, which are of type `node`. Type `node` and other declarations necessary for using the list manipulation functions are given in the file `list.h`:

```
/*----------------------------------------------------*/
/* list.h: Integer List Manipulation Routines    */
/*         Declarations File                      */
/*----------------------------------------------------*/


struct node {
   int value;
   struct node *next;
};

void add(), delete();
int in_list(), empty();

/*----------------------------------------------------*/
```

File `list.h` is included in the file containing definitions of the list manipulation functions; it must also be included in files that contain references to these functions.

The list manipulation functions are

```
/*--------------------------------------------------*/
/* add, delete, in_list, empty: Integer list        */
/*                              manipulation         */
/*                              routines             */
/*--------------------------------------------------*/

#include <stdio.h>
#include "list.h"

#define TRUE    1
#define FALSE   0

void add(phead, i)        /* address of list must be */
                          /* passed, i.e., pointer   */
                          /* to the head of the list */
struct node **phead;      /* note the double         */
                          /* indirection*/
int i;
{
   struct node *t;
   char *malloc();        /* storage allocator */

   /* search for the value "i" in the list */
     t = *phead;
     while (t != NULL && t->value != i)
       t = t->next;

   if (t == NULL) { /* insert "i" in the list        */
                    /* because it is not in the      */
                    /* list                          */
     /* allocate storage for one element */
       t = (struct node *)
                 malloc(sizeof(struct node));
     /* put the value "i" in this element */
       t->value = i;
     /* insert element at the head of the list       */
       t->next = *phead; *phead = t;
   }
}

/*--------------------------------------------------*/

void delete(phead, i)
```

```
struct node **phead;
int i;
{
   struct node *t, *temp;
   int free();

   if (*phead == NULL)
      ;      /* empty list */
   else {
      if ((*phead)->value == i) {
        /* first element in the list is to be */
        /* deleted */
         temp = *phead;
         *phead = (*phead)->next;
         free((char *) temp);
      }
      else {
        t = *phead;
        while (t->next!=NULL && t->next->value!=i)
           t = t->next;
        if (t->next != NULL) {
           temp = t->next;
           t->next = t->next->next;
           free((char *) temp);
        }
      }
   }
}

/*-----------------------------------------------*/

int in_list(phead, i)
struct node **phead;
int i;
{
   struct node *t;

   for (t = *phead; t != NULL; t = t->next)
      if (t->value == i)
         return TRUE;
   return FALSE;

}
```

```
/*----------------------------------------------------*/

int empty(phead)
struct node **phead;
{
    return *phead == NULL;
}

/*----------------------------------------------------*/
```

### 5.3 Class Buffer

The problem is to implement a class `buffer` that can be used to define circular character buffers of size `128`. The following operations are to be provided for `buffer` class objects:

| | |
|---|---|
| `empty()` | return `TRUE` if the buffer is empty; otherwise return `FALSE`. |
| `clear()` | clear the buffer; this function must also be used to initialize the buffer. |
| `put(c)` | add character `c` to the buffer if the buffer is not full and return 0 to indicate success; otherwise return -1 indicating failure. |
| `get()` | if the buffer is not empty, then return the next character in the buffer; otherwise return -1 indicating failure. |

Class `buffer` is declared as

```
#define SIZE    128

class buffer {
    int s[SIZE];
    int in, out, count;
public:
    int empty();
    void clear();
    int put(char);
    int get();
};
```

Functions of class `buffer` are implemented as

```
#define TRUE    1
#define FALSE   0
#define FAILURE (-1)
#define SUCCESS 0
/*--------------------------------------------------*/

int buffer.empty()
{
  return count == 0;
    /* could have also written this statement */
    /* simply as "return !count"; why? */
}

/*--------------------------------------------------*/

void buffer.clear()
{
  in = out = count = 0;
}

/*--------------------------------------------------*/

int buffer.put(char c)
{
  if (count == SIZE)
    return FAILURE;
  else {
    s[in] = c;
    in = (in + 1) % SIZE;   /* wrap around when    */
                            /* the end of the      */
                            /* buffer is reached   */
    count++;
    return SUCCESS;
  }
}

/*--------------------------------------------------*/

int buffer.get()
{
```

```
    char result;

    if (count == 0)
      return FAILURE;
    else {
      result = s[out];
      out = (out + 1) % SIZE;    /* wrap around */
      count--;
      return result;
    }
}

/*--------------------------------------------------------*/
```

## 6. Problems

1.  Modify the stack implementation (the one that uses files to provide data abstraction) so that the stack functions do not terminate the program when the user attempts to add an element to a full stack, delete an element from an empty stack and so on. Instead, the functions should return - 1 in such situations and 0 under normal conditions.

2.  In the implementation of the stack function `push`, instead of comparing the value of `next` with `MAX_SIZE`, I could have used the stack function `full` to determine whether or not the stack was full. Similarly, in the implementation of `pop` I could have used `empty`. What are the pros and cons of the two approaches?

3.  Function `clear`, in the symbol table example, clears the symbol table by setting variable `last` to 0. The storage locations pointed to by elements of the symbol table array `st` will not be reused (that is, they are effectively lost) because the symbol table is not explicitly deallocated (e.g., by using the deallocation function `free`). Modify `clear` so that it deallocates the elements of `st` before setting `last` to 0.

4.  Why was it necessary to impose a maximum limit on the number of items in the symbol table example? Is it possible to do away with the restriction of 200 items in the symbol table by using a list, instead of an array, to implement the symbol table? Implement the symbol table by using a list; make sure that this change is not visible to the users of these functions; i.e., syntactically and semantically, the functions have the same effect as far as the user is concerned.

5.  Modify the class `stack` example so that lists are used to store the *stack* elements. What are the pros and cons of using a list versus an array to

store elements?

6.  What modifications are necessary so that the `stack` can be used to store both `int` and `float` values? *Hint*: Use unions.

# Chapter 7

# Exceptions

An *exception* is an event that occurs unexpectedly or infrequently, such as division by zero or the premature interruption of program execution. Like Pascal, FORTRAN and ALGOL 60, but unlike PL/I and Ada, C does not provide exception handling facilities.

In languages without exception handling facilities, other methods must be used to indicate exceptions and to handle exceptions. The most common method is to have functions return *status codes* or "funny values" to indicate exceptional conditions [Lee 1983]. If the value returned by a function indicates that an exception has occurred during the function call, then appropriate action is taken. However, the status code technique does not allow the detection and handling of processor exceptions such as one raised by an attempt to divide by zero; nor can this technique help detect and handle exceptions raised from the program environment, e.g., an exception raised by a user wanting to terminate program execution prematurely. The status code technique must be supplemented by some other mechanism, possibly provided by the operating system.

Two techniques are used for handling exceptions in C:

1. *Status Codes*: by convention, a – 1 value is often returned by functions to indicate that an exception occurred during function execution. For example, function `getc` returns a – 1 if it encounters an end-of-file.

2. *UNIX Signals*:[50] An exception handler is established by instructing the UNIX system to invoke a specific C function (the *exception handler*) upon the receipt of a signal. C programs set up signal handlers by means of a library function that interacts with the UNIX system. Signals can be generated by the hardware or the software.

---

50. The UNIX *signal* mechanism is an asynchronous inter-process communication mechanism. Among other things, signals are used to indicate the occurrence of exceptions. To conform with UNIX terminology, the words *signal* and *exception* will be used interchangeably when there is no confusion about the meaning; e.g., both a signal handler and an exception handler mean the same thing.

UNIX signals are generally used to handle [Lee 1983]

1.  exceptions raised from the environment that affect program execution; e.g., the *delete* character is used to generate a signal indicating that the currently executing program should terminate.

2.  exceptions that are detected by the hardware, e.g., illegal memory reference.

3.  exceptions that could have been handled by returning status codes.

Signals are generated automatically as a result of program errors or are sent explicitly by one process to another.[51]

The use of status codes to indicate exceptions is straightforward and has been illustrated in many of the examples in earlier chapters. This chapter will focus on the use of UNIX signals to handle exceptions. A word of caution—C programs using signals may not be portable to another operating system without some changes.

## 1. The Different Signals

Many different kinds of signals can be handled in C programs running on a UNIX system. These are declared in the header file `<signal.h>`. Some of the signals that are handled on the *UNIX System (Release 5.0)* [AT&T UNIX (Release 5.0) 1982] are

---

51. The user typing the *delete* character to interrupt a currently executing process causes the keyboard handler to generate an appropriate signal.

| name | number | comments |
|------|--------|----------|
| SIGHUP | 1 | hangup |
| SIGINT | 2 | interrupt |
| SIGQUIT | 3 | quit |
| SIGILL | 4 | illegal instruction (not reset when caught) |
| SIGTRAP | 5 | trace trap (not reset when caught) |
| SIGIOT | 6 | IOT instruction |
| SIGEMT | 7 | EMT instruction |
| SIGFPE | 8 | floating point exception |
| SIGKILL | 9 | kill (cannot be caught or ignored) |
| SIGBUS | 10 | bus error |
| SIGSEGV | 11 | segmentation violation |
| SIGSYS | 12 | bad argument to system call |
| SIGPIPE | 13 | write on a pipe with no one to read it |
| SIGALRM | 14 | alarm clock |
| SIGTERM | 15 | software termination signal |
| SIGUSR1 | 16 | user-defined signal 1 |
| SIGUSR2 | 17 | user-defined signal 2 |
| SIGCLD | 18 | death of a child process |
| SIGPWR | 19 | power failure |

Exceptions such as those resulting from arithmetic overflow and division by zero are implementation-dependent. For example, most implementations of C ignore integer overflow [Ritchie 1980].

Unlike languages with explicit facilities for exception handling, which allow an unlimited number of exceptions to be declared and handled, only a limited number of different exceptions can be handled in C; moreover, only two exceptions can be declared by the user.

## 2. Setting Up Signal/Exception Handlers

The UNIX system function `signal` is called to establish a signal handler, i.e., an exception handler. It has the specification

```
#include <sys/signal.h>

  int (*signal(sig, func))()
  int sig;
  int (*func)();
```

Function `signal` has two formal parameters: `sig`, which specifies the signal to be handled, and `func`, which is a pointer to a function that specifies how the signal is to be handled; `func` is the signal handler that is invoked upon the receipt of signal `sig`. Function `signal` returns the previous value of `func` for the specified signal `sig`, except in case of an error when it returns − 1.

The actual parameter corresponding to `func` can be one of three values: `SIG_DFL`, `SIG_IGN` or a *pointer to a function*. The actions prescribed by these values are as follows:[52]

| **value of** func | **action** |
|---|---|
| `SIG_DFL` | terminate process upon receipt of a signal |
| `SIG_IGN` | ignore signal |
| *function address* | execute the specified function upon receipt of the signal |

The following program segment illustrates the association of the signal handler *handler* with the signal *signal_name*:

```
#include <signal.h>      /* signal declarations */
{
   .
   .
   .
   /* associate signal with its handler */
     signal(signal_name, handler);
   .
   .
   .
}
```

Another paradigm[53] is the following one, which associates a signal handler with a signal only if the user has not previously specified that the signal is to be ignored; the use of this paradigm is necessary only in contexts in which a user may have specified that a signal is to be ignored:

---

52. A *process* is a component of a program that executes in parallel with the rest of the program. Processes are discussed in detail in Chapter 8 titled *Concurrent Programming*.

53. This paradigm was brought to my attention by John Linderman, a colleague at AT&T Bell Labs.

```
#include <signal.h>
{
   int (*old)();
   .
   .
   .
   if ((old = signal(signal_name, SIG_IGN)) != SIG_IGN)
     signal(signal_name, handler);
   .
   .
   .
}
```

A reference to the original signal handler is saved in the variable `old` for possible reassociation with signal *signal_name* later. If the original signal handler is to be not saved, then the above *if* statement can be written as

```
if (signal(signal_name, SIG_IGN) != SIG_IGN)
   signal(signal_name, handler);
```

The signal handler *handler* should be of the form

```
int handler(i)        /* Handle signal "i" */
int i;
{
   .
   .
   .
   /* Reset signal; i.e., reassociate signal "i" */
   /* with its handler */
     signal(i, handler);
   .
   .
   .
}
```

When a signal for which an exception handler has been specified is received, normal program execution is suspended and control is transferred to the exception handler. A signal is passed as an argument to its exception handler. Upon normal completion of the exception handler, program execution is

resumed at the point where it was interrupted.  Program execution may not be
resumed in some cases, e.g.,

- the exception handler may terminate the program by calling function
  `exit`.

- the exception handler may force program execution to be resumed at a
  point other than the point of interruption by calling the function `longjmp`
  (non-local *goto*).

In the exception handler, it is necessary to reassociate the signal with the
handler because most signals are automatically reset so that the default action
is performed when the signal next occurs.[54]

**2.1 An Example Illustrating the Use of Signals to Handle Floating Point Errors**

The problem is to write a program that computes the real roots of a quadratic
equation.  The program should print an appropriate error message if it is
aborted as a result of a floating point exception such as a floating point divide
by zero or a floating point overflow.  Floating point exceptions generate the
signal `SIGFPE`.

The two roots, $r_1$ and $r_2$, of a quadratic equation

$$a x^2 + b x + c = 0.0$$

are given by the equations

$$r_1 = \frac{-b - \sqrt{b^2 - 4.0 a c}}{2.0 a}$$

and

$$r_2 = \frac{-b + \sqrt{b^2 - 4.0 a c}}{2.0 a}$$

These roots will be real only if

$$b^2 - 4.0 a c > 0.0$$

The program to compute the roots is

---

54. In the new version of **Berkeley** UNIX (i.e., version 4.2) it is not necessary to reassociate the signal with the handler because the handler association is not affected when a signal is handled.

```
/*-------------------------------------------------*/
/* main: A program to compute the real roots       */
/*        of a quadratic equation                  */
/*-------------------------------------------------*/

#include <stdio.h>
#include <signal.h>    /* on Unix 5.0 use    */
                       /* "<sys/signal.h> "*/
#include <math.h>      /* contains declaration for */
                       /* function "sqrt" */

main()
{
   float a, b, c;
   float r1, r2;
   float temp;

   int float_error();

   /* set up the exception handler */
     signal(SIGFPE, float_error);

   printf("Type 3 coefficients separated by blanks:");
   if (scanf("%f %f %f", &a, &b, &c) != 3) {
     printf("Error: No input or incomplete input\n");
     exit(1);
   }


   if (a == 0.0) {
     printf("Equation is not quadratic");
     printf(" because the first coefficient is 0\n");
     exit(1);
   }

   if (b * b - 4.0 * a * c < 0.0) {
     printf("Quadratic equation has no real roots\n");
     exit(1);
   }

   temp = (float) sqrt(b * b - 4.0 * a * c);

   r1 = (- b + temp) / (2.0 * a);
```

```
   r2 = (- b - temp) / (2.0 * a);

   printf("The two roots are %g and %g\n", r1, r2);
}
/*-------------------------------------------------*/


/*-------------------------------------------------*/
/* float_error: floating point exception handler */
/*-------------------------------------------------*/

int float_error(i)
int i;
{
   printf("Floating point exception raised!\n");
   exit(1);
}
/*-------------------------------------------------*/
```

The floating point exception handler function `float_error` cannot print
the values of the variables a, b and c because it cannot access them; these
variables are local to the function `main`. However, if they were made global
to `main`, i.e., if they were made external variables, then they would become
accessible from `float_error`, making it possible to print their values to
provide the user with better information.

If an exception handler is not provided in this program, then it will abort with
a cryptic error message upon the occurrence of a floating point error.

The above program uses the function `sqrt` that is contained in the math
library `libm`; consequently, it must be compiled with the math library `libm`.
More accurately, because the math library is precompiled, the roots program
(assume that it is contained in file `roots.c`) must be linked and loaded with
the math library, e.g.,

```
cc -o roots roots.c -lm
```

## 3. Generating/Sending Signals

Signals can be generated implicitly or explicitly. Signals are generated
implicitly in a program by the underlying software or hardware when some
unusual condition occurs, e.g., a floating point divide by zero, floating point
overflow or the user typing the *delete* character at the terminal.

Signals are generated explicitly when a process sends a signal to another process or itself by calling function `kill`, which has the specification

```
int kill(pid, sig)
int pid, sig;
```

Argument `pid` is the process identification number of the process to which the signal `sig` is being sent.

## 4. Examples

The calculator example given in Chapter 1 will be modified so that it can handle exceptions resulting from both implicitly and explicitly generated signals. Three versions of the calculator example will be presented to illustrate exception handling semantics.

### 4.1 Calculator Example with Exception Handling (Version 1)

The problem is to modify the calculator example given in Chapter 1 so that it can handle floating point exceptions and premature termination signals; a premature termination signal can be sent to the currently executing process by typing a *delete* character at the terminal. In case the program is sent a termination signal, a confirmation should be requested from the user; if the user answers affirmatively, then the program should terminate; otherwise, the program should continue execution.

The calculator program, modified to handle exceptions, is

```
/*----------------------------------------------------*/
/* main: A Simple Calculator with Exception           */
/*        Handling (version 1)                        */
/*----------------------------------------------------*/

#include <stdio.h>
#include <signal.h>   /* on Unix 5.0 use  */
                       /* "<sys/signal.h>" */

#define PROMPT ':'

main()
{
  int float_error(), term_inter();
  float a, b;
  char opr;
  float result;

  /* set up the interrupt/exception handlers */
    signal(SIGFPE, float_error);
    signal(SIGINT, term_inter);

  while(putchar(PROMPT),scanf("%f%c%f",&a,&opr,&b)!=EO

    switch (opr) {
      case '+': result = a + b; break;
      case '-': result = a - b; break;
      case '*': result = a * b; break;
      case '/': result = a / b; break;
      default:
        printf("ERROR **** illegal operator\n");
        exit(1);
    }

    printf("result is %g\n", result);
  }
  exit(0);
}

/*----------------------------------------------------*/
/* float_error: floating point error handler          */
/*----------------------------------------------------*/
```

```
int float_error(i)
int i;     /* signal being handled */
{
   signal(SIGFPE, float_error);

   printf("You have raised a floating point error\n");
   printf("such as dividing by 0.0; the result of\n");
   printf("this operation will not be meaningful\n");
}
/*-------------------------------------------------*/

/*-------------------------------------------------*/
/* term_inter: handler for handling user-          */
/*             generated interrupts from the       */
/*             keyboard, i.e., del" or "break"      */
/*             characters                          */
/*-------------------------------------------------*/

int term_inter(i)
int i;     /* signal being handled */
{
   int c;

   signal(SIGINT, term_inter);

   printf("Do you really want to quit? Y or N:");

   c = getchar();
   switch (c) {
   case 'Y': case 'y': exit(0);
   default: printf("continue\n");
   }

}
/*-------------------------------------------------*/
```

### 4.2  Calculator Example with Exception Handling (Version 2)

A floating point error may cause the above version of the calculator program to go into an infinite loop because on some computers the instruction causing the error is executed again upon return from the exception handler.

This infinite loop problem can be avoided by ensuring that the floating point error does not occur again upon return from the exception handler. A simple way of doing this is to change the values of the operands of the operation causing the floating point exception in the exception handler. In this example, the operation causing the exception can be one of +, -, * or /; changing the values of their operands, a and b, to 1.0 will ensure that the floating point exception will not be raised upon return from the exception handler float_error. Variables a and b must be made global, i.e., external, to allow the exception handler float_error to change their values:[55]

```
/*----------------------------------------------------*/
/* main: A Simple Calculator with Exception           */
/*       Handling (version 2)                         */
/*----------------------------------------------------*/

#include <stdio.h>
#include <signal.h>    /* on Unix 5.0 use  */
                       /* "<sys/signal.h>" */

#define PROMPT ':'

float a, b;
char opr;
float result;

main()
{
   int float_error(), term_inter();

   /* set up the interrupt/exception handlers */
     signal(SIGFPE, float_error);
     signal(SIGINT, term_inter);
```

---

55. *Warning*: This solution is implementation dependent because it relies on the fact that upon return from the signal handler float_error, new values of variables a and b will be used upon resumption of normal program execution. Whether or not the new values are used depends upon the code generated by the C compiler. For example, if the compiler has stored the value of variable b in a register, then changing its value in the signal handler may not lead to the use of the new value upon resumption of normal program execution.

The Berkeley UNIX [Berkeley UNIX 1981] C compiler uses the new values of a and b, but the AT&T UNIX [AT&T UNIX (Release 5.0) 1982] C compiler does not use the new values. For the latter compiler, the longjmp strategy illustrated in the next version of the calculator must be used; this strategy is better because it is not implementation dependent.

```
while(putchar(PROMPT),scanf("%f%c%f",&a,&opr,&b)!=EOF)

    switch (opr) {
      case '+': result = a + b; break;
      case '-': result = a - b; break;
      case '*': result = a * b; break;
      case '/': result = a / b; break;
      default:
        printf("ERROR **** illegal operator\n");
        exit(1);
    }

    printf("result is %g\n", result);
  }
  exit(0);
}

/*------------------------------------------------*/
/* float_error: floating point error handler      */
/*------------------------------------------------*/

int float_error(i)
int i;     /* signal being handled */
{
  signal(SIGFPE, float_error);

  printf("You have raised a floating point error\n");
  printf("such as dividing by 0.0; the result of\n");
  printf("this operation will not be meaningful\n");

  /* change the operands so that a floating point */
  /* exception is not raised */
    a = b = 1.0;
}
/*------------------------------------------------*/

/*------------------------------------------------*/
/* term_inter: handler for handling user          */
/*             generated interrupts from the      */
/*             keyboard, i.e., del" or "break"    */
/*             characters                         */
/*------------------------------------------------*/

int term_inter(i)
```

```
int i;      /* signal being handled */
{
  int c;

  signal(SIGINT, term_inter);

  printf("Do you really want to quit? Y or N:");

  c = getchar();
  switch (c) {
  case 'Y': case 'y': exit(0);
  default: printf("continue\n");
  }

}
/*-----------------------------------------------*/
```

### 4.3 Calculator Example with Exception Handling (Version 3)

Although the latest modifications eliminated problems with the exception handler `float_error`, there are still some problems with the second exception handler `term_inter`. Suppose the user interrupts the program with a `del` character when the program is trying to read more data and then responds negatively to the "quit" query. After the error handler returns, `scanf` will return `EOF`, causing program termination. Program termination can be prevented by using `setjmp` to save the environment at the point where execution should be resumed and then using `longjmp` (non-local goto) in the interrupt handler to resume execution; the call `longjmp(env, 0)` restores the program environment saved in the buffer `env` by the last call to `setjmp`.

```
/*------------------------------------------------*/
/* main: A Simple Calculator with Exception       */
/*       Handling (version 3)                     */
/*------------------------------------------------*/

#include <stdio.h>
#include <signal.h>    /* on Unix 5.0 use  */
                       /* "<sys/signal.h>" */
#include <setjmp.h>

#define PROMPT ':'

float a, b;
char opr;
float result;

jmp_buf env;  /* buffer used to save the program */
              /* state that is to be used when   */
              /* resuming program execution upon */
              /* return from the terminal        */
              /* exception handler "term_inter"  */

main()
{
  int float_error(), term_inter();
  int setjmp();

  /* set up the interrupt/exception handlers */
     signal(SIGFPE, float_error);
     signal(SIGINT, term_inter);

  /* save start area */
    setjmp(env);

while(putchar(PROMPT),scanf("%f%c%f",&a,&opr,&b)!=EOF)

    switch (opr) {
      case '+': result = a + b; break;
      case '-': result = a - b; break;
      case '*': result = a * b; break;
      case '/': result = a / b; break;
      default:
        printf("ERROR **** illegal operator\n");
```

```
         exit(1);
      }

      printf("result is %g\n", result);
   }
   exit(0);
}

/*------------------------------------------------*/
/* float_error: floating point error handler     */
/*------------------------------------------------*/

int float_error(i)
int i;    /* signal being handled */
{
   signal(SIGFPE, float_error);

   printf("You have raised a floating point error\n");
   printf("such as dividing by 0.0; the result of\n");
   printf("this operation will not be meaningful\n");

   /* change the operands so that a floating point */
   /* exception is not raised */
      a = b = 1.0;

}
/*------------------------------------------------*/

/*------------------------------------------------*/
/* term_inter: handler for handling user          */
/*             generated interrupts from the      */
/*             keyboard, i.e., del" or "break"     */
/*             characters                          */
/*------------------------------------------------*/

int term_inter(i)
int i;    /* signal being handled */
{
   int c;
   void longjmp();

   signal(SIGINT, term_inter);

   printf("Do you really want to quit? Y or N:");
```

```
    c = getchar();
    switch (c) {
    case 'Y': case 'y': exit(0);
    default: printf("continue\n"); longjmp(env, 0);
    }

}
/*---------------------------------------------------*/
```

## 5. Problems

1. In the calculator program, what happens when a user types the `del` character instead of the typing `Y` or `N` in response to the question

   > `Do you really want to quit? Y or N:`

   printed by the exception handler `term_inter`? Try to verify your answer by executing the calculator program on your computer.

2. Modify the final version of the calculator program so that the exception handler `float_error` returns by executing `longjmp`.

3. Describe an example program where it is advantageous or necessary to ignore signals; i.e., the signal handler `SIG_IGN` has been associated with one or more signals.

# Chapter 8

# Concurrent Programming

A *concurrent program* is a program built from sequential components, called *processes*, which execute in parallel. Concurrent programming is desirable for many reasons [Hoare 1978; Gehani 1983b]:

- Concurrent programming facilities provide notational convenience and conceptual elegance in writing operating systems, real-time systems, database systems and simulation programs, all of which may have many events occurring concurrently.

- Inherently concurrent algorithms are best expressed with the concurrency explicitly stated; otherwise, the structure of the algorithm may be lost.

- Concurrent programming can reduce program execution time because genuine multiprocessing hardware can be used to execute different parts of a program in parallel.

- Concurrent programming can reduce program execution time because lengthy input/output operations and program execution by the CPU (central processing unit) can proceed in parallel.

A programming language that does not provide facilities for concurrent programming discourages programmers from inventing concurrent solutions for their problems.

The C language does not provide concurrent programming facilities; nevertheless, concurrent programs can still be written in C:

> *In case of C under UNIX, concurrency and interprocess communication, like I/O, is supplied by UNIX kernel calls, and is not part of the C language proper. However, it is a fine example of a language in current use that in practice does offer concurrency* [Pratt 1983].

Concurrent programs are written in C by using library functions that call upon the underlying operating system to provide concurrency. Dennis Ritchie, the designer of C, intentionally did not incorporate concurrent programming facilities in C for several reasons [Ritchie 1978]:

1. One of the design goals of C was to keep the language small.

2. Providing concurrent programming facilities in a programming language is inappropriate because it makes the hard task of language design even more difficult.

3. Incorporating concurrent programming facilities in programming languages is inappropriate because these facilities tend to make strong assumptions about the underlying operating system, while in practice there may be a poor match between these facilities and the operating system.

## 1. Concurrent Programming in C Under the UNIX Operating System

A concurrent C program consists of two or more complete sequential C programs executing in parallel. An executing program is called a *process* in C. Processes interact with each other to accomplish the common objective of the concurrent C program. Process interaction consists of data communication and synchronization.

Concurrency is introduced into a C program by performing the following actions:

1. An identical copy of a process is created by calling the `fork` function.

2. This new process is converted to the desired process by using the `execl` function to overlay some other program image (executable version of the program, i.e., the `a.out` file produced by the C compiler) on top of the code being executed by the new process.[56]

3. Interprocess communication is established by using the UNIX *pipe* facility. A pipe may informally be described as a mechanism that allows the output of one process to be made the input of another process without the use of temporary files. Although pipes are the primary interprocess communication mechanism, *signals* and files can also be used.

## 2. Creating a Process Using the `fork` Library Function

A new process is created by executing the `fork` system call; the process created by `fork` is nearly, but not quite, identical to the process that executes the `fork` system call. The new process (i.e., the *child* process) and the creating process (i.e., the *parent* process) differ in the following aspects:

---

56. Overlaying the new process with another program image is, strictly speaking, not necessary because the new process can continue to execute the original program—possibly a different section of the program.

1. The parent and child processes have different *process identification numbers* (*pids*). This difference distinguishes the parent and the child processes.

2. The value returned by fork is different in the two processes. In the parent process, the value returned by fork is the process identification number of the child, while in the child process, the value returned is 0.

3. The child process inherits all the open files and pipes of its parent; however, the child has its own copy of the file and pipe descriptors.

For example, successful execution of the fork system call in the *switch* statement

```
switch (pid = fork()) {
case 0: /* child process */
   .
   .
   .

case -1: /* parent process--unsuccessful in */
         /* creating a new process */
   .
   .
   .

default: /* parent process--successful in */
         /* creating a new process */
   .
   .
   .
}
```

creates a new process; the parent process will continue by executing the alternative labeled default while the child process will start by executing the alternative labeled case 0. If fork is unable to create a new process, then it returns -1 and the process invoking fork continues by executing the alternative labeled case -1.

A parent process can wait for its child processes to terminate by means of the library function wait.

There are two strategies for structuring concurrent programs in which the parent and child processes have to perform different tasks:

1. The child process executes the same program as the parent process. However, each process executes a different part of the program. For example, the child process executes only the code in the alternative

labeled `case 0` and the parent process executes only the code in the alternative labeled `default`.

2. The parent process continues executing the original program while the child process executes another program that is overlaid on it.

The first strategy suffers from some disadvantages: it wastes memory because it contains code that will not be executed; moreover, it may lead to unpredictable errors because both the parent and child processes can update the same files and read from and write to the same pipes. The concurrent program is not modular because each process contains irrelevant code and because each process can access files and pipes that are relevant only to the other process.

The second strategy suffers from the disadvantage that establishing communication between the two processes requires much effort; fortunately, much of this effort is straightforward and routine. On the positive side, this strategy allows independently written programs to be executed in parallel and, at the same time, cooperate with each other in accomplishing a common goal. The examples in this book will be based on the second strategy for structuring concurrent programs.

## 3. The `execl` Library Function for Overlaying Processes

Once the child process has been created, it can be made to execute a desired program P with the help of the `execl` library function. The effect of

$$execl(\textit{full name of } P, \ P, \ 0)$$

is to overlay the process executing the call with the specified program P (to be more precise, P is a file which is a compiled and ready-to-execute version of a C program). The actual parameter *full name of* P specifies the location of the program P in the UNIX file system (in UNIX terminology, it is the path name of file P).[57]

As a more detailed example, consider the program segment

---

57. For `execl` function details please read the description of the *exec* commands in Appendix A titled *Some Library Functions*.

```
switch (pid = fork()) {
case 0: /* child process */
     .

     .

     .
   execl("/a1/nhg/acb/count", "count", 0);
     .

     .

     .
case -1: /* parent process--unsuccessful in */
         /* creating a new process */
     .

     .

     .
default: /* parent process--successful in */
         /* creating a new process */
     .

     .

     .
}
```

The process created by `fork` will execute the compiled program named `count` whose complete name is /a1/nhg/acb/count.

## 4. Pipes—A Synchronous Communication Mechanism

A *pipe* is a one-way synchronous communication channel that is used by two processes to communicate and synchronize with each other. If information is to be sent in both directions, then two pipes must be used. One process writes at the *write* end of a pipe while the second process reads from the *read* end of the pipe. A pipe automatically buffers information between the two processes.

Pipes are similar to files, but there are some differences:

- An attempt to write into a "full" pipe causes the writing process to be delayed until the pipe is not full, i.e., until the process at the read end of the pipe reads from the pipe. Similarly, an attempt to read from an "empty" pipe is delayed until the pipe becomes non-empty, i.e., until the process at the write end of the pipe writes into the pipe. Delaying a process attempting to write to a full pipe and delaying a process attempting to read from an empty pipe are the primary means of synchronization in concurrent C programs.

- Pipes must be accessed sequentially whereas files may be accessed randomly (provided the files being accessed reside on disk).

Prior to the creation of a new process, pipes must be set up in the parent process; *pipe descriptors* (similar to file descriptors) must be allocated. Pipe descriptors identify the read and write ends of the pipe. As mentioned earlier, a child process inherits pipes, files and data from its parent process; the file and pipe descriptors in the child process are copies of the file and pipe descriptors of the parent process.

### 4.1 Setting Up a Pipe

Pipes are set up by executing the `pipe` system call. As an illustration of the use of `pipe`, suppose that file descriptors 0, 1 and 2 have been allocated initially and that they are associated with the streams `stdin`, `stdout` and `stderr`, respectively; no other file descriptors have been allocated.

| 0 | 1 | 2 |
|---|---|---|
| std. input file | std. output file | std. error file |

Now assume that p has been defined a two-element integer array:

```
int p[2];
```

Then the system call

```
pipe(p);
```

allocates the two next highest file descriptors, i.e., 3 and 4, to be used as pipe descriptors:

| 0 | 1 | 2 | 3 | 4 |
|---|---|---|---|---|
| std. input file | std. output file | std. error file | $p_{read}$ | $p_{write}$ |
| | | | p[0] | p[1] |

File descriptor p[0] represents the read end of the pipe and file descriptor p[1] represents the write end of the pipe. Function `pipe` returns 0 if it is successful and -1 otherwise.

System calls `read` and `write` can be used to read from and write to the pipe. Alternately, a stream can be associated with each end of the pipe by using function `fdopen` and then all functions, such as `putc` and `getc`, that are used with streams can be used with pipes. For example, the write end of pipe p can be converted to a stream pointed to by `fp` as follows:

```
FILE *fdopen(), *fp;
.
.
.
fp = fdopen(p[1], "w");
```

Characters can now be written to the pipe by using functions that are used to write to streams, e.g.,

```
putc(c, fp);
```

## 4.2 Redirection of Standard Input/Output

As I mentioned earlier, establishing communication between two processes executing different programs requires much effort. Let us now see how this communication is established. Suppose that

- the child process executes an independently written program that reads from the standard input stream `stdin` and writes to the standard output stream `stdout`; i.e., it uses the macro `getchar` and the function `printf`.

- the parent and child processes are to communicate by using two pipes p and q; i.e., the parent process supplies data to the child process via pipe p and it expects results via q.

How is communication to be established between the child and parent processes? The child process expects to get its input from `stdin`, but when executing in parallel the input will be supplied by the parent process via pipe p; similarly, the child process must send its output to pipe q instead of `stdout`. How are these differences to be reconciled?

One way of solving this problem is to *redirect standard input and output* in the child process. The standard input file is made synonymous with the read end of pipe p; i.e., the file descriptor 0 is made to refer to the read end of the pipe p; similarly, file descriptor 1 is associated with the write end of the pipe q.

Assuming that the pipes p and q have been established, i.e., the calls

```
pipe(p);
pipe(q);
```

have been made, the standard input and output file descriptors are associated with the pipes by changing the following associations of the file and pipe descriptors in the child process

| 0 | 1 | 2 | 3 | 4 | 5 | 6 |
|---|---|---|---|---|---|---|
| std. input file | std. output file | std. error file | $p_{read}$ | $p_{write}$ | $q_{read}$ | $q_{write}$ |
|  |  |  | p[0] | p[1] | q[0] | q[1] |

to

| 0 | 1 | 2 | 3 | 4 | 5 | 6 |
|---|---|---|---|---|---|---|
| $p_{read}$ | $q_{write}$ | std. error file | $p_{read}$ | $p_{write}$ | $q_{read}$ | $q_{write}$ |
|  |  |  | p[0] | p[1] | q[0] | q[1] |

Changing the file and pipe descriptor associations in the child process has no effect on the file and pipe descriptor associations in the parent process (initially the child and parent processes have the same file and pipe descriptor associations).

In the child process, the write end of pipe p (p[1]) and the read end of pipe q (q[0]) will not be used. Moreover, descriptor 0 will be used to access the read end of pipe p instead of pipe descriptor p[1] and descriptor 1 will be used to access the write end of pipe q instead of pipe descriptor q[0]. Consequently, pipe descriptors p[0], p[1], q[0] and q[1] can be all deallocated, i.e., closed. Deallocating a descriptor severs the association between a file and its descriptor:

| 0 | 1 | 2 |
|---|---|---|
| $p_{read}$ | $q_{write}$ | std.<br>error<br>file |

Deallocating descriptors

1. allows the deallocated descriptors to be allocated and used elsewhere (only 20 file or pipe descriptors can be open at any time [AT&T UNIX (Release 5.0) 1982]).[58]

2. prevents inadvertent use of descriptors that should not be used (an error will be diagnosed if an attempt is made to use a descriptor that has been deallocated).

3. allows the reading end of a pipe to sense an end of pipe (EOF) when all the descriptors used to write to a pipe are closed; any open descriptor that refers to the write end of a pipe will prevent an EOF from being sensed at the read end, even though the descriptor may never be used to write to the pipe.

The following sequence of system calls is used to sever file descriptor 0 from standard input file, associate it with the read end of pipe p, and then close the descriptor p [ 0 ] [Bourne 1982]:

---

58. The number of file or pipe descriptors that can be open at any time is implementation dependent.

```
close(0);        /* file descriptor 0 is          */
                 /* deallocated by closing the    */
                 /* file associated with it, i.e., */
                 /* standard input                */

dup(p[0]);       /* make the lowest available file */
                 /* descriptor, i.e., 0,          */
                 /* synonymous with p[0], i.e.,   */
                 /* the read end of the pipe "p"  */

close(p[0]);     /* close descriptor p[0] because */
                 /* no process will read from pipe */
                 /* "p" directly by using pipe    */
                 /* descriptor p[0], but will     */
                 /* instead read from it by using */
                 /* descriptor 0 */
```

Functions, such as scanf and getchar, that read from the standard input stdin can now be used to read from pipe p.

Similarly, file descriptor 1 is associated with the write end of pipe p by the following sequence of system calls:

```
close(1); dup(q[1]); close(q[1]);
```

Both of the above sequences of system calls rely on the fact that descriptors 0 and 1 are allocated; otherwise system call close will fail.

## 5. Examples

I will illustrate concurrent programming in C by means of two simple examples. In the first example, a request to copy a file results in a process being created to do the actual file copy while the parent process continues execution without waiting for the child process to complete file copy; i.e., the file copying is done in parallel with the process requesting the copy. There is no communication between the parent and the child process. In the second example, a child process is created to count characters for the parent process. Bidirectional communication is established between the parent and child processes by using two pipes: one pipe is used by the parent process to send characters to the child process; the other pipe is used by the parent process to receive the character total from the child process.

## 5.1  Asynchronous or Parallel File Copy

Write a function acopy that asynchronously copies one file to another; i.e., acopy does not make its caller wait while the file is being copied. Function acopy checks to ensure that the two files are accessible and then creates a new process that does the file copy in parallel with its caller. The new process executes the program copy with the full name /a1/nhg/acb/copy.

Function acopy can be abstractly described as

*check to determine if the source and destination files can be opened*
*for reading and writing, respectively*
*create a process to do the actual file copying and return without*
*waiting for this process*

```
/*---------------------------------------------------*/
/* acopy: Asynchronously copies one file to          */
/*        another                                    */
/*---------------------------------------------------*/

#include <stdio.h>

int acopy(src, dest)    /* asynchronous copy file    */
                        /* "src" to "dest"; return   */
                        /* -1 if an error occurs;    */
                        /* otherwise return 0        */
char *src, *dest;
{
  FILE *fopen(), *fs, *fd;
  int fclose();
  int fork(), pid;

  if ((fs = fopen(src, "r")) == NULL) {
    printf("acopy: cannot open file %s\n", src);
    return -1;
  }
  if ((fd = fopen(dest, "w")) == NULL) {
    printf("acopy: cannot open file %s\n", dest);
    fclose(fs);
    return -1;
  }
  fclose(fs);
```

```
fclose(fd);

switch (pid = fork()) {
case 0: /* child process that will copy the    */
        /* file in parallel with the program    */
        /* calling this function */
   execl("/a1/nhg/acb/copy","copy",src,dest,0);
       /* if "execl" executes successfully it */
       /* will not return */
   printf("acopy: exec failed\n");
   return -1;
case -1: /* parent process--unsuccessful in    */
         /*creating a new process */
   printf("acopy: cannot fork a process\n");
   return -1;
default: /* parent process--successful return */
   return 0;
   }
}

/*-------------------------------------------------*/
```

As a minor optimization, the *return* statement has been used in this *switch* statement instead of the *break* statement.

Program copy, the program executed by the child process created by acopy, is a compiled version of the file copy.c:

```
/*-------------------------------------------------*/
/* copy: Copy file "a" to file "b"                 */
/*-------------------------------------------------*/

#include <stdio.h>

main(argc, argv)    /* files to be copied are      */
                    /* passed as arguments to      */
                    /* this function from the      */
                    /* command line. File in       */
                    /* "argv[1]" is to be copied   */
                    /* to "argv[2]"                */
int argc;
char *argv[];
{
  FILE *fopen(), *fs, *fd;
  int fclose();
  int c;

  fs = fopen(argv[1], "r");  /* open file for */
                             /* reading       */
  fd = fopen(argv[2], "w");  /* open file for */
                             /* writing       */

  while ((c = fgetc(fs)) != EOF)
    fputc(c, fd);

  fclose(fs);
  fclose(fd);
}

/*-------------------------------------------------*/
```

File copy.c is compiled as

```
cc -o copy copy.c
```

to produce the executable form copy.

## 5.2  Parallel Counting of the Non-Formatting Characters in a File

A file contains formatting commands and text.  The formatting commands all start with a period in column one and are terminated by the newline character. The problem is to write a program that counts the number of characters in the text, i.e., the number of characters in the file minus the characters in the formatting commands.

Two processes are used in the solution: process `textcount` reads the text file and deletes the formatting commands while passing the text lines on to the second process `count`; process `count` counts the characters and on reaching the end of the text sends the character total to the first process.  Two pipes, p and q, are set up for communication between the two processes.  Pipe p is used by `textcount` to send text characters to `count`.  Pipe q is used by `count` to send the character total to `textcount`.

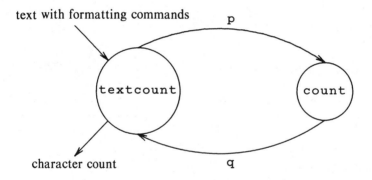

text with formatting commands          p

`textcount`                    `count`

character count                          q

Counting Characters in Parallel

Program `count` is implemented as

```
/*----------------------------------------------------*/
/* count: determines the total number of              */
/*          characters in a file                      */
/*----------------------------------------------------*/

#include <stdio.h>

main()
{
   int count = 0;

   while (getchar() != EOF)
     count++;
   printf("%d\n", count);
}

/*-------------------------------------------------*/
```

Program count expects its input from stdin and writes its output to stdout. Consequently, the process that executes count must redirect input and output so that count reads input from pipe p and writes its output to pipe q.

```
/*--------------------------------------------------*/
/* textcount: Count the number of characters in   */
/*            the file after deleting all the      */
/*            text formatting commands, lines      */
/*            that begin with a "." in column 1    */
/*--------------------------------------------------*/

#include <stdio.h>

#define R  0  /* stdin and subscript for     */
              /* read end  of the pipe       */
#define W  1  /* stdout and subscript for    */
              /* write end of the pipe       */
#define TRUE     1
#define FALSE    0
#define PERIOD   '.'

main()
{
   int pid;            /* process id returned by fork */
   int p[2], q[2]; /* the two pipes; pipe "p"     */
                   /* will be used to send the    */
                   /* text with the formatting    */
                   /* commands stripped to        */
                   /* "count"; pipe "q" will be   */
                   /* used to receive the total   */
                   /* number of characters from   */
                   /* "count"*/
   FILE *fdopen(), *fp;

   int c;
   int newline = TRUE;    /* initially at the     */
                          /* beginning of a new   */
                          /* line */
   int total;

   /* create a new process for counting the       */
   /* characters*/
     pipe(p);     /* p[R] is the read end, p[W] is */
                  /* the write end                 */
     pipe(q);     /* q[R] is the read end, q[W] is */
                  /* the write end                 */
     switch (pid = fork()) {
```

```
case 0:
  /* set up the pipes */
  /* child will read from pipe "p" and write */
  /* into pipe "q"; consequently, the write   */
  /* end of "p" and the read end of "q" are    */
  /* closed; the standard input of the child   */
  /* is made synonymous with the read end of   */
  /* "p" and the write end of "q" is made       */
  /* synonymous with standard output.           */
  /* File descriptor 0 = standard input.        */
  /* File descriptor 1 = standard output.       */

    close(p[W]);
    close(R); dup(p[R]); close(p[R]);
        /* standard input of child made */
        /* synonymous with p[R] */

    close(q[R]);
    close(W); dup(q[W]); close(q[W]);
        /* standard output of child made */
        /* synonymous with q[W] */

  execl("/a1/nhg/acb/count", "count", 0);
  printf("textcount: exec failed");
  exit(1);
case -1: /* parent process--unsuccessful in */
         /* creating a new process*/
  printf("textcount: cannot fork a process");
  exit(1);
default:
  close(p[R]); close(q[W]);
  fp = fdopen(p[W],"w");
                /* convert to stream */
}

/* strip the formatting commands and send the */
/* rest of the text to "count"; formatting      */
/* commands begin with PERIOD in column 1       */
  while ((c = getchar()) != EOF) {
    switch (newline) {
    case TRUE:
      if (c == '\n') /* null line */
        putc(c, fp);
      else if (c == PERIOD)
```

```
            /* skip the line */
            while ((c=getchar())!=EOF&&c!='\n')
               ;
          else {
            putc(c, fp);
            newline = FALSE;
          }
          break;
        default:
          putc(c, fp);
          if (c == '\n')
            newline = TRUE;
        }
    }

  fclose(fp);     /* the write end of the pipe        */
                  /* must be closed so the process    */
                  /* at the read end of the pipe      */
                  /* can sense an EOF                 */

  /* after the end of standard input has been         */
  /* reached, the input from pipe "q" can be          */
  /* redirected to standard input; i.e.,              */
  /* standard input of parent is made synonymous      */
  /* with q[R]                                        */
    close(R); dup(q[R]); close(q[R]);

  scanf("%d", &total);
  printf("Total number of characters %d\n", total);

  exit(0);
}

/*-----------------------------------------------------*/
```

## 6. Problems

1. Modify the *parallel character counting* example of the last section so that
   the output of count goes directly to standard output instead of being
   sent back to textcount via a pipe:

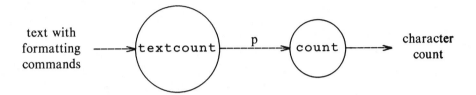

## Counting Characters in Parallel

2.  *(For readers familiar with the UNIX system):* The *parallel character counting* example can be written in a simpler and more general way by using the UNIX command language pipe notation ¦. For example, if program `strip` removes the formatting commands and program `count` counts the number of characters read by it, then these two programs can be "plumbed" together to run in parallel as

    `strip` <*data-file* ¦ `count`

    Compare this version with the example program given. Why is the example program much more complicated than the version written using the command language pipe notation?

3.  Functions `tbl`, `eqn` and `troff` all read input from `stdin` and write to `stdout`. Write a program that runs all three programs in parallel such that the output of `tbl` is the input of `eqn` and the output of `eqn` is the input of `troff`:

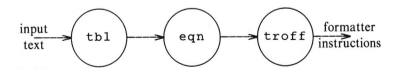

## Formatting in Parallel

# Chapter 9

# The C Preprocessor

A *preprocessor* is a tool used to process a program prior to compiling it. Preprocessors have been used to extend languages and to provide extra-language capabilities. Although innumerable preprocessors have been built to enhance the capabilities of programming languages, they are usually non-standard and provide ad hoc facilities; few languages have provided a preprocessor as part of their standard environment. Two examples of major languages that provide preprocessors as part of their environment are C and PL/I.

The C preprocessor provides facilities for defining macros (constant definition being a special case), file inclusion and conditional compilation. The C preprocessor is called automatically when the C compiler is invoked by the command `cc`.

A program can be processed by just the preprocessor by using the `-E` option with the C compiler command `cc`; the program is not compiled:

`cc -E` *file-name*

The output of the preprocessor is placed on the standard output stream `stdout`. Running the preprocessor on a program without compiling it allows the programmer to examine the effect of preprocessor definitions and macro calls.

Preprocessor instructions are usually different from the instructions of the associated language. For example, C preprocessor instructions begin with the character # in column 1. C preprocessor instructions can appear anywhere in a program. The effect of these instructions lasts until the end of the file containing them unless their effect is undone by other instructions.

## 1. Macro Definition and Invocation

A *macro facility* allows an identifier to be associated with a text string; all subsequent occurrences of this identifier are replaced with the associated string. C preprocessor macro definitions are of two forms, simple and parameterized:

```
#define identifier  token-string
#define identifier ( x₁ , x₂ , ... , xₙ )  token-string
```

where a *token* is an identifier, a keyword, an operator, a separator such as a parenthesis or a square bracket, or a string of characters that does not contain any separators.

The replacement string *token-string* can be continued on the next line by appending the backslash character \ at the end of the line to be continued.

### 1.1 Invoking Macros

Occurrence of the macro name causes an invocation of the macro. The replacement string is rescanned for more macro calls. Note that recursive macros cannot be made to terminate because it is not possible to include a preprocessor conditional instruction inside a macro definition; an occurrence of a macro name as a substring of a larger string (the macro name is not a token) will not invoke the macro.

### 1.2 Simple Macro Definitions

The first form of a macro definition causes all subsequent occurrences of *identifier* to be replaced by *token-string*.

Some examples of simple macro definitions are

```
#define NULL    0
#define EOF     (-1)
#define GET     getc(stdin)
```

After the above macro definitions have been processed, every occurrence of NULL, EOF and GET will be replaced by the corresponding right hand side. For example, every occurrence of

```
GET
```

will be replaced by the string

```
getc(stdin)
```

Macros can be used to make limited changes in the syntax of a language. For example, the macro definitions

```
#define begin      {
#define end        }
```

can be used to make C programs take on a Pascal-like appearance. Using these definitions, a *while* statement can be written as

```
while (e)
begin
   .
   .
   .
end
```

### 1.3 Parameterized Macro Definitions

The second form of the macro definition is a parameterized version of the first form. Prior to the replacement of *identifier* by the *token-string*, all occurrences of the formal parameters in *token-string* are replaced by the corresponding actual parameters. Actual parameters in a macro must be separated by commas.

Some examples of parameterized macro definitions are

```
#define getchar()        getc(stdin)
#define putchar(x)       putc(x,stdout)
#define MAX(x,y)         ((x)>(y)?(x):(y))
#define MIN(x,y)         ((x)>(y)?(y):(x))
#define UPPER(c)         ((c)-'a'+'A')
                         /* "c" must be lower case */
#define LOWER(c)         ((c)-'A'+'a')
                         /* "c" must be upper case */
```

Definitions of the macros `getchar` and `putchar` are taken from file `stdio.h`; macros `MAX` and `MIN` return the maximum and minimum parameter values, respectively; macros `UPPER` and `LOWER` return the lower or upper case character corresponding to their arguments, respectively. (The reason for including so many parentheses in the definitions of `MAX`, `MIN`, `UPPER` and `LOWER` is discussed in the next section.)

A parameterized macro call is similar to a function call. As an example of parameterized calls, consider the program fragment

```
while ((c = getchar()) != EOF)
    putchar(UPPER(c));
```

The preprocessor transforms this program fragment to

```
while ((c = getc(stdin)) != EOF)
    putc(((c)-'a'+'A'),stdout);
```

## 1.4 Defining Constants

The most common use of the C preprocessor is to define constants in C
programs; simple macro definitions are used for this purpose. Constant
definitions are usually of the form

```
#define constant-name      literal or constant-name
#define constant-name      (constant-expression)
```

Some examples of constant definitions are

```
#define NULL    0
#define EOF     (-1)

#define TRUE    1
#define FALSE   0
```

If a constant is defined to have as its value a constant expression, then it is wise
to surround the expression by parentheses. As an example, consider the
constant definition

```
#define E        5+10
```

Use of the constant E in expressions can produce strange results. For example
although the expression

```
E+10
```

evaluates correctly to 25, expression

```
E*10
```

will not evaluate to 150 as expected; instead, it evaluates to 105 because E is replaced by 5 + 1 0, which produces the expression

5 + 1 0 ∗ 1 0

This problem arises because the C preprocessor does not understand constant definitions; actually, the C preprocessor does know much about C at all. Constant definitions are just macro definitions.

## 1.5  In-line Code Generation

Function calls incur an overhead because registers must be saved and argument values must be copied, and because jumps must be made to the function body and back to the calling program. For small functions, especially those that are called repeatedly, this overhead can be significant. Consequently, a programmer may be tempted to avoid using functions despite their advantages (such as control abstraction) and to manually replace each function call by the body of the function. This manual replacement has several disadvantages; for example, the code becomes hard to read and understand and it becomes difficult to modify. Manual replacement can be discouraged by providing a facility by which a programmer can inform the compiler that calls to some functions should be replaced by the corresponding function body, i.e., a facility for *in-line code generation*. Such a facility is provided by the C preprocessor macros.

UPPER and LOWER were defined as the macros

```
#define UPPER(c)        ((c)-'a'+'A')
#define LOWER(c)        ((c)-'A'+'a')
```

instead of functions so that code for them is generated in-line. This is appropriate because UPPER and LOWER perform very small tasks. In this case, the in-line code generated for the expressions represented by UPPER and LOWER is less than that generated for a function call.

It is important to note that in-line code generation can, in some cases, lead to a significant increase in the storage required by the program itself.

## 1.6  Removing Macro Definitions

The preprocessor instruction

```
#undef    identifier
```

causes the definition of *identifier* to be forgotten. Removing the definition of an identifier can be used to control *conditional compilation* (discussed in the Section 3); it may also be used to prevent the preprocessor from grumbling about redefinitions.

## 2. File Inclusion

Arbitrary files can be textually included in a C program by means of the *include* instruction. The capability to include files textually in a program allows common constant, data, type and function declarations and definitions to be kept in separate files. These common declarations and definitions can then be used in many programs by one or more programmers. Keeping common declarations and definitions in separate files and then *including* them in C programs is a popular style used for writing C programs. A common example is the inclusion of the standard input/output declarations file `stdio.h`.

The instruction for textual inclusion of files, *include*, has two forms. Execution of the first form

```
#include "fname"
```

causes the instruction to be replaced by the contents of the file `fname` prior to the compilation of the program. The preprocessor expects to find `fname` in the directory containing the source file; otherwise, it looks for the file in some standard or prespecified places. Execution of the second form

```
#include <fname>
```

has a similar effect except that the preprocessor does not look for file `fname` in the directory containing the source file; instead, it just expects to find `fname` in the standard or prespecified places. For example, on the UNIX system the standard place for finding many files is the directory `/usr/include`; the complete name of the specified file `fname` is `/usr/include/fname`.

Instructions to include files can be nested. Finally, specification of the standard and prespecified places is not part of the language and is implementation dependent.

## 3. Conditional Compilation

*Conditional compilation* is the selective compilation of only those portions of programs that satisfy some conditions. For example, only those portions of a program that are necessary for a desired version of a system may be compiled.

Some advantages of conditional compilation are

1. It provides a compile-time parameterization facility. For example, such a facility can be used to generate programs with different kinds of structures.

2. It leads to storage efficiency because extraneous code need not be kept around at run-time.

3. Decisions can be made at compile-time rather than at run-time. This is often more efficient (but less flexible).

The preprocessor *if* instruction is used for conditional compilation. It has two forms—with or without the *else* part:

*if-header*
*lines$_{true}$*
`#endif`

and

*if-header*
*lines$_{true}$*
`#else`
*lines$_{false}$*
`#endif`

where

1. *if-header* is a preprocessor control line.

2. *lines$_{true}$* and *lines$_{false}$* are lines of arbitrary text.

The preprocessor control line *if-header* contains a condition that evaluates to true or false causing the interpretation of *lines$_{true}$* or *lines$_{false}$*, respectively. The preprocessor control line *if-header* has three forms:

`#if` *constant-expression*
`#ifdef` *identifier*
`#ifndef` *identifier*

In the first form, the condition is specified by the *constant-expression*, which is true or false depending upon whether it is non-zero or zero, respectively. In the second form, the condition is true if *identifier* has been defined previously (and not subsequently undefined) by means of a *define* instruction; otherwise, it is false. In the third form, the condition is true if *identifier* has not been defined previously (or was defined, but then subsequently undefined) by means of a *define* instruction; otherwise, it is false.

One example of conditional compilation is the instruction

```
#ifndef MAX_STK_SIZE
#define MAX_STK_SIZE     128
#endif
```

This instruction provides for a default value for MAX_STK_SIZE if a value has not been provided by the user.

Another example of conditional compilation is the definition of the identifier BUFSIZ (taken from stdio.h [AT&T UNIX (Release 5.0) 1982]):

```
#if u370
#define BUFSIZ   4096
#endif
#if vax || u3b
#define BUFSIZ   1024
#endif
#if pdp11
#define BUFSIZ   512
#endif
```

The value of the constant BUFSIZ depends upon which one of the identifiers u370, vax u3b or pdp11 has been defined (assuming that only such one identifier will be defined).

As a final example, consider the declaration of the type FILE (also taken from stdio.h):

```
typedef struct {
#if vax ¦¦ u3b
  int _cnt;
  unsigned char *_ptr;
#else
  unsigned char *_ptr;
  int _cnt;
#endif
  unsigned char *_base;
  char _flag;
  char _file;
} FILE;
```

If the identifiers vax and u3b have been defined, then type FILE will be declared as

```
typedef struct {
  int _cnt;
  unsigned char *_ptr;
  unsigned char *_base;
  char _flag;
  char _file;
} FILE;
```

otherwise, it will be declared as

```
typedef struct {
  unsigned char *_ptr;
  int _cnt;
  unsigned char *_base;
  char _flag;
  char _file;
} FILE;
```

Notice that both versions of structure FILE have the same components; however, the order in which the first two components appear is different. This declaration exploits the fact that structure components have addresses that increase as their declarations are read from left-to-right [Ritchie 1980]. According to my colleague John Linderman, on most machines, it is possible to generate more efficient references to the first element of a structure than to other elements. Therefore, it is likely that the first version of FILE leads to more efficient code for the VAX (DEC) and 3B (AT&T) computers while the second version leads to more efficient code for the IBM computers.

## 4. Concluding Remarks

Although preprocessors extend the facilities provided by the programming language, their use is not without disadvantages:

- the use of a preprocessor requires an extra pass over the program text; the program must be analyzed one extra time.

- the error messages produced by the compiler may not correspond directly to the original program (because the compiler translates the output of the preprocessor, not the original program). The C preprocessor makes special efforts to eliminate this problem.

## 5. Example

To illustrate the power of the C preprocessor, a *generic* function will be defined. A *generic* function is a template of an ordinary (non-generic) function. In addition to normal kinds of parameters, generic functions also take data types and function names as parameters. Ordinary functions are created from generic functions by instantiating them with appropriate actual parameters. Generic functions can be implemented in C by using the preprocessor.

Two advantages of having a generic facility in a programming language are [Gehani 1983b]

1. *Reduced Programming Effort*: It is less work to write and maintain one generic function instead of several ordinary functions.

2. *More Manageable Programs*: Programs become smaller because only one generic function needs to be written for several ordinary functions.

The problem is to write a *generic* function (actually a macro) to exchange elements. This generic function can be instantiated to create ordinary functions. For example, suppose that the generic swap function is named GENERIC_SWAP. Then ordinary swap functions swap_int and swap_float to exchange elements of type int and float, respectively, may be created by the macro calls

```
GENERIC_SWAP(swap_int, int)
GENERIC_SWAP(swap_float, float)
```

Function `GENERIC_SWAP` is defined as

```
#define GENERIC_SWAP(NAME, ELEM_TYPE) void NAME(a, b)\
                     ELEM_TYPE *a, *b;\
                     {\
                         ELEM_TYPE t;\
                         t = *a;\
                         *a = *b;\
                         *b = t; \
                     }
```

The above instantiations will result in the creation of the ordinary functions

```
void swap_int(a, b)
int *a, *b;
{
    int t;
    t = *a;
    *a = *b;
    *b = t;
}

void swap_float(a, b)
float *a, *b;
{
    float t;
    t = *a;
    *a = *b;
    *b = t;
}
```

which can be called directly.

## 6. Problems

1. What are the pros and cons of defining constants using a preprocessor, as in C, versus a *constant* definition facility in a programming language such as that provided in languages like Ada, Pascal and Fortran 77?

2. Why was it necessary to use so many parentheses in the definitions of **MAX** and **MIN**? Why are the following definitions not correct?

```
#define MAX(x,y)          x>y?x:y
#define MIN(x,y)          x>y?y:x
```

3. Write a macro `ADD` that generates a program segment to add the corresponding elements of two arrays and put the result in the corresponding elements of a third array. For example,

   ```
   ADD(x, y, z, n)
   ```

   will generate instructions so that

   ```
   x[i] = y[i] + z[i];
   ```

   for values of i between 0 and n-1. *Hint*: A local loop variable must be defined.

4. When would it be undesirable to use macros (for in-line code generation) instead of functions?

5. Write macro definitions that can be used to implement an ALGOL-like *if* statement of the form
   ```
   if expression
     then ...
     else ...;
   ```
   Can you give a definition of the form

   ```
   #define if       if(
   ```

   or will you have to use another keyword for *if*, e.g.,

   ```
   #define IF       if(
   ```

6. Write a generic sort function `GENERIC_SORT` that takes as parameters the sort function name, the array element type and the comparison operator. An example of an instantiation using `GENERIC_SORT` is

   ```
   GENERIC_SORT(int_sort, int, <)
   ```

   that produces an ordinary sort function `int_sort` to sorts `int` arrays in non-decreasing order.

What will be the result of the instantiation

```
GENERIC_SORT(int_sort, int, >)
```

7. Write a program that implements some of the capabilities of the C preprocessor, e.g., the *define* statements.

# Chapter 10

# One Final Example

## 1. A Simple Query Database Example

The example involves writing a set of functions that can be used to interrogate the employee database of a small company (about 50 employees).[59] The employee information is kept in a file that is used by function `initialize_db` to initialize the database. This file contains lines of the form

name(19) room#(7) extension#(4) designation(11) companyid(5) signature(3) logid(3) mailid(49)

The fields in the data lines are separated by a blank; numbers in parentheses indicate the length of the field (these numbers are not actually stored in the file). The fields represent the following information:

| | |
|---|---|
| name | name in the form *lastname, first_initial, middle_initial* |
| room# | office number |
| extension# | telephone number |
| designation | organizational rank |
| companyid | company identification number |
| signature | a three character password |
| logid | computer system identification |
| mailid | name of mail directory |

Some sample lines from the database file are

---

59. This problem is based on a database that was built as part of a prototype electronic form system [Gehani 1983a]; the system was designed as a test bed for an office environment where employees use electronic forms that can be mailed by one employee to another. The database was used to fill in some information in the forms automatically and to authenticate other information.

```
Limb,J.O.         3D479    2582   DeptHead      30479   LIM   jol   /a1/jol
Allen,R.B.        3D443    4755   MTS           30443   ALL   rba   /a1/rba
Gehani,N.H.       3D414    4461   MTS           30414   GEH   nhg   /a1/nhg
Maxemchuk,N.F.    3D402    6240   MTS           30402   MAX   nfm   /a1/nfm
Sharma,D.K.       3A402    2914   MTS           31402   SHA   dks   /a1/dks
Super,S.S.        3D400    2583   Supervisor    30400   SUP   sss   /a1/sss
```

The functions to be implemented are

| function | comments |
|---|---|
| `initialize_db(db_file)` | initialize the database to the file `db_file` |
| `print_db( )` | print the database for debugging |
| `emp_ext(n)` | returns a pointer to a string containing the extension of person named n |
| `emp_room(n)` | returns a pointer to a string containing the room of the person named n |
| `emp_desig(n)` | returns a pointer to a string containing the designation of the person named n |
| `emp_compid(n)` | returns a pointer to a string containing the company id of the person named n |
| `emp_sig(n)` | returns a pointer to a string containing the signature of the person named n |
| `emp_logid(n)` | returns a pointer to a string containing the login id of the person named n |
| `get_desig(l_id)` | returns a pointer to a string containing the designation of the person with logid `l_id` |
| `get_sig(l_id)` | returns a pointer to a string containing the signature of the person with logid `l_id` |
| `get_maild(l_id)` | returns a pointer to a string containing the mail directory of the person with logid `l_id` |

where the functions with parameters expect strings as arguments. All functions
return the value NULL if the specified argument is not in the database.

Based on anticipated use, it is expected that one employee query is followed by several other queries about the same employee. In other words, the database query sequence can be partitioned into subsequences such that each subsequence consists of queries about the same person. This information may be used to optimize retrieval of information from the database.

### 1.1 Database Design Strategy

Because the database is small it will be kept in main memory; the file containing the employee information will be read into objects of type emp. Elements of array db will point to these objects. Variable size will be used to represent the current size of the database. Both variables db and size will be global to all the database functions; however, to restrict their visibility to just the database functions, they will be defined as static:

```
static emp *db[MAX_DB];
static int size;
```

Storage for the emp objects will be allocated as needed.

Function search_db is called by most of the other functions to search the database. Function search_db uses the employee name as the key to search the database; it sets the global variable cur to the index of the appropriate element, if any, of the database array db. Consequently, in most cases,[60] element db[cur] points to the employee involved in the last successful query. To take advantage of the clustering of queries, search_db first examines the employee information pointed to by db[cur] to determine if this employee is the one being sought. If db[cur] points to information about the employee in question, then search_db returns 1; otherwise, search_db examines the database sequentially; if the employee is in the database, then it sets cur to the index of the element of db that point to information about the employee and returns 1; otherwise it returns 0.

Variable cur is defined as

```
static int cur = 0;
```

---

60. Some functions such as get_desig do not call search_db to search the database because they do not search the database using the employee name as the key.

## 1.2  The Database Functions

The functions are straightforward and self explanatory:

```
#include <stdio.h>

         /* LAYOUT of the database file */

#define LN 20    /* length(name)+1 for null char    */
#define LR 8     /* length(room)+1 for null char     */
#define LE 5     /* length(extension)+1 for null     */
                 /* char                             */
#define LD 12    /* length(designation)+1 for        */
                 /* null char                        */
#define LC 6     /* length(company id)+1 for         */
                 /* null char                        */
#define LS 4     /* length(signature)+1 for          */
                 /* null char                        */
#define LL 4     /* length(login id)+1 for null      */
                 /* char                             */
#define LM 50    /* length(mail directory)+1 for     */
                 /* null char                        */

#define MAX_DB  100      /* max size of database */


/* some string functions from library "libc" */
/* which is automatically loaded */
  char *strcpy();
  int strlen(), strcmp();

/* structure emp defines layout of the employee */
/* database file */

  typedef struct {
    char name[LN];
    char room[LR];
    char ext[LE];
    char desig[LD];
    char compid[LC];
    char sig[LS];
    char logid[LL];
    char maild[LM];
  } emp;
```

```
static emp *db[MAX_DB];
            /* db is an array of pointers to the */
            /* database records*/

static int cur = 0;
            /* contains a pointer to the last    */
            /* employee looked up--for reasons   */
            /* of efficiency. It is assumed      */
            /* that one employee query is        */
            /* followed by several other         */
            /* queries about the same employee. */
            /* Initially "cur" points to the     */
            /* first person in the database      */

static int size = 0;
            /* size contains the number of       */
            /* records in the database           */


/*---------------------------------------------------*/
/* initialize_db(db_file): Initialize database to*/
/*                        the file "db_file"     */
/*---------------------------------------------------*/

initialize_db(db_file)
char *db_file;
{
   FILE *fopen(), *fp;
   char *malloc();     /* storage allocator */
   int i;      /* i is used to step through the */
               /* database */

   if ((fp = fopen(db_file,"r")) == NULL) {
     printf("initialize_db: cannot open");
     printf("file %s\n", db_file);
     exit(1);
   }

   for (i = 0; ; i++) {
     if (i == MAX_DB) {
        printf("initialize_db: Warning");
        printf("--database size = MAX_DB; extra\n");
        printf("--records in file will not be read\n");
        break;
```

```
  }
/* allocate storage */
  if ((db[i]=(emp *)malloc(sizeof(emp)))==NULL) {
    printf("initialize_db: no more storage");
    printf(" available\n");
    exit(1);
  }

  if (fscanf(fp,"%s%s%s%s%s%s%s%s",db[i]->name,
       db[i]->room,db[i]->ext,db[i]->desig,
       db[i]->compid,db[i]->sig,db[i]->logid,
       db[i]->maild) == EOF)
    break;
  }
size = i;
fclose(fp);

}
/*-------------------------------------------------*/

/*-------------------------------------------------*/
/* print_db: Print the database for debugging   */
/*-------------------------------------------------*/

print_db()
{
  int i;

  for(i = 0; i < size; i++)
    printf("--%s %s %s %s %s %s %s \n",
         db[i]->name,db[i]->room,db[i]->ext,
         db[i]->desig,db[i]->compid,db[i]->sig,
         db[i]->logid);
}
/*-------------------------------------------------*/

/*-------------------------------------------------*/
/* search_db(n): Internal function that sets the */
/*               static variable "cur" to be the */
/*               index of element of database    */
/*               "db" that contains the string   */
/*               "n" in its name field. It       */
/*               returns 1 if successful and 0    */
/*               otherwise.                       */
```

```
/*-------------------------------------------------*/

static int search_db(n)
char n[];
{
  if (strcmp(n, db[cur]->name) == 0)
    return 1;

  for(cur = 0; cur < size; cur++)
    if (strcmp(n, db[cur]->name) == 0)
      return 1;
  cur = 0;
  return 0;
}

/*-------------------------------------------------*/

/*-------------------------------------------------*/
/* strsave(s): Allocate storage for string "s"    */
/*             and return a pointer to this        */
/*             address                             */
/*-------------------------------------------------*/

char *strsave(s)
char s[];
{
  char *p, *malloc();

  if ((p = malloc((unsigned) strlen(s) + 1)) == NULL) {
    printf("strsave: lack of dynamic storage\n");
    exit(1);
  }
  else
    strcpy(p, s);
  return p;
}

/*-------------------------------------------------*/

/*-------------------------------------------------*/
/* emp_ext(n): Returns a pointer to the extension*/
/*             of person "n"; if "n" is not found*/
/*             then NULL is returned               */
/*-------------------------------------------------*/
```

```
char *emp_ext(n)
char n[];
{
   return search_db(n)?strsave(db[cur]->ext):NULL;
}



/*---------------------------------------------------*/

/*---------------------------------------------------*/
/* get_desig(l_id): Returns a pointer to the         */
/*                  designation of person with       */
/*                  logid "l_id"; otherwise NULL      */
/*                  is returned                       */
/*---------------------------------------------------*/

char *get_desig(l_id)
char l_id[];
{
   int i;

   for(i = 0; i < size; i++)
     if (strcmp(db[i]->logid, l_id) == 0)
       return strsave(db[i]->desig);
   return NULL;
}

/*---------------------------------------------------*/
```

Functions emp_room, emp_desig, emp_compid, emp_sig and emp_logid have not been given because they are all similar to function emp_ext. Likewise, functions get_sig and get_mailid have not been given because they are similar to function get_desig.

## 2. Problems

1. Function strsave is used to make a copy of the query answer and it is the address of this copy that is returned to the program making the query. What is the harm in returning the address (in the database db) of the query answer? What is the problem with this strategy? Suggest another strategy.

2. Suggest ways of increasing the efficiency of the database functions.

3. Extend the database example to allow changes to the database, e.g., addition of new entries or modification of the existing entries. Note that any modifications to the database must eventually be written to the file where the database information is stored permanently. Consequently, a function that writes the current contents of the database to a file must also be provided.

4. Many of the database functions are similar, e.g., `ext`, `room`, `desig`, `compid`, `sig` and `logid`. Using the preprocessor facilities, write a generic function from which these functions can be instantiated.

5. Write a program to recognize strings generated by the following grammar written in extended BNF[61] (i.e., the program should determine whether or not the given input string is a valid expression)

> *statement* $\longrightarrow$ *variable* = *expression*
> *variable* $\longrightarrow$ *letter* { *letter-or-digit* }
> *expression* $\longrightarrow$ *term* { + *term* }
> *term* $\longrightarrow$ *factor* { * *factor* }
> *factor* $\longrightarrow$ *variable* | ( *expression* )

where *letter* stands for one the upper case letters and *letter-or-digit* stands for one of the upper case letters or a digit.

*Hints*: Recursion will simplify the task of writing the syntax recognizer. Write one function for each term on the left hand side of the productions.

---

61. Extended BNF notation is used for defining the syntax of programming languages:

| | |
|---|---|
| [a] | specifies the optional occurrence of item *a*. |
| {a} | specifies 0 or more occurrences of item *a*. |
| a | b | specifies either item *a* or item *b*. |
| a $\longrightarrow$ b | is a *production* specifying that item *a* really stands for item *b*. |

# Appendix A

# Some Library Functions

Many functions that are taken for granted by C programmers are actually library functions that are not part of the C language itself, but are part of its standard environment. In this chapter, I will describe some of the commonly used functions contained in two libraries provided by the UNIX system: the standard C Library `libc` and the math library `libm`. Functions belonging to `libc` will be described in detail while those belonging to the `libm` will be mentioned briefly. A complete list of these functions can be found in the *UNIX Reference Manual* [Berkeley UNIX 1981, AT&T UNIX (Release 5.0) 1982, AT&T UNIX (System V) 1982].

## 1. UNIX System Calls and The Standard C Library `libc`

UNIX reference manuals are usually divided into sections. Functions described in Section 2 of a UNIX reference manual are called *system calls* because they invoke the underlying UNIX system to achieve their effect. Functions described in Section 3 also may invoke the UNIX system, but only by calling the functions described in Section 2. Sections 2 and 3 functions are found in the library `libc` on the UNIX system; functions identified as belonging to Section 3S constitute the standard input/output environment (`stdio`).

Declarations of these functions are given in the *include* files specified in their specifications. For example, declarations of functions in the standard input/output package `stdio` are given in the file named `/usr/include/stdio.h` on most UNIX systems; these declarations can be included in a C program by means of the C preprocessor instruction

```
#include <stdio.h>
```

The function descriptions given here are modified versions of excerpts from the corresponding descriptions in the *UNIX Reference Manual* [AT&T UNIX (Release 5.0) 1982]. They have been modified to remove the irrelevant and non-essential parts of the descriptions, e.g., descriptions of bugs. The number (and the optional letter) following the function names indicates the section of the *UNIX Reference Manual* [AT&T UNIX (Release 5.0) 1982] where these functions are described in detail.

------------------------------------------------------------

# ALARM(2)
### (set a process's alarm clock)

Function `alarm` instructs the calling process's alarm clock to send the signal `SIGALRM` to the calling process after the number of real time seconds specified by `sec` have elapsed (see description of `signal` for more details). It has the specification

```
unsigned alarm(sec);
unsigned sec;
```

Alarm requests are not stacked; successive calls reset the calling process's alarm clock.

If `sec` is 0, any previously made alarm request is canceled. Function `alarm` returns the amount of time previously remaining in the calling process's alarm clock.

------------------------------------------------------------

# CLOSE(2)
### (close a file descriptor)

Given a file descriptor `fildes`, such as one returned from an `open`, `creat`, `dup` or `pipe` call, a call to the function `close`, specified as

```
int close(fildes)
int fildes;
```

closes the file descriptor indicated by `fildes`.

Function `close` will fail if `fildes` is not a valid open file descriptor. Upon successful completion, 0 is returned. Otherwise, −1 is returned.

All files are closed automatically on *exit*, but because there is a limit on the number of open files per process, the use of `close` is necessary for programs that deal with many files.

------------------------------------------------------------

---

# CREAT(2)
### (create a new file or rewrite an existing one)

Function `creat` is specified as

```
•
int creat(path, mode)
char *path;
int mode;
```

A call to function `creat` creates a new ordinary file or prepares to rewrite an existing file named by the path name pointed to by the parameter `path`.

Upon successful completion, a non-negative integer, namely the file descriptor, is returned. Otherwise, −1 is returned.

---

# DUP(2)
### (duplicate an open file descriptor)

Given a file descriptor returned from an `open`, `pipe`, or `creat` call, a call to the function `dup`, specified as

```
int dup(fildes)
int fildes;
```

returns a new file descriptor having the following in common with the original:

- same open file (or pipe).
- same file pointer (i.e., both file descriptors share one file pointer).
- same access mode (read, write or read/write).

The new file descriptor is set to remain open across `exec` system calls. The file descriptor returned is the lowest one available.

Function `dup` will fail if `fildes` is not a valid open file descriptor or if 20 file descriptors are currently open. Upon successful completion, a non-negative integer, namely the file descriptor, is returned. Otherwise, −1 is returned.

---

------------------------------------------------------------

# EXEC(2)
### (execute a file)

A process can be made to execute any desired program by using one the *exec*
functions: `execl`, `execv`, `execle`, `execve`, `execlp` and `execvp`.
The specifications of these functions are

```
int execl(path, arg0, arg1, ..., argn, 0)
char *path, *arg0, *arg1, ..., *argn;

int execv(path, argv)
char *path, *argv[];

int execle(path, arg0, arg1, ..., argn, 0, envp)
char *path, *arg0, *arg1, ..., *argn, *envp[];

int execve(path, argv, envp)
char *path, *argv[], *envp[];

int execlp(file, arg0, arg1, ..., argn, 0)
char *file, *arg0, *arg1, ..., *argn;

int execvp(file, argv)
char *file, *argv[];
```

All forms of the *exec* function transform the calling process into a new process.
The new process is constructed from a file which is a compiled and ready to
execute version of a program; this file is called the "new process file." There
can be no return from a successful execution of an *exec* function because the
calling process is overlaid by the new process.

When a C program is executed, it is called as follows:

```
main(argc, argv, envp)
int argc;
char **argv, **envp;
```

where `argc` is the argument count and `argv` is an array of character
pointers to the arguments themselves; `argc` is conventionally at least one and
the first member of the array `argv` points to a string containing the name of

the file.[62]

Argument path points to a path name that identifies the new process file. Argument file is the name of the new process file.

Arguments arg0, arg1, ..., argn are pointers to null-terminated character strings. These strings constitute the argument list available to the new process. By convention, at least arg0 must be present and point to a string that is the same as path (or its last component).

Argument argv is an array of character pointers to null-terminated strings. These strings constitute the argument list available to the new process. By convention, argv must have at least one member, and it must point to a string that is the same as path (or its last component); argv is terminated by a null pointer.

Argument envp is an array of character pointers to null-terminated strings. These strings constitute the environment for the new process. Argument envp is terminated by a null pointer. For execl and execv, the C run-time start-off routine places a pointer to the calling process's environment in the global cell:

```
extern char **environ;
```

and it is used to pass the calling process's environment to the new process.

File descriptors open in the calling process remain open in the new process, except for those whose close-on-exec flag is set; For those file descriptors that remain open, the file pointer is unchanged.

Signals set to terminate the calling process will be set to terminate the new process. Signals set to be ignored by the calling process will be set to be ignored by the new process. Signals set to be caught by the calling process will be set to terminate new process.

If *exec* returns to the calling process an error has occurred; the return value will be −1.

---

62. When defining the main function, arguments can be omitted as follows: envp can be omitted, or argv and envp can be omitted, or all three arguments can be omitted. The implication of omitting an argument is that the value passed for the omitted argument, when invoking main, will not be accessible in main.

---

# EXIT, _EXIT(2)
### (terminate process)

Calling function `exit` is the normal means of terminating a process. It is specified as

```
void exit(status)
int status;
```

Function `exit` terminates the calling process with the following consequences: all of the file descriptors open in the calling process are closed; if the parent process of the calling process is executing a `wait`, it is notified of the calling process's termination. The C function `exit` may cause cleanup actions before the process exits. Function `_exit`, specified as

```
void _exit(status)
int status;
```

circumvents all cleanup.

---

---

# FORK(2)
### (create a new process)

Function `fork` is used to create a new process. Its specification is

```
int fork( )
```

The new process (child process) is an "exact" copy of the calling process (parent process). However, there are some differences; e.g.,

- the child process has a unique process *id*.

- the child process has a different parent process *id* (i.e., the process *id* of the parent process).

- the child process has its own copy of the parent's file descriptors. Each of the child's file descriptors shares a common file pointer with the corresponding file descriptor of the parent.

Function `fork` will fail and no child process will be created if the system-imposed limits on the total number of processes or on the total number of processes under execution by a single user are exceeded.

Upon successful completion, `fork` returns 0 to the child process and returns the process *id* of the child process to the parent process. Otherwise, −1 is returned to the parent process and no child process is created.

---

---

# KILL(2)
### (send a signal to a process)

Function kill has the specification

```
int kill(pid, sig)
int pid, sig;
```

Function kill sends the signal sig to the process specified by the process number pid. Upon successful completion, 0 is returned. Otherwise, −1 is returned.

---

---

# LSEEK(2)
(move read/write file pointer)

Function lseek is used to position the file pointer at a particular location in a file prior to reading or writing. It has the specification

```
long lseek(fildes, offset, whence)
int fildes;
long offset;
int whence;
```

Parameter fildes is a file descriptor returned from a creat, open or dup system call. Function lseek sets the file pointer associated with fildes as follows:

| value of whence | file pointer set to |
|---|---|
| 0 | offset bytes |
| 1 | current location plus offset |
| 2 | size of the file plus offset |

Upon successful completion, the resulting pointer location as measured in bytes from the beginning of the file is returned.

Function lseek will fail and the file pointer will remain unchanged if fildes is not an open file descriptor, if it is associated with a pipe, whence is not 0, 1 or 2 or if the resulting file pointer would become negative.

Some devices are incapable of seeking. The value of the file pointer associated with such a device is undefined.

Upon successful completion, a non-negative integer indicating the file pointer value is returned. Otherwise, −1 is returned.

---

--------------------------------------------------------

# OPEN(2)
(open file for reading or writing)

Function `open`, which is used to open files for reading or writing, has the specification

```
#include <fcntl.h>

int open(path, oflag [, mode])
char *path;
int oflag, mode;
```

Parameter `path` points to a path name naming a file. Function `open` opens a file descriptor for the named file and sets the file status flags according to the value of `oflag`. Values for parameter `oflag` are constructed by or-ing flags from the following list (only one of the first three flags below may be used):

O_RDONLY        Open for reading only.

O_WRONLY        Open for writing only.

O_RDWR          Open for reading and writing.

O_NDELAY        This flag may affect subsequent reads and writes. When opening a FIFO with O_RDONLY or O_WRONLY set:

- *If* O_NDELAY *is set*: An `open` for reading-only will return without delay. An `open` for writing-only will return an error if no process currently has the file open for reading.

- *If* O_NDELAY *is clear*: An `open` for reading-only will block until a process opens the file for writing. An `open` for writing-only will block until a process opens the file for reading.

When opening a file associated with a communication line:

- *If* O_NDELAY *is set*: An `open` will return without waiting for carrier.

|  | • *If* O_NDELAY *is clear*: The open will block until carrier is present. |
|---|---|
| O_APPEND | If set, the file pointer will be set to the end of the file prior to each write. |
| O_CREAT | If the file exists, this flag has no effect. Otherwise, the file's owner ID is set to the process's effective user ID the file's group ID is set to the process's effective group ID, and the low-order 12 bits of the file mode are set to the value of mode modified as follows: |

- All bits set in the process's file mode creation mask are cleared.

- The *save text image after execution bit* of the mode is cleared.

| O_TRUNC | If the file exists, its length is truncated to 0 and the mode and owner are unchanged. |
|---|---|
| O_EXCL | If O_EXCL and O_CREAT are set, open will fail if the file exists. |

Upon successful completion, a non-negative integer, the file descriptor, is returned. The file pointer used to mark the current position within the file is set to the beginning of the file. The new file descriptor is set to remain open across exec system calls. No process may have more than 20 file descriptors open simultaneously.

Upon successful completion, a non-negative integer, namely a file descriptor, is returned. Otherwise, a value of −1 is returned and errno is set to indicate the error.

------------------------------------------------------------

----------------------------------------------------------------

# PAUSE(2)
### (suspend process until signal)

Function `pause` suspends the calling process until it receives a signal. The signal must be one that is not currently set to be ignored by the calling process. It has the specification

```
pause()
```

If the signal causes termination of the calling process, `pause` will not return. If the signal is *caught* by the calling process and control is returned from the signal catching-function (see description of `signal` for more details), the calling process resumes execution from the point of suspension with a return value of −1 from `pause`.

----------------------------------------------------------------

# PIPE(2)
### (create an interprocess channel)

Function `pipe`, which has the specification

```
int pipe(fildes)
int fildes[2];
```

creates an I/O mechanism called a pipe and returns two file descriptors, `fildes[0]` and `fildes[1]`. Descriptor `fildes[0]` is opened for reading and descriptor `fildes[1]` is opened for writing.

Writes of up to 5120 bytes of data are buffered by the pipe before the writing process is blocked. A read using the file descriptor `fildes[0]` accesses the data written to `fildes[1]` on a first-in-first-out basis.

A call to function `pipe` will fail if 19 or more file descriptors are currently open, because no process may have more than 20 file descriptors open simultaneously.

Upon successful completion, 0 is returned. Otherwise, −1 is returned.

----------------------------------------------------------------

------------------------------------------------------------

# READ(2)
### (read from file)

The specification of read is

```
int read(fildes, buf, nbyte)
int fildes;
char *buf;
unsigned nbyte;
```

Function read attempts to read nbyte bytes from the file associated with fildes into the buffer pointed to by buf. Descriptor fildes should have been obtained from a creat, open, dup, or pipe system call.

On devices capable of seeking, the read starts at a position in the file given by the file pointer associated with fildes. Upon return from read, the file pointer is incremented by the number of bytes actually read.

Devices that are incapable of seeking always read from the current position. The value of a file pointer associated with such a file is undefined.

Upon successful completion, read returns the number of bytes actually read and placed in the buffer; this number may be less than nbyte if the file is associated with a communication line or if the number of bytes left in the file is less than nbyte bytes; 0 is returned when an end-of-file has been reached.

A call to function read will fail if fildes is not a valid file descriptor open for reading or if buf points outside the allocated address space.

Upon successful completion, a non-negative integer is returned indicating the number of bytes actually read. Otherwise, a −1 is returned.

------------------------------------------------------------

------------------------------------------------------------

# SIGNAL(2)
(specify what to do upon receipt of a signal)

Function `signal` allows the calling process to choose one of three ways in which it is possible to handle the receipt of a specific signal. It is specified as

```
#include <sys/signal.h>

int (*signal(sig, func))()
int sig;
int (*func)();
```

Argument `sig` specifies the signal and argument `func` specifies the choice. Argument `sig` can be assigned any one of the following except `SIGKILL`:

| signal | number | explanation |
|--------|--------|-------------|
| SIGHUP | 1 | hangup |
| SIGINT | 2 | interrupt |
| SIGQUIT | 3 | quit |
| SIGILL | 4 | illegal instruction (not reset when caught) |
| SIGTRAP | 5 | trace trap (not reset when caught) |
| SIGIOT | 6 | IOT instruction |
| SIGEMT | 7 | EMT instruction |
| SIGFPE | 8 | floating point exception |
| SIGKILL | 9 | kill (cannot be caught or ignored) |
| SIGBUS | 10 | bus error |
| SIGSEGV | 11 | segmentation violation |
| SIGSYS | 12 | bad argument to system call |
| SIGPIPE | 13 | write on a pipe with no one to read it |
| SIGALRM | 14 | alarm clock |
| SIGTERM | 15 | software termination signal |
| SIGUSR1 | 16 | user defined signal 1 |
| SIGUSR2 | 17 | user defined signal 2 |
| SIGCLD | 18 | death of a child |
| SIGPWR | 19 | power fail |

Argument `func` is `SIG_DFL`, `SIG_IGN` or a *function address*. The actions prescribed by these values of are as follows:

| value of `func` | action |
|---|---|
| `SIG_DFL` | terminate process upon receipt of a signal |
| `SIG_IGN` | ignore signal |
| *function address* | execute specified function upon receipt of a signal |

Upon successful completion, `signal` returns the previous value of `func` for the specified signal `sig`. Otherwise, −1 is returned.

---------------------------------------------------------------

----------------------------------------------------------

# WAIT(2)
### (wait for child process to stop or terminate)

Execution of function `wait` suspends the calling process until it receives a signal that is to be caught (see the description of `signal` for more details) or any one of the calling process's child processes terminates. If a child process stopped or terminated prior to the call on `wait`, return is immediate. Function `wait` has the specification

```
int wait(stat_loc)
int *stat_loc;

int wait ((int *)0)
```

If `stat_loc` (taken as an integer) is non-zero, 16 bits of information called *status* are stored in the low order 16 bits of the location pointed to by `stat_loc`. The *status* bits can be used to differentiate between stopped and terminated child processes.[63] Moreover, if the child process terminated, status identifies the cause of termination and passes useful information to the parent. This is accomplished in the following manner:

1. If the child process stopped, the high order 8 bits of status will contain the number of the signal that caused the process to stop and the low order 8 bits will be set equal to 0177.

2. If the child process terminated due to an `exit` call, the low order 8 bits of status will be zero and the high order 8 bits will contain the low order 8 bits of the argument that the child process passed to `exit`.

3. If the child process terminated due to a signal, the high order 8 bits of status will be zero and the low order 8 bits will contain the number of the signal that caused the termination. In addition, if the low order seventh bit is set, a *core image* will have been produced.

If a parent process terminates without waiting for its child processes to terminate, the parent process *id* of each child process is set to 1. This means

---

63. Stopped processes occur when a process is executing in the trace mode [AT&T UNIX (Release 5.0) 1982].

the initialization process inherits the child processes.

A call to function `wait` will immediately return −1 if the calling process has no existing unwaited-for child processes or `stat_loc` points to an illegal address.

If `wait` returns due to the receipt of a signal, then −1 is returned to the calling process. If `wait` returns due to a stopped or terminated child process, then the process *id* of the child is returned to the calling process. Otherwise, −1 is returned.

------------------------------------------------------------

-------------------------------------------------------

# WRITE(2)
(write to a file)

Function `write` has the specification

```
int write(fildes, buf, nbyte)
int fildes;
char *buf;
unsigned nbyte;
```

Function `write` attempts to write nbyte bytes from the buffer pointed to by `buf` to the file associated with `fildes`. Argument `fildes` is a file descriptor obtained from a `creat`, `open`, `dup` or `pipe` system call.

On devices capable of seeking, the actual writing of data proceeds from the position in the file indicated by the file pointer. Upon return from `write`, the file pointer is incremented by the number of bytes actually written.

On devices incapable of seeking, writing always takes place starting at the current position. The value of a file pointer associated with such a device is undefined.

A call to function `write` will fail and the file pointer will remain unchanged if one or more of the following are true:

- `fildes` is not a valid file descriptor open for writing.

- an attempt is made to write to a pipe that is not open for reading by any process.

- An attempt is made to write a file that exceeds the process's file size limit or the maximum file size.

- `buf` points outside the process's allocated address space.

If a `write` requests that more bytes be written than there is room for, only as many bytes as there is room for will be written. For example, suppose there is space for 20 bytes more in a file before reaching a limit. A write of 512 bytes will return 20. The next write of a non-zero number of bytes will give a failure return. Writes to a full pipe will block until space becomes available.

Upon successful completion, the number of bytes actually written is returned. Otherwise, −1 is returned.

-------------------------------------------------------

# ABORT(3)
### (generate an IOT fault)

Function `abort` causes an IOT signal to be sent to the process. This usually results in termination with a core dump. It has the specification

```
int abort( )
```

It is possible for `abort` to return control if `SIGIOT` is caught or ignored, in which case the value returned is that of the `kill` system call.

# ABS(3)
### (return integer absolute value)

Function `abs`, which has the specification

```
int abs(i)
int i;
```

returns the absolute value of its integer operand.

---

# ISALPHA, ISUPPER, ISLOWER, ISDIGIT, ISALNUM, ISSPACE ISPUNCT, ISPRINT, ISCNTRL, ISASCII(3)
### (character classification macros)

The character classification macros `isalpha`, `isupper`, etc., classify ASCII-coded integer values by table lookup. Their definitions are in the file `/usr/include/ctype.h` and can be included in a program by using the *include* instruction:

```
#include <ctype.h>
```

Each macro is a predicate returning nonzero for true, zero for false and has a specification of the form

```
int istype(c)
int c;
```

where *type* can be one of `alpha`, `upper`, `lower`, `digit`, `alnum`, `space`, `print`, `punct`, `cntrl` and `ascii`. Macro `isascii` is defined on all integer values; the rest are defined only where `isascii` is true and on the single non-ASCII value `EOF`:

| function | explanation |
|---|---|
| `isalpha(c)` | c is a letter |
| `isupper(c)` | c is an upper case letter |
| `islower(c)` | c is a lower case letter |
| `isdigit(c)` | c is a digit |
| `isalnum(c)` | c is an alphanumeric character |
| `isspace(c)` | c is a space, tab, carriage return, newline or formfeed |
| `ispunct(c)` | c is a punctuation character |
| `isprint(c)` | c is a printing character |
| `iscntrl(c)` | c is a delete character (0177) or an ordinary control character (less than 040) |
| `isascii(c)` | c is an ASCII character, code less than 0200 |

---

------------------------------------------------------------

# FCLOSE, FFLUSH(3S)
## (close or flush a stream)

Function `fclose` causes any buffered data for the named `stream` to be written out, and the `stream` to be closed.  Its specification is

```
#include <stdio.h>

int fclose(stream)
FILE *stream;
```

A call to `fclose` is performed automatically for all open files upon calling `exit`.

Function `fflush` causes any buffered data for the named `stream` to be written to that file.  Its specification is

```
#include <stdio.h>

int fflush(stream)
FILE *stream;
```

The `stream` remains open after the execution of `fflush`.

------------------------------------------------------------

------------------------------------------------------------

# FOPEN, FREOPEN, FDOPEN(3S)
## (open a stream)

Functions `fopen`, `freopen` and `fdopen` are used to open streams. They
have the specifications

```
#include <stdio.h>

FILE *fopen(filename, type)
char *filename, *type;

FILE *freopen(filename, type, stream)
char *filename, *type;
FILE *stream;

FILE *fdopen(fildes, type)
int fildes;
char *type;
```

Function `fopen` opens the file named by `filename` and associates a
`stream` with it. Function `fopen` returns a pointer to the `FILE` structure
associated with the `stream`.

Argument `filename` points to a character string that contains the name of
the file to be opened.

Argument `type` is a character string having one of the following values:

| type | explanation |
|------|-------------|
| r | open for reading |
| w | truncate or create for writing |
| a | append; open for writing at end of file, or create for writing |
| r+ | open for update (reading and writing) |
| w+ | truncate or create for update |
| a+ | append; open or create for update at end-of-file |

A call to function `freopen` substitutes the named file in place of the open
`stream`. The original `stream` is closed, regardless of whether the open

ultimately succeeds. Function `freopen` returns a pointer to the `FILE` structure associated with `stream`.

Function `freopen` is typically used to attach the preopened `streams` associated with `stdin`, `stdout` and `stderr` to other files.

Function `fdopen` associates a `stream` with a file descriptor obtained from `open`, `dup`, `creat`, or `pipe`, which will open files, but not return the pointers to a `FILE` structure `stream` that are necessary input for many of the Section 3S library routines. The `type` of `stream` must agree with the mode of the open file.

When a file is opened for update, both input and output may be done on the resulting `stream`. However, output may not be directly followed by input without an intervening `fseek` or `rewind`, and input may not be directly followed by output without an intervening `fseek`, `rewind`, or an input operation that encounters end-of-file.

When a file is opened for append (i.e., when `type` is a or a+), it is impossible to overwrite information already in the file. Function `fseek` may be used to reposition the file pointer to any position in the file, but when output is written to the file, the current file pointer is disregarded. All output is written at the end of the file and causes the file pointer to be repositioned at the end of the output. If two separate processes open the same file for append, each process may write freely to the file without fear of destroying output being written by the other. The output from the two processes will be intermixed in the file in the order in which it is written.

--------------------------------------------------------------

---------------------------------------------------------------

# FREAD, FWRITE(3S)
### (binary input/output)

Binary input/output is done using the functions `fread` and `fwrite`. These
functions have the specification

```
#include <stdio.h>

int fread(ptr, size, nitems, stream)
char *ptr;
int size, nitems;
FILE *stream;

int fwrite(ptr, size, nitems, stream)
char *ptr;
int size, nitems;
FILE *stream;
```

Function `fread` copies, into an array beginning at `ptr`, `nitems` items of
data from the named input `stream`, where an item of data is a sequence of
bytes (not necessarily terminated by a null byte) of length `size`. A call to
function `fread` stops appending bytes if an end-of-file or error condition is
encountered while reading `stream`, or if `nitems` items have been read.
Function `fread` leaves the file pointer in `stream`, if defined, pointing to the
byte following the last byte read if there is one. Function `fread` does not
change the contents of `stream`.

Function `fwrite` appends at most `nitems` items of data from the array
pointed to by `ptr` to the named output `stream`. Function `fwrite` stops
appending when it has appended `nitems` items of data or if an error
condition is encountered on `stream`. Function `fwrite` does not change the
contents of the array pointed to by `ptr`.

The variable `size` is typically `sizeof(*ptr)` where the pseudo-function
`sizeof` specifies the length of an item pointed to by `ptr`. If `ptr` points to
a data type other than `char`, it should be cast into a pointer to `char`.

---------------------------------------------------------------

-------------------------------------------------------

# FSEEK, REWIND, FTELL(3S)
(reposition a file pointer in a stream)

Functions `fseek`, `rewind` and `ftell` are used for randomly accessing streams. They have the specifications

```
#include <stdio.h>

int fseek(stream, offset, ptrname)
FILE *stream;
long offset;
int ptrname;

void rewind(stream)
FILE *stream;

long ftell(stream)
FILE *stream;
```

Function `fseek` sets the position of the next input or output operation on the `stream`. The new position is at the signed distance `offset` bytes from the beginning, from the current position, or from the end of the file, depending upon whether `ptrname` has the value 0, 1, or 2.

Function `rewind(stream)` is equivalent to `fseek(stream, 0L, 0)`, except that no value is returned.

Functions `fseek` and `rewind` undo any effects of `ungetc`.

After `fseek` or `rewind`, the next operation on a file opened for update may be either input or output.

Function `ftell` returns the offset of the current byte relative to the beginning of the file associated with the named `stream`.

-------------------------------------------------------

---

# GETC, GETCHAR, FGETC, GETW(3S)
## (get character or word from stream)

Macros `getc` and `getchar` and functions `fgetc` and `getw` are used to get characters and words from streams; their specifications are

```
#include <stdio.h>

int getc(stream)
FILE *stream;

int getchar()

int fgetc(stream)
FILE *stream;

int getw(stream)
FILE *stream;
```

Macro `getc` returns the next character (i.e., byte) from the named input `stream`. It also moves the file pointer, if defined, ahead one character in `stream`. Because `getc` is a macro, it cannot be used if a function is necessary; for example, one cannot have a function pointer point to it.

Macro `getchar` returns the next character from the standard input stream, `stdin`. As in the case of `getc`, `getchar` is a macro.

Function `fgetc` is similar to `getc`, but is a genuine function. Function `fgetc` runs more slowly than `getc`, but takes less space per invocation.

Function `getw` returns the next word (i.e., integer) from the named input `stream`. The size of a word varies from machine to machine. It returns the constant `EOF` upon end-of-file or error. Function `getw` increments the associated file pointer, if defined, to point to the next word. Function `getw` assumes no special alignment in the file.

---

-------------------------------------------------------

# GETS, FGETS(3S)
(get a string from a stream)

Functions `gets` and `fgets` are used to read strings from streams. They have the specifications

```
#include <stdio.h>

char *gets(s)
char *s;

char *fgets(s, n, stream)
char *s;
int n;
FILE *stream;
```

Function `gets` reads characters from the standard input stream, `stdin`, into the array pointed to by `s`, until a new-line character is read or an end-of-file condition is encountered. The new-line character is discarded and the string is terminated with a null character.

Function `fgets` reads characters from the `stream` into the array pointed to by `s`, until `n-1` characters are read, a new-line character is read and transferred to `s`, or an end-of-file condition is encountered. The string is then terminated with a null character.

-------------------------------------------------------

---

# MALLOC, FREE, REALLOC, CALLOC(3)
### (main memory allocator)

Functions `malloc` and `free` provide a simple general-purpose memory allocation package. They have the specifications

```
char *malloc(size)
unsigned size;

void free(ptr)
char *ptr;
```

Function `malloc` returns a pointer to a block of at least `size` bytes suitably aligned for any use.

The argument to `free` is a pointer to a block previously allocated by `malloc`; after `free` is performed, this space is made available for further allocation, but its contents are left undisturbed.

Undefined results will occur if the space assigned by `malloc` is overrun or if some random number is handed to `free`.

Function `malloc` allocates the first big enough contiguous reach of free space found in a circular search from the last block allocated or freed, coalescing adjacent free blocks as it searches.

Function `realloc` changes the size of the block pointed to by `ptr` to `size` bytes and returns a pointer to the (possibly moved) block. The contents are unchanged up to the lesser of the new and old sizes. If no free block of `size` bytes is available in the storage arena, then `realloc` asks `malloc` to enlarge the arena by `size` bytes and then moves the data to the new space. Function `realloc` has the specification

```
char *realloc(ptr, size)
char *ptr;
unsigned size;
```

Function `realloc` also works if `ptr` points to a block freed because the last call of `malloc`, `realloc`, or `calloc`; thus, sequences of `free`, `malloc` and `realloc` can exploit the search strategy of `malloc` to do storage compaction.

Function `calloc` allocates space for an array of `nelem` elements of size `elsize`. The space is initialized to zeros. Function `calloc` has the specification

```
char *calloc(nelem, elsize)
unsigned nelem, elsize;
```

Each of the allocation routines returns a pointer to space suitably aligned (after possible pointer coercion) for storage of any type of object.

Routines `malloc`, `realloc` and `calloc` return a `NULL` pointer if there is no available memory.

-------------------------------------------------------------------

---------------------------------------------------------

# POPEN, PCLOSE(3S)
(initiate pipe to/from a process)

Function `popen` creates a pipe between the calling program and the command to be executed. The arguments to `popen` are pointers to null-terminated strings containing, respectively, a shell command line and an I/O mode, either `r` for reading or `w` for writing. The value returned is a stream pointer such that one can write to the standard input of the command, if the I/O mode is `w`, by writing to the file `stream`; and one can read from the standard output of the command, if the I/O mode is `r`, by reading from the file `stream`. Function `popen` has the specification

```
#include <stdio.h>

FILE *popen(command, type)
char *command, *type;
```

A stream opened by `popen` should be closed by `pclose`, which waits for the associated process to terminate and returns the exit status of the command. Function `pclose` has the specification

```
#include <stdio.h>

int pclose(stream)
FILE *stream;
```

Because open files are shared, a type `r` command may be used as an input filter and a type `w` as an output filter.

---------------------------------------------------------

---

# PRINTF, FPRINTF, SPRINTF(3S)
### (print formatted output)

The three functions printf, fprintf, and sprintf are used for formatted output. They have the specifications

```
#include <stdio.h>

int printf(format [, arg] ... )
char *format;

int fprintf(stream, format [, arg] ... )
FILE *stream;
char *format;

int sprintf(s, format [, arg] ... )
char *s, format;
```

Function printf places output on the standard output stream stdout. Function fprintf places output on the named output stream. Function sprintf places "output", followed by the null character \0 in consecutive bytes starting at *s; it is the user's responsibility to ensure that enough storage is available. Each function returns the number of characters transmitted (not including the \0 in the case of sprintf), or a negative value if an output error was encountered.

Each of these functions converts, formats, and prints its args under control of the format. The format is a character string that contains two types of objects: plain characters, which are simply copied to the output stream, and conversion specifications, each of which results in fetching of zero or more args. The results are undefined if there are insufficient args for the format. If the format is exhausted while args remain, the excess args are simply ignored.

Each conversion specification is introduced by the character %. After the %, the following appear in sequence:

1. Zero or more *flags*, which modify the meaning of the conversion specification.

2. An optional decimal digit string specifying a minimum *field width*. If the converted value has fewer characters than the field width, it will be

padded on the left (or right, if the left-adjustment flag (see below) has been given) to the field width;

3.  A *precision* that gives the minimum number of digits to appear for the d, o, u, x, or X conversions, the number of digits to appear after the decimal point for the e and f conversions, the maximum number of significant digits for the g conversion, or the maximum number of characters to be printed from a string in s conversion. The precision takes the form of a period (.) followed by a decimal digit string: a null digit string is treated as zero.

4.  An optional letter l specifying that a following d, o, u, x, or X conversion character applies to a long integer arg.

5.  A character that indicates the type of conversion to be applied.

A field width or precision may be indicated by an asterisk (*) instead of a digit string. In this case, an integer arg supplies the field width or precision. The arg that is actually converted is not fetched until the conversion letter is seen, so the args specifying field width or precision must appear *before* the arg (if any) to be converted.

The flag characters and their meanings are

    −      The result of the conversion will be left-justified within the field.

    +      The result of a signed conversion will always begin with a sign (+ or −).

    blank  If the first character of a signed conversion is not a sign, a blank will be prefixed to the result. This implies that if the blank and + flags both appear, the blank flag will be ignored.

    #      This flag specifies that the value is to be converted to an *alternate form*. For c, d, s, and u conversions, the flag has no effect. For o conversion, it increases the precision to force the first digit of the result to be a zero. For x (X) conversion, a non-zero result will have 0x (0X) prefixed to it. For e, E, f, g, and G conversions, the result will always contain a decimal point, even if no digits follow the point (normally, a decimal point appears in the result of these conversions only if a digit follows it). For g and G conversions, trailing zeros will *not* be removed from the result (as they normally are).

The conversion characters and their meanings are

    d, o, u, x, X    The integer arg is converted to signed decimal, unsigned octal, decimal, or hexadecimal notation (x and X), respectively; the letters abcdef are used for x conversion and the letters ABCDEF for X conversion. The precision specifies the minimum number of digits to appear; if the value being converted can be represented in fewer digits, it will be expanded with leading zeroes. The default precision is 1. The result of converting a zero value with a precision of zero is a null string.

f      The float or double arg is converted to decimal notation in the style [-]ddd.ddd, where the number of digits after the decimal point is equal to the precision specification. If the precision is missing, 6 digits are output; if the precision is explicitly 0, no decimal point appears.

e,E      The float or double arg is converted in the style [-]d.ddde±dd, where there is one digit before the decimal point and the number of digits after it is equal to the precision; when the precision is missing, 6 digits are produced; if the precision is zero, no decimal point appears. The E format code will produce a number with E instead of e introducing the exponent. The exponent always contains at least two digits.

g,G      The float or double arg is printed in style f or e (or in style E in the case of a G format code), with the precision specifying the number of significant digits. The style used depends on the value converted: style e will be used only if the exponent resulting from the conversion is less than −4 or greater than the precision. Trailing zeroes are removed from the result; a decimal point appears only if it is followed by a digit or if the # flag was given.

c      The character arg is printed.

s      The arg is taken to be a string (character pointer) and characters from the string are printed until a null character (\0) is encountered or the number of characters indicated by the precision specification is reached. If the precision is missing, it is taken to be infinite, so all characters up to the first null character are printed. If the string pointer arg has the value zero, the result is undefined. A *null* arg will yield undefined results.

%                           Print a %; no argument is converted.

In no case does a non-existent or small field width cause truncation of a field; if the result of a conversion is wider than the field width, the field is simply expanded to contain the conversion result. Characters generated by `printf` and `fprintf` are printed as if `putc` had been called.

Two examples of the use of `printf` are

- To print a date and time in the form

```
Sunday, July 3, 10:02
```

  where `weekday` and `month` are pointers to null-terminated strings:

```
printf("%s, %s %d, %.2d:%.2d", weekday,
                          month, day, hour, min);
```

- To print $\pi$ to 5 decimal places:

```
printf("pi = %.5f", 4*atan(1.0));
```

--------------------------------------------------------------

------------------------------------------------------------

# PUTC, PUTCHAR, FPUTC, PUTW(3S)
(put character or word on a stream)

Macros `putc` and `putchar`, and functions `fputc` and `putw` are used to output a character or a word. They have the specifications

```
#include <stdio.h>

int putc(c, stream)
char c;
FILE *stream;

int putchar(c)
char c;

int fputc(c, stream)
char c;
FILE *stream;

int putw(w, stream)
int w;
FILE *stream;
```

Macro `putc` writes the character c to the output `stream` (at the position where the file pointer, if defined, is pointing). Macro `putchar(c)` is defined as `putc(c, stdout)`.

Function `fputc` behaves like `putc`, but is a function rather than a macro. Function `fputc` runs more slowly than `putc`, but takes less space per invocation.

Function `putw` writes the word (i.e., integer) w to the output `stream` (at the position at which the file pointer, if defined, is pointing). The size of a word is the size of an integer and varies from machine to machine. Function `putw` neither assumes nor causes special alignment in the file.

Output streams, with the exception of the standard error stream `stderr`, are by default buffered if the output refers to a file and line-buffered if the output refers to a terminal. The standard error output stream `stderr` is by default unbuffered, but use of `freopen` (see description of `fopen` for more details) will cause it to become buffered or line-buffered. When an output stream is unbuffered, information is queued for writing on the destination file or terminal as soon as written; when it is buffered, many characters are saved up and written as a block; when it is line-buffered, each line of output is queued for writing on the destination terminal as soon as the line is completed (that is, as soon as a new-line character is written or terminal input is requested).

-------------------------------------------------------

# PUTS, FPUTS(3S)
(put a string on a stream)

Function puts writes the null-terminated string pointed to by s, followed by a new-line character, to the standard output stream stdout. It has the specification

```
#include <stdio.h>

int puts(s)
char *s;
```

Function fputs writes the null-terminated string pointed to by s to the named output stream. It has the specification

```
#include <stdio.h>

int fputs(s, stream)
char *s;
FILE *stream;
```

Neither function writes the terminating null character; both functions return EOF on error.

-------------------------------------------------------

-------------------------------------------------------

# QSORT(3)
### (quicker sort)

Function `qsort` is an implementation of the quick sort algorithm. It sorts a table of data in place. Function `qsort` has the specification

```
void qsort((char *) base, nel, sizeof(*base), compar)
unsigned int nel;
int (*compar)( );
```

Argument `base` points to the element at the base of the table. Argument `nel` is the number of elements in the table. Argument `compar` is the name of the comparison function, which is called with two arguments that point to the elements being compared. The function must return an integer less than, equal to, or greater than zero depending upon whether the first argument is to be considered less than, equal to, or greater than the second.

-------------------------------------------------------

------------------------------------------------------

# SCANF, FSCANF, SSCANF(3S)
(convert formatted input)

Functions `scanf`, `fscanf` and `sscanf` are used for formatted input. These functions have the specifications

```
#include <stdio.h>

int scanf(format [, pointer ] ... )
char *format;

int fscanf(stream, format [, pointer] ... )
FILE *stream;
char *format;

int sscanf(s, format [, pointer] ... )
char *s, *format;
```

Function `scanf` reads from the standard input stream `stdin`. Function `fscanf` reads from the named input `stream`. Function `sscanf` reads from the character string `s`. Each function reads characters, interprets them according to a format, and stores the results in its arguments. Each expects, as arguments, a control string `format` described below, and a set of `pointer` arguments indicating where the converted input should be stored.

The control string usually contains conversion specifications, which are used to direct interpretation of input sequences. The control string may contain

1. White-space characters (blanks, tabs, new-lines, or form-feeds) which, except in two cases described below, cause input to be read up to the next non-white-space character.

2. An ordinary character (not %), which must match the next character of the input stream.

3. Conversion specifications consisting of the character %, an optional assignment suppressing character *, an optional numerical maximum field width, an optional 1 or h indicating the size of the receiving variable, and a conversion code.

A conversion specification directs the conversion of the next input field; the result is placed in the variable pointed to by the corresponding argument, unless assignment suppression was indicated by *. The suppression of assignment provides a way of describing an input field that is to be skipped. An input field is defined as a string of non-space characters; it extends to the next inappropriate character or until the field width, if specified, is exhausted.

The conversion code indicates the interpretation of the input field; the corresponding pointer argument must usually be of a restricted type. For a suppressed field, no pointer argument should be given. The following conversion codes are legal:

%  a single % is expected in the input at this point; no assignment is done.

d  a decimal integer is expected; the corresponding argument should be an integer pointer.

u  an unsigned decimal integer is expected; the corresponding argument should be an unsigned integer pointer.

o  an octal integer is expected; the corresponding argument should be an integer pointer.

x  a hexadecimal integer is expected; the corresponding argument should be an integer pointer.

e,f,g  a floating point number is expected; the next field is converted accordingly and stored through the corresponding argument, which should be a pointer to a float. The input format for floating point numbers is an optionally signed string of digits, possibly containing a decimal point, followed by an optional exponent field consisting of an E or an e, followed by an optionally signed integer.

s  a character string is expected; the corresponding argument should be a character pointer pointing to an array of characters large enough to accept the string and a terminating \0, which will be added automatically. The input field is terminated by a white-space character.

c  a character is expected; the corresponding argument should be a character pointer. The normal skip over white space is suppressed in this case; to read the next non-space character, use %1s. If a field width is given, the corresponding argument should refer to a character array; the indicated number of characters is read.

[  indicates string data and the normal skip over leading white space is suppressed. The left bracket is followed by a set of characters, which we will call the *scanset*, and a right bracket; the input field is the maximal sequence of input characters consisting entirely of characters in the scanset. The circumflex, (^), when it appears as the first character in the scanset, serves as a complement operator and redefines the scanset as the set of all characters *not* contained in the remainder of the scanset string. There are some conventions used in the construction of the scanset. A range of characters may be represented by the construct *first-last*, thus [0123456789] may be expressed [0-9]. Using this convention, *first must be lexically less than or equal to last*, or else the dash will stand for itself. The dash will also stand for itself whenever it is the first or the last character in the scanset. To include the right square bracket as an element of the scanset, it must appear as the first character (possibly preceded by a circumflex) of the scanset, and in this case it will not be syntactically interpreted as the closing bracket. The corresponding argument must point to a character array large enough to hold the data field and the terminating \0, which will be added automatically.

The conversion characters d, u, o, and x may be preceded by l or h to indicate that a pointer to long or to short rather than to int is in the argument list. Similarly, the conversion characters e, f, and g may be preceded by l to indicate that a pointer to double rather than to float is in the argument list.

Conversion by function scanf terminates at EOF, at the end of the control string, or when an input character conflicts with the control string. In the latter case, the offending character is left unread in the input stream.

Function scanf returns the number of successfully matched and assigned input items; this number can be zero in the event of an early conflict between an input character and the control string. If the input ends before the first conflict or conversion, EOF is returned. Some examples of the use of scanf are

1.  Using the definitions

    ```
    int i; float x; char name[50];
    ```

    the scanf call

    ```
    scanf("%d%f%s", &i, &x, name);
    ```
    with the input line
    ```
    25 54.32E-1 thompson
    ```

will assign 25 to i, 5.432 to x and thompson\0 to name.

2. Using the variable definitions given above, the call

```
scanf("%2d%f%*d %[0-9]", &i, &x, name);
```

with the input line

```
56789 0 123 56a72
```

will assign 56 to i, 789.0 to x, skip 0 123, and place the string 56\0 in name. The next call to getchar (see description of getc for more details) will return a.

------------------------------------------------------------

---

# SETJMP, LONGJMP(3)
## (non-local goto)

Functions `setjmp` and `longjmp` are useful for dealing with errors and interrupts encountered in a low-level subroutine of a program. Their specifications are

```
#include <setjmp.h>

int setjmp(env)
jmp_buf env;

void longjmp(env, val)
jmp_buf env;
int val;
```

Function `setjmp` saves its stack environment in `env` (whose type, `jmp_buf`, is defined in the `<setjmp.h>` header file), for later use by `longjmp`. It returns the value 0.

Function `longjmp` restores the environment saved by the last call of `setjmp` with the corresponding `env` argument. After `longjmp` is completed, program execution continues as if the corresponding call of `setjmp` (which must not itself have returned in the interim) had just returned the value `val`. Function `longjmp` cannot cause `setjmp` to return the value 0. If `longjmp` is invoked with a second argument of 0, `setjmp` will return 1. All accessible data have values as of the time `longjmp` was called.

---

------------------------------------------------------

# SLEEP(3)
### (suspend execution for interval)

Function s l e e p, which is specified as,

```
unsigned sleep(seconds)
unsigned seconds;
```

suspends execution of the current process for the number of seconds specified by the argument.

The actual suspension time may be less than that requested for two reasons:

1.  scheduled wakeups occur at fixed 1-second intervals (on the second, according to an internal clock);

2.  any caught signal will terminate the s l e e p following execution of that signal's catching routine.

The suspension time may be longer than requested by an arbitrary amount due to the scheduling of other activity in the system. The value returned by s l e e p will be the *unslept* amount (the requested time minus the time actually slept) in case the caller had an alarm set to go off earlier than the end of the requested s l e e p time, or there was premature arousal due to another caught signal.

The routine is implemented by setting an alarm signal and pausing until it (or some other signal) occurs. The previous state of the alarm signal is saved and restored. The calling program may have set up an alarm signal before calling s l e e p; if the s l e e p time exceeds the time until such alarm signal, the process sleeps only until the alarm signal would have occurred, and the caller's alarm catch routine is executed just before the s l e e p routine returns, but if the s l e e p time is less than the time until such alarm, the prior alarm time is reset to go off at the same time it would have without the intervening s l e e p.

------------------------------------------------------

---------------------------------------------------------

# STRCAT, STRNCAT, STRCMP, STRNCMP, STRCPY, STRNCPY, STRLEN, STRCHR, STRRCHR, STRPBRK STRSPN, STRCSPN, STRTOK(3)
### (string operations)

The string functions operate on null-terminated strings. They have the specifications

```
#include <string.h>

char *strcat(s1, s2)
char *s1, *s2;

char *strncat(s1, s2, n)
char *s1, *s2;
int n;

int strcmp(s1, s2)
char *s1, *s2;

int strncmp(s1, s2, n)
char *s1, *s2;
int n;

char *strcpy(s1, s2)
char *s1, *s2;

char *strncpy(s1, s2, n)
char *s1, *s2;
int n;

int strlen(s)
char *s;

char *strchr(s, c)
char *s, c;

char *strrchr(s, c)
char *s, c;

char *strpbrk(s1, s2)
```

```
char *s1, *s2;

int strspn(s1, s2)
char *s1, *s2;

int strcspn(s1, s2)
char *s1, *s2;

char *strtok(s1, s2)
char *s1, *s2;
```

The arguments s1, s2 and s point to strings (arrays of characters terminated by a null character). The functions strcat, strncat, strcpy and strncpy all alter s1. These functions do not check for overflow of the array pointed to by s1.

Function strcat appends a copy of string s2 to the end of string s1. Function strncat appends at most n characters. Each returns a pointer to the null-terminated result.

Function strcmp compares its arguments and returns an integer less than, equal to, or greater than 0, depending upon whether s1 is lexicographically less than, equal to, or greater than s2. Function strncmp makes the same comparison, but looks at up to n characters.

Function strcpy copies string s2 to s1, stopping after the null character has been copied. Function strncpy copies exactly n characters, truncating s2 or adding null characters to s1 if necessary. The result will not be null-terminated if the length of s2 is n or more. Each function returns s1.

Function strlen returns the number of characters in s, not including the terminating null character.

Function strchr (strrchr) returns a pointer to the first (last) occurrence of character c in string s, or a NULL pointer if c does not occur in the string. The null character terminating a string is considered to be part of the string.

Function strpbrk returns a pointer to the first occurrence in string s1 of any character from string s2, or a NULL pointer if no character from s2 exists in s1.

Function strspn (strcspn) returns the length of the initial segment of string s1 which consists entirely of characters from (not from) string s2.

Function strtok considers the string s1 to consist of a sequence of zero or more text tokens separated by spans of one or more characters from the separator string s2. The first call (with pointer s1 specified) returns a pointer to the first character of the first token, and will have written a null character into s1 immediately following the returned token. The function keeps track of its position in the string between separate calls, so that on subsequent calls (which must be made with the first argument a NULL pointer) will work through the string s1 immediately following that token. In this way subsequent calls will work through the string s1 until no tokens remain. The separator string s2 may be different from call to call. When no token remains in s1, a NULL pointer is returned.

For user convenience, all these functions are declared in the optional <string.h> header file.

---

---

# TMPFILE(3S)
## (create a temporary file)

Function tmpfile creates a temporary file and returns a corresponding
FILE pointer. Its specification is

```
#include <stdio.h>

FILE *tmpfile()
```

The file will automatically be deleted when the process using it terminates.
The file is opened for update.

---

# TMPNAM, TEMPNAM(3S)
## (create a name for a temporary file)

Functions tmpnam and tempnam generate file names that can safely be used
for a temporary file. These functions generate a different file name each time
they are called. They have the specifications

```
#include <stdio.h>

char *tmpnam(s)
char *s;

char *tempnam(dir, pfx)
char *dir, *pfx;
```

Function tmpnam always generates a file name using the path-name defined
as P_tmpdir in file stdio.h. If s is NULL, tmpnam leaves its result in
an internal static area and returns a pointer to that area. The next call to
tmpnam will destroy the contents of the area. If s is not NULL, it is
assumed to be the address of an array of at least L_tmpnam bytes, where
L_tmpnam is a constant defined in file stdio.h; tmpnam places its result
in that array and returns s.

Function `tempnam` allows the user to control the choice of a directory. The argument `dir` points to the path-name of the directory in which the file is to be created. If `dir` is `NULL` or points to a string that is not a path-name for an appropriate directory, the path-name defined as `P_tmpdir` in file `stdio.h` file is used. If that path-name is not accessible, `/tmp` is used as a last resort. This entire sequence can be up-staged by providing an environment variable `TMPDIR` in the user's environment, whose value is a path-name for the desired temporary-file directory.

Many applications prefer their temporary files to have certain favorite initial letter sequences in their names. Use the `pfx` argument for this. This argument may be `NULL` or point to a string of up to five characters to be used as the first few characters of the temporary-file name.

Function `tempnam` uses `malloc` to get space for the constructed file name, and returns a pointer to this area. Thus, any pointer value returned from `tempnam` may serve as an argument to `free` (see the description of `malloc` for more details). If `tempnam` cannot return the expected result for any reason, i.e., `malloc` failed, or none of the above mentioned attempts to find an appropriate directory was successful, a `NULL` pointer will be returned.

-------------------------------------------------------------------

---

# UNGETC(3S)
(push character back into input stream)

It has the specification

```
#include <stdio.h>

int ungetc(c, stream)
char c;
FILE *stream;
```

Function `ungetc` inserts the character `c` into the buffer associated with an input `stream`. That character, c, will be returned by the next `getc` call on that `stream`. Function `ungetc` returns c, and leaves the file `stream` unchanged.

One character pushback is guaranteed provided something has been read from the stream and the stream is actually buffered.

If c equals `EOF`, `ungetc` does nothing to the buffer and returns `EOF`.

Function `fseek` erases all memory of inserted characters.

---

## 2. Math Library `libm`

The math library contains the following functions:

1. Bessel functions (`j0`, `j1`, `jn`, `y0`, `y1` and `yn`).

2. Error and complementary error functions (`erf` and `erfc`).

3. • Exponential (`exp`),
   • Logarithm (`log` and `log10`),
   • Power (`pow`) and
   • Square root (`sqrt`).

4. • Floor (`floor`),
   • Ceiling (`ceil`),
   • Floating point remainder (`fmod`) and
   • Floating point absolute value (`fabs`).

5. Gamma function (`gamma`).

6. Length of the hypotenuse, i.e., Euclidean distance function (`hypot`).

7. Hyperbolic functions (`sinh`, `cosh` and `tanh`).

8. Trigonometric functions (`sin`, `cos`, `tan`, `asin`, `acos`, `atan` and `atan2`).

# Appendix B
## Some C Tools

The UNIX operating system provides a very rich and fertile environment for writing C programs. It provides the C programmer with a wide range of tools that facilitate program development. For example, there are tools that allow C programs to be checked for errors, compiled,[64] formatted nicely and maintained.

Use of these tools, with the exception of the C compiler, is optional; however, using these tools is easy and quite productive; consequently most C programmers gravitate towards using them more and more. Only some of the commonly used tools will be described here. A more complete list of tools can be found in the *UNIX Reference Manual* [Berkeley UNIX 1981, AT&T UNIX (Release 5.0) 1982, AT&T UNIX (System V) 1983].

## 1. `lint`: The C Program Checker [Johnson 1978b]

The C program checker `lint` detects features of C programs that cause bugs or make programs difficult to port from one computer to another. It checks for incorrect type usage more strictly than the C compilers. It finds potential errors and sources of errors such as unreachable statements, loops that are not entered at the top and automatic variables that have been defined but not used. Functions are checked to determine if they are called with the appropriate types of actual parameters, if they return values in some places but not in others, if they are called with varying numbers of arguments and if the values returned by them are used (functions used as subroutines).

The program checker `lint` is invoked as

`lint [-abchnpuvx]` *file*$_1$`.c` *file*$_2$`.c` ... *file*$_n$`.c`

By default, it is assumed that all the files are to be loaded together; they are checked for mutual compatibility.

---

64. Compilers are tools!

Any number of the following options may be used:

h          Apply a number of heuristic tests to detect bugs, improve style and reduce waste.

b          Report *break* statements that cannot be reached.

v          Suppress complaints about unused arguments in functions.

x          Report variables referred to by `extern` declarations but never used.

a          Report assignments of `long` values to `int` variables.

c          Complain about casts that have questionable portability.

u          Do not complain about functions and variables used and not defined, or defined and not used (this is suitable for running `lint` on a subset of files out of a larger program).

n          Do not check compatibility against the standard library.

Function `exit` and other functions that do not return upon completion are not understood and lead to incorrect error messages.

Certain comments in a C program change the behavior of `lint`:

`/*NOTREACHED*/`      at appropriate points, stops comments about unreachable code.

`/*VARARGSn*/`        suppresses the usual checking for variable number of arguments in the following function declaration. The data types of the first *n* arguments are checked; a missing *n* is taken to be 0.

`/*NOSTRICT*/`        shuts off strict type checking in the next expression.

`/*ARGSUSED*/`        turns on the `-v` option for the next function.

`/*LINTLIBRARY*/`     at the beginning of a file shuts off complaints about unused functions in this file.

## 2. cc: The C Compiler [AT&T Unix (Release 5.0)]

The UNIX C compiler accepts several types of arguments. Arguments whose names end with `.c` are taken to be C source programs; they are compiled, and each object program is left in a file whose name is the same as that of the C source file but with a `.o` substituted for the `.c`.[65] If a single C program is compiled and loaded all at once, then an a.out file is produced and the .o file is deleted.

Other arguments are taken to be either loader option arguments, C-compatible object programs, typically produced by an earlier cc run, or perhaps libraries of C-compatible routines. These programs, together with the results of any compilations specified, are loaded (in the order given) to produce an executable program with the name a.out.

The C compiler is invoked as

cc [ *options* ] *file*$_1$ *file*$_2$ · · · *file*$_n$

The following options are interpreted by cc:

-c     Suppress the loading phase of the compilation and force an object file to be produced even if only one program is compiled.

-w     Suppress warning diagnostics.

-O     Invoke an object-code improver.

-E     Run only the macro preprocessor on the named C programs and send the result to the standard output.

-C     Prevent the macro preprocessor from eliding comments.

-o *output*   Name the final output file *output*. If this option is used, file a.out will be left undisturbed.

## 3. cb: The C Beautifier

The C program beautifier cb takes as input a C program from the standard input stream and produces a program with spacing and indentation that displays the structure of the program. This program is written on to the standard output stream. It is invoked as

cb  <*file*$_{input}$  >*file*$_{output}$

---

65. On the UNIX system, to be more precise, the object file (the file with the .o suffix) is left in the current directory.

Consider the following program written without any indentation:

```
#include <stdio.h>
int x[3] = {1, 2, 3};
main()
{
void swap();
swap (&x[1], &x[2]);
printf( "%d", x[1]);
}
void swap(a, b)
int *a, *b;
{
int t;
t = *a;
*a = *b;
*b =t;
}
```

The C beautifier transforms this into the following form, which is more readable than the original form:

```
#include <stdio.h>
int x[3] = {
        1, 2, 3};
main()
{
        void swap();
        swap (&x[1], &x[2]);
        printf( "%d", x[1]);
}
void swap(a, b)
int *a, *b;
{
        int t;
        t = *a;
        *a = *b;
        *b =t;
}
```

You might prefer to use your own program layout style instead of that produced by cb. The important thing is not that a particular style must be used by every programmer, but that a programmer use a style that enhances program readability, not just for the programmer, but also for others who may have to look at the resulting program.

## 4. make: Program Group Maintainer [Feldman 79]

The advantages of designing a software system in a modular fashion are widely recognized. However, such an approach poses one practical problem. When a module (C source file) is changed, how does one keep track of all the other modules affected by this change? This problem is especially severe in the early stages of program construction because modules are changed frequently to correct errors, and in response to changing program specifications and better understanding of the problem being solved.

There are two obvious, but inelegant, solutions to the above problem: either all system modules can be recompiled whenever a module is modified or only the affected modules can be selectively recompiled. The first solution wastes resources and is time consuming because often only a few modules need to be recompiled. The second solution is prone to errors, especially when there are a large number of modules and the modules are modified frequently. Forgetting to recompile even one module or using an incorrect recompilation sequence will produce an incorrect version of the system.

The make program solves the above problem by automating the selective recompilation process; the programmer does not have to remember which modules are affected by a change and the order in which these modules are to be recompiled. Program make uses information supplied by the user indicating dependencies between the files; it also uses the time the file was last modified, which it gets from the file system. The make program also has built-in knowledge about relationships between several kinds of objects. For example, it knows that any file with an .o suffix can be created by compiling the corresponding C file that has the same prefix, but a .c suffix.

As an example illustrating the use of the make program, consider a program sort that is produced using the following five files:

| module | function performed by the module |
|--------|----------------------------------|
| sort | contains the executable form of the complete sort program. |
| main.c | contains the main program that reads input from the standard input stream, calls function qksort (contained in file qksort.c) with an array containing the input elements and then writes the sorted array on the standard output stream. |

| | |
|---|---|
| qksort.c | contains function qksort that does the sorting; calls function part for partitioning an array, and calls function swap for exchanging two elements. |
| part.c | contains function part. |
| swap.c | contains function swap. |
| defs | contains definitions used by main.c; included in main.c by means of the preprocessor *include* statement. |

Dependencies between the files are used to specify the actions that should be taken when the files are modified. Dependencies between program sort and these modules (or their compiled versions) are illustrated by the following diagram:

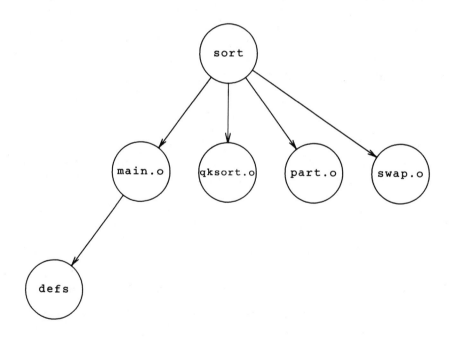

The dependencies between the files used in the construction of sort and the actions that should be taken when the files are modified are specified as follows:

```
sort:   main.o qksort.o part.o swap.o
        cc -o sort main.o qksort.o part.o swap.o
main.o: defs
```

The first line states that `sort` depends upon `main.o`, `qksort.o`, `part.o` and `swap.o`. The third line states that `main.o` depends upon the file `defs`. Dependencies between the object files and the corresponding C source files need not be explicitly specified. As mentioned earlier, this information is built into `make`.

This dependency information and the associated actions are placed in a file named `makefile`. Whenever any one of the modules is changed, executing the command

```
make
```

ensures that `sort` is up-to-date by compiling all files that need to be recompiled.

If all modules were up-to-date and `sort` did actually represent the latest version, then `make` will print

```
'sort' is up to date
```

and stop. If all the object files are the latest versions and a new version of `sort` has not been created, then the second line of the dependency file given above, which specifies how program `sort` is created,

```
cc -o sort main.o qksort.o part.o swap.o
```

is executed. If any object module is not the latest version, then its latest version must be compiled. A new version of the object module is automatically compiled from the corresponding source code (i.e., `main.c`, `qksort.c`, `part.c` and `swap.c`). Suppose that the definitions file `defs` has been modified. Now `sort` depends upon `main.o`, which in turn depends upon `defs`. Consequently, `main.o` is first recompiled; then line 2 of the above dependency file is executed to construct an updated version of `sort`.

As another example, consider a shortened version of `makefile` used in the construction of an electronic form system prototype [Gehani 1983a]:[66]

```
#macros definitions have the form NAME = string;
#macros are invoked as $(NAME)
#non-comment lines longer than a line may be
#continued on the next line provided the backslash
#character is used to escape a newline, i.e., it
#is the last character in the line

LINT =                  lint

CFLAGS =                -O      #C compiler option for
                                #producing optimized code
BEEP =                  "^G"    #the non-printing character
                                #control G is used to make a
                                #beeping sound at the
                                #terminal


FILES =                 Makefile        \
                        createmask      \
                        enhncemsk.c     \
                        mask_pre.c      \
                        tra.disp.tbl    \
                        help_pos.c      \
                        forms           \
                        emp.db          \
                        emp.dbrt.c      \
                        formI.c         \
                        str.h           \
                        tra.fld.defs    \
                        tra.pre.c       \
                        tra.post.c      \
                        tra.acc_rts     \
                        acc_rts.c       \
                        tra.fld.types   \
                        tra.error.c     \
```

---

66. The beginning of a comment is signaled by the character # and terminated by the end of the line. Although a comment can begin anywhere there is one exception: lines containing only comments can be placed between commands (which update a target) provided they start in column 1.

```
                         tra.template     \
                         tra.number       \
                         tra.actions.c    \
                         hpsub.c


INTP =                   formI.o          \
                         hpsub.o          \
                         tra.pre.o        \
                         tra.post.o       \
                         acc_rts.o        \
                         tra.error.o      \
                         tra.actions.o    \
                         emp.dbrt.o


MASK =                   createmask       \
                         enhncemsk        \
                         mask_pre

formI:                   $(INTP)  #macro call that lists
#                                 the files that "formI"
#                                 is dependent upon
                         $(CC) $(CFLAGS) -o formI $(INTP)
#                                 macro call $(CC) is
#                                 equivalent to "cc"; loads
#                                 and links all the files
#                                 $(INT) into an executable
#                                 file "formI"; CC is a
#                                 predefined macro

formI.o tra.pre.o tra.post.o \
tra.error.o tra.actions.o:         tra.fld.defs

tra.mask:                $(MASK) tra.disp.tbl
                         @echo "creating tra.mask"
#                                 character @ suppresses printing
#                                 of the command itself
                         createmask tra
                         @echo $(BEEP)   #beep to attract
#                                         attention of the user

enhncemsk:               enhncemsk.c
                         $(CC) $(CFLAGS) enhncemsk.c -o enhncemsk
                         @echo $(BEEP)
```

```
mask_pre:          mask_pre.c
                   $(CC) $(CFLAGS) mask_pre.c -o mask_pre
                   @echo $(BEEP)

lnt:               *.c     #check files for type errors
                   $(LINT) *.c
                   touch lnt
                   @echo $(BEEP)

print:             $(FILES)       #print all recently
#                                 modified files
#                                 (specified by $?)
                   pr $? ¦ lpr    #the output of "pr" is
#                                 sent to the line
#                                 printer "lpr" for
#                                 printing via pipe "¦"
                   touch print
                   @echo $(BEEP)
```

Files lnt and print are *null* files used for determining the last time the corresponding list of source files were checked for errors and printed, respectively.

The command

```
make name
```

executes the commands associated with the target *name* if file *name* is out of date. If the target is not specified, then make assumes is to be the first target in makefile. The commands used to keep the electronic form system and its program listings up-to-date are

| command | effect |
|---------|--------|
| `make` | ensure that program `formI` is up-to-date |
| `make formI` | same as above—because `formI` is the first label |
| `make tra.mask` | create the mask for form type `tra` |
| `make enhncemsk` | ensure that the program `enhncemsk` is up-to-date |
| `make lnt` | ensure that the file `lnt` is up-to-date; the effect of this is to force the application of `lint` to all the C programs |
| `make print` | print all files that have been modified |

Now for some more details about the `make` program. It is invoked as

`make` [ `-f` *makefile* ] [ *option* ] [ *names* ]

Program `make` executes the commands in *makefile* to update one or more target *names*. The target names are usually program names that have been specified to depend upon other files in the *makefile*. If no `-f` option is present, then the files `makefile` and `Makefile` are tried in that order. If *makefile* is `-`, the standard input is taken. More than one `-f` option may be given. Program `make` updates a target if it depends on prerequisite files that have been modified because the target was last modified, or if the target does not exist.

File *makefile* contains a sequence of entries that specify dependencies. The first line of an entry is a blank-separated list of targets, then a colon, then a list of prerequisite files. Text following a semicolon, and all following lines that begin with a tab, are shell commands to be executed to update the target. If a name appears on the left of more than one *colon* line, then it depends on all of the names on the right of the colon on those lines, but only one command sequence may be specified for it. If a double colon `::` instead of a colon then the command sequence following that line is performed only if the name is out of date with respect to the names to the right of the double colon, and is not affected by other double colon lines on which that name may appear.

Comments begin with the character `#` and are terminated by the end-of-line.

Some options that may be used are

-n          Trace and print, but do not execute the commands to
            update the targets.

-t          Update the modified date of the targets without executing
            any commands.

# Appendix C
# ANSI Standard C

The programming language C is currently in the process of being standardized. An ANSI Technical Committee (X3J11) is currently working on a standard for C.[67] It is expected that the version of C to be adopted as the standard will be presented to ANSI in late 1984. Adoption of C as an ANSI standard is scheduled for late 1985.

Most of the changes contemplated to C [Ritchie 1980] are minor. Some of the changes are

| | |
|---|---|
| Keywords | • Keyword const has been added and the keyword entry has been deleted. |
| Character Constants | • Multi-character constants can be specified. |
| Strings | • Adjacent string literals will be concatenated into a single string literal. |
| Arithmetic Conversions | • Floating point arithmetic may be done in single precision. |
| Types | • The type const has been added.<br>◦ Type equivalence is defined; two types are the same if their component types are the same. |
| Operators | • sizeof yields an unsigned integer constant of a suitable size. |
| Expressions | • Unary plus has been added.<br>• Pointers of different types may not be mixed. |

---

67. The IEEE has also initiated an effort to standardize C.

| | |
|---|---|
| Declarations | • Type modifier unsigned may be used with long, short or char. |
| | • The types of function formal parameters may be specified in function declarations. |
| Initialization | • An automatic aggregate may be initialized. |
| External Function Definitions | • Formal parameters of type float will not be automatically changed to double. |
| | • A function name may be used as a formal parameter. |
| Main Program | Every program running under the control of an operating system will be required to have the function named main; this function will be executed first in every program. |
| Preprocessor | • An arbitrary number of spaces or horizontal tabs may precede or follow the # character in the preprocessor instructions. |
| | • The unary operator defined has been added. |
| | • The #elif directive has been added. |

# Appendix D

## ASCII Table

ASCII (American Standard Code for Information Exchange)

### ASCII Table in Octal

| | | | | | | | | | | | | | | | |
|---|---|---|---|---|---|---|---|---|---|---|---|---|---|---|---|
| 000 | nul | 001 | soh | 002 | stx | 003 | etx | 004 | eot | 005 | enq | 006 | ack | 007 | bel |
| 010 | bs | 011 | ht | 012 | nl | 013 | vt | 014 | np | 015 | cr | 016 | so | 017 | si |
| 020 | dle | 021 | dc1 | 022 | dc2 | 023 | dc3 | 024 | dc4 | 025 | nak | 026 | syn | 027 | etb |
| 030 | can | 031 | em | 032 | sub | 033 | esc | 034 | fs | 035 | gs | 036 | rs | 037 | us |
| 040 | sp | 041 | ! | 042 | " | 043 | # | 044 | $ | 045 | % | 046 | & | 047 | ' |
| 050 | ( | 051 | ) | 052 | * | 053 | + | 054 | , | 055 | - | 056 | . | 057 | / |
| 060 | 0 | 061 | 1 | 062 | 2 | 063 | 3 | 064 | 4 | 065 | 5 | 066 | 6 | 067 | 7 |
| 070 | 8 | 071 | 9 | 072 | : | 073 | ; | 074 | < | 075 | = | 076 | > | 077 | ? |
| 100 | @ | 101 | A | 102 | B | 103 | C | 104 | D | 105 | E | 106 | F | 107 | G |
| 110 | H | 111 | I | 112 | J | 113 | K | 114 | L | 115 | M | 116 | N | 117 | O |
| 120 | P | 121 | Q | 122 | R | 123 | S | 124 | T | 125 | U | 126 | V | 127 | W |
| 130 | X | 131 | Y | 132 | Z | 133 | [ | 134 | \ | 135 | ] | 136 | ^ | 137 | _ |
| 140 | ` | 141 | a | 142 | b | 143 | c | 144 | d | 145 | e | 146 | f | 147 | g |
| 150 | h | 151 | i | 152 | j | 153 | k | 154 | l | 155 | m | 156 | n | 157 | o |
| 160 | p | 161 | q | 162 | r | 163 | s | 164 | t | 165 | u | 166 | v | 167 | w |
| 170 | x | 171 | y | 172 | z | 173 | { | 174 | \| | 175 | } | 176 | ~ | 177 | del |

## ASCII Table in Hexadecimal

| 00 nul | 01 soh | 02 stx | 03 etx | 04 eot | 05 enq | 06 ack | 07 bel |
|--------|--------|--------|--------|--------|--------|--------|--------|
| 08 bs  | 09 ht  | 0a nl  | 0b vt  | 0c np  | 0d cr  | 0e so  | 0f si  |
| 10 dle | 11 dc1 | 12 dc2 | 13 dc3 | 14 dc4 | 15 nak | 16 syn | 17 etb |
| 18 can | 19 em  | 1a sub | 1b esc | 1c fs  | 1d gs  | 1e rs  | 1f us  |
| 20 sp  | 21 !   | 22 "   | 23 #   | 24 $   | 25 %   | 26 &   | 27 '   |
| 28 (   | 29 )   | 2a *   | 2b +   | 2c ,   | 2d -   | 2e .   | 2f /   |
| 30 0   | 31 1   | 32 2   | 33 3   | 34 4   | 35 5   | 36 6   | 37 7   |
| 38 8   | 39 9   | 3a :   | 3b ;   | 3c <   | 3d =   | 3e >   | 3f ?   |
| 40 @   | 41 A   | 42 B   | 43 C   | 44 D   | 45 E   | 46 F   | 47 G   |
| 48 H   | 49 I   | 4a J   | 4b K   | 4c L   | 4d M   | 4e N   | 4f O   |
| 50 P   | 51 Q   | 52 R   | 53 S   | 54 T   | 55 U   | 56 V   | 57 W   |
| 58 X   | 59 Y   | 5a Z   | 5b [   | 5c \   | 5d ]   | 5e ^   | 5f _   |
| 60 `   | 61 a   | 62 b   | 63 c   | 64 d   | 65 e   | 66 f   | 67 g   |
| 68 h   | 69 i   | 6a j   | 6b k   | 6c l   | 6d m   | 6e n   | 6f o   |
| 70 p   | 71 q   | 72 r   | 73 s   | 74 t   | 75 u   | 76 v   | 77 w   |
| 78 x   | 79 y   | 7a z   | 7b {   | 7c \|  | 7d }   | 7e ~   | 7f del |

# Appendix E

# Implementation-Dependent Characteristics

**Character Set**

|  | DEC PDP-11 | DEC VAX-11 | AT&T 3B series | IBM 370 | Motorola 68000 |
|---|---|---|---|---|---|
| character set | ASCII | ASCII | ASCII | EBCDIC | ASCII |

**Storage Typically Allocated for Fundamental Types (in bits)**
**by**
**C compilers on various machines**

|  | DEC PDP-11 | DEC VAX-11 | AT&T 3B series | IBM 370 | Motorola 68000 |
|---|---|---|---|---|---|
| char | 8 | 8 | 8 | 8 | 8 |
| int | 16 | 32 | 32 | 32 | 8 or 16 |
| short | 16 | 16 | 16 | 16 | 16 |
| long | 32 | 32 | 32 | 32 | 32 |
| float | 32 | 32 | 32 | 32 | 32 |
| double | 64 | 64 | 64 | 64 | 32 or 64 |
| pointers | 16 | 32 | 32 | 32 | 32 |

# Annotated Bibliography

Ada 1983. *Reference Manual for the Ada Programming Language.* United States Department of Defense (January).

Anderson, B. 1980. Type Syntax in the Language C: an object lesson in syntactic innovation. *SIGPLAN Notices*, v15, no. 3 (March). Criticizes the C syntax for declaring types; argues that the syntax is cryptic and hard to read in contrast to the syntax for type declarations in languages like ALGOL 68 or Pascal.

AT&T UNIX (Release 5.0) 1982. *UNIX System User's Manual (Release 5.0).* AT&T Bell Laboratories, Murray Hill, N.J. 07974.

AT&T UNIX (System V) 1983. *UNIX System V Reference Manuals.* AT&T Technologies, 1983.

Berkeley UNIX 1981. *UNIX Programmer's Manual (4.1 BSD).* Computer Science Division, Department of Electrical Engineering and Computer Science, University of California, Berkeley, CA 94720.

Bourne, S. R. 1982. *The UNIX System.* Addison-Wesley Publishing Co. A detailed and comprehensive guide to the UNIX operating system and the facilities available on it.

Bowles, K. L. 1977. *Problem Solving Using PASCAL.* Springer-Verlag.

Brinch Hansen, P. 1973. Concurrent Programming Concepts. *ACM Computing Surveys*, v6, no. 4 (December), pp. 223-245.

Brinch Hansen, P. 1975. The Programming Language Concurrent Pascal. *IEEE Transactions on Software Engineering*, vSE-1, no. 2 (June).

Byte Magazine 1983. Special Issue of *Byte* magazine on the C programming language, v8, no. 8 (August).

Christian, K. 1983. *The UNIX Operating System.* John Wiley. Chapter 15 discusses the relationship between C and the UNIX operating system.

Collinson, R. P. A. 1981. Comments on Style in C. UKC Computing Lab-7, Computing Lab, Kent University, Canterbury, England.

Dahl, O. J., E. W. Dijkstra and C. A. R. Hoare 1972. *Structured Programming.* Academic Press. A classic book on the disciplined and methodological approach to programming that has come to be known as *structured programming.*

The book contains three articles. In the first article, "Notes on Structured Programming," Dijkstra outlines the methods and discipline used by him in programming. Abstraction is a very powerful tool in mastering complexity and should be used in the design of programs. Programs are developed using *invariants* and stepwise refinement using the three types of decomposition—*concatenation, selection* and *repetition.*

Hoare, in the second article titled "Notes on Data Structuring," applies the above principles to the design of data structures. The abstract versions of the program should rely only on the logical properties of the abstract versions of the data structures and not on details of the implementations of the abstract data structures. Implementation details of the abstract data structures should be postponed as long as possible, preferably until the writing of code, because this helps make a program independent of its implementation.

In the final article, "Hierarchical Program Structures," Hoare and Dahl talk about the connection between the design of data structures and the design of programs. The *class* concept of Simula 67 and coroutines are advocated as important program development ideas.

Dijkstra, E. W. 1968. Goto Statement Considered Harmful. *CACM*, v11 (March), pp. 147-148. Dijkstra argues that the good programming constructs are those that allow the understanding of a program in time proportional to its length. In trying to understand a program containing *goto*s used in an undisciplined manner, the reader of the program is repeatedly forced to jump from one part of a program to another; the reader must follow the execution path of the program to understand the program. This slows program understanding. Dijkstra convincingly argues that constructs such as the *if-then-else* statement and the *while* loop do not cause such slowdowns.

Dijkstra, E. W. 1972. Notes on Structured Programming. In *Structured Programming* edited by O. J. Dahl, E. W. Dijkstra and C. A. R. Hoare, Academic Press.

Dijkstra, E. W. 1976. *A Discipline of Programming.* Prentice-Hall.

Evans Jr., A. 1984. A Comparison of Programming Languages: Ada, Pascal, C. In *Comparing and Assessing Programming Languages* edited by Alan Feuer and Narain Gehani, Prentice-Hall [Feuer and Gehani 1984]. The three programming languages are compared against a set of requirements for systems programming and with each other.

Feldman, S. I. 1979. Make—A Program for Maintaining Computer Programs. *Software—Practice and Experience*, v9, pp. 255-265. A tool for maintaining latest versions of programs that consist of many modules (actually files in C).

Feuer, A. 1982. *C Puzzle Book.* Prentice-Hall. A work book that contains convoluted problems, called puzzles, that aim to test and enhance the student's understanding of the operators in C.

Feuer, A. and N. Gehani 1982. A Comparison of the Programming Languages C and Pascal. *ACM Computing Surveys*, v14, no. 1 (March), pp. 73-92. Also in *Comparing and Assessing Programming Languages* edited by Alan Feuer and Narain Gehani, Prentice-Hall [Feuer and Gehani 1984]. The two languages are summarized and compared objectively. Topics covered include their design philosophies, their handling of data types, the programming facilities provide, the impact of these facilities on the quality of programs, and how useful are the facilities for programming in a variety of application domains.

Feuer, A. and N. Gehani (Editors) 1984. *Comparing and Assessing Programming Languages.* Prentice-Hall. Contains papers that compare and assess programming languages with a special focus on the languages Ada, C and Pascal.

Fitzhorn, P. A. and G. R. Johnson 1981. C: Toward a Concise Syntactic Description. *SIGPLAN Notices*, v16, no. 12 (December), pp. 14-21. The syntax of C [Kernighan and Ritchie 1978, Ritchie 1980] is not complete and not defined rigorously; e.g., the syntax for

1. function definitions and declarations is incomplete.

2. statements is not clear

3. data and function types is not separated clearly.

A syntax of C that remedies these concerns is given. Unfortunately, because of printing problems, the syntax given in this paper is not readable. A more readable version, with some more comments, can be found in *SIGPLAN Notices*, v17, no. 8, pp. 84-95, August 1982.

Gannon, J. D. 1975. Language Design to Enhance Program Reliability. Technical Report CSRG-47, University of Toronto.

Gannon, J. D. 1977. An Experimental Evaluation of Data Type Conventions. *CACM*, v20, no. 8 (August).

Gehani, N. 1977. Units of Measure as a Data Attribute, *Computer Languages*, v2, pp. 93-111.

Gehani, N. H. 1981. Program Development by Stepwise Refinement and Related Topics. *Bell System Technical Journal*, v60, no. 3 (March), pp. 347-378. Takes another look at stepwise refinement in the context of recent developments in programming languages and programming methodology such as abstract data types, formal specifications, and multiversion programs. Offers explicit suggestions for the refinement process.

Gehani, N. H. 1983a. An Electronic Form System: An Experience in Prototyping. *Software—Practice & Experience*, v13, pp. 479-486.

Gehani, Narain 1983b. *Ada: An Advanced Introduction Including Reference Manual for the Ada Language.* Prentice-Hall. The author first gives a quick introduction to the conventional aspects of the Ada language—features found in existing programming languages such as Pascal, C, PL/I, ALGOL 60 or FORTRAN, and then focuses on its novel aspects—data encapsulation, concurrency, exception handling, generic facilities, program structure and representation clauses. Interesting differences between the Ada language and other languages are pointed out. The book contains many realistic examples including some large ones, all of which have been tested on an Ada compiler.

Gries, D. 1976. An Illustration of Current Ideas on the Derivation of Correctness Proofs and Correct Programs. *IEEE Transactions on Software Engineering* v2, no. 4, pp. 238-243. Explains how to develop correct programs. A non-trivial example (a line justifier) is developed hand in hand with its correctness proof.

Gries, D. 1979. **cand** and **cor** before **and then or else** in Ada. Technical Report TR79-402, Department of Computer Science, Cornell University, Ithaca, N. Y. 14853. This paper contains an argument for the use of the semicolon as a statement terminator rather than a separator. The following quote says it all: "From the standpoint of tradition, grammar, theory, elegance and style, the semicolon deserves its place as a separator. To use the PL/I blunder of the semicolon as a terminator is, in my mind, intolerable. The grounds for this are very weak: a badly done experiment and the fact that it is supposed to help the compiler recover after errors."

Halfant, M. 1983. The UNIX C Compiler in a CP/M Environment. *Byte*, v8, no. 8 (August), pp. 243-267. A look at how compatible the standard C compiler is when it is used under CP/M (taken from *Byte*).

Hamming, R. W. 1973. *Numerical Methods for Scientists and Engineers* (second edition). McGraw Hill.

Hancock, L. and M. Krieger 1982. *The C Primer.* McGraw Hill.

Harbison, S. P. and G. L. Steele, Jr. 1983. *The C Language Reference Manual.* Tartan Labs. A detailed reference manual for the C language prepared for the ANSI standardization committee. The authors emphasize on good programming conventions and describe differences between different implementations of C.

Hoare, C. A. R. 1962. Quicksort. *Computer Journal*, v5, no. 1, pp. 10-15.

Hoare, C. A. R. 1973. Hints on Programming Language Design *ACM SIGACT/SIGPLAN Symposium of Principles on Programming*

*Languages* (October), Boston, Mass.

Hoare, C. A. R. and N. Wirth 1973. An Axiomatic Definition of the Programming Language Pascal, *Acta Informatica* v2, pp. 335-355.

Hoare, C. A. R. 1978. Towards a Theory of Parallel Programming. In *Programming Methodology, a Collection of Articles by Members of WG2.3* edited by D. Gries, Springer-Verlag. Proposes parallel programming constructs with objectives such as security from error, efficiency, simplicity and breadth of application. Introduces the idea of critical regions.

Horowitz, E. 1983. *Fundamentals of Programming Languages.* Computer Science Press.

Horning, J. J. 1979. Effects of Programming Languages on Reliability. In *Computing Systems Reliability* edited by T. Anderson and B. Randell, Cambridge University Press. The first part of the paper is a comprehensive survey of programming language features (e.g., types and the treatment of types) that aid in the development of correct programs. Acknowledging the fact that faults and exceptional situations are inevitable in real programs, the author discusses language features (e.g., exception handling) for writing fault tolerant programs in the second part. The final part of the paper is a discussion of language features that encourage program correctness proofs.

Houston, J., J. Broderick and L. Kent 1983. Comparing C Compilers for CP/M-86. *Byte*, v8, no. 8 (August), pp. 82-106.

Pascal 1980. Second Draft Proposal of the ISO Pascal Standard (January 1981). *Pascal News*, no. 20.

Jensen, K. and N. Wirth 1974. *The Pascal User Manual and Report.* Springer-Verlag.

Johnson, S. C. and B. W. Kernighan 1973. The Programming Language B. Unpublished notes.

Johnson, S. C. 1978a. A Portable Compiler: Theory and Practice. *Fifth Annual ACM Symposium on Principles of Programming Languages* (January), Tucson, Arizona. Overview of the construction of a C compiler with goals such as easy compiler portability, production of reasonable quality object code and use of the latest results in code generation.

Johnson, S. C. 1978b. Lint, a C Program Checker.

Johnson, S. C. and B. W. Kernighan 1983. The C Language and Models for Systems Programming. *Byte*, v8, no. 8 (August), pp. 48-60. A happy medium between low- and high-level languages. C provides a model for efficient programming (taken from *Byte*).

Joyce, J. 1983a. A C Language Primer, Part 1: Constructs and Conventions. *Byte*, v8, no. 8 (August), pp. 64-78.

Joyce, J. 1983b. A C Language Primer, Part 2: Tool Building in C. *Byte*, v8, no. 9 (September), pp. 289-302.

Katzenelson, J. 1983a. Introduction to Enhanced C. *Software—Practice and Experience*, v13, no. 7 (July), pp. 551-576. A set oriented extensible C-like language.

Katzenelson, J. 1983b. Higher Level Programming and Data Abstractions—A Case Study Using Enhanced C. *Software—Practice and Experience*, v13, no. 7 (July), pp. 577-595.

Kernighan, B. W. and P. J. Plauger 1974. *The Elements of Programming Style*. McGraw-Hill. Contains many simple and elegant suggestions of how to write good programs. Lots of examples.

Kernighan, B. W. and P. J. Plauger 1976. *Software Tools*. Addison-Wesley. The book explains how to write good programs that make good tools. These tools are intended for use in the construction of other programs. Real, nontrivial examples are given.

Kernighan, B. W. and P. J. Plauger 1981. *Software Tools in Pascal*. Addison-Wesley.

Kernighan, B. W. and D. M. Ritchie 1978. *The C Programming Language*. Prentice-Hall. Excellent introduction and the standard reference to the C language; contains *The C Reference Manual*.

Kernighan, B. W. and M. D. McIlroy (Editors) 1979. *UNIX Programmer's Manual, Seventh Edition*. AT&T Bell Laboratories, Murray Hill, N.J. 07974.

Kern, C. O. 1983. Five C Compilers for CP/M-80. *Byte*, v8, no. 8 (August), pp. 110-130. How C compilers for the CP/M-80 operating system stack up (taken from *Byte*).

Kernighan, B. W. and R. Pike 1984. *The UNIX Programming Environment*. Prentice-Hall.

Lalonde, W. R. and J. R. Pugh 1983. A Simple Technique for Converting from a Pascal Shop to a C Shop. *Software—Practice and Experience*, v13, pp. 771-775. The C preprocessor *define* statement is used to allow a programmer to write C programs that superficially look like Pascal programs. However, a programmer is still required to know a certain amount of C in order to use this Pascal facility.

Lear, E. 1964. *The Nonsense Books of Edward Lear*. The New American Library.

Lee, P. A. 1983. Exception Handling in C Programs. *Software—Practice and Experience*, v13, no. 5 (May), pp. 389-405. Only limited exception handling facilities are provided in C. General exception handling facilities, based on the exception handling facilities in the Ada language, are provided in C by means of a software package—no modifications to the C compiler or the C preprocessor are required. The author describes this package and discusses practical experience in using it.

Linhart, J. 1983. Managing Software Development with C. *Byte*, v8, no. 8 (August), pp. 172-182. Choosing a good programming environment can affect programming ease and code quality more than you might imagine (taken from *Byte*).

Liskov, B. and S. N. Zilles 1974. Programming with Abstract Data Types. *SIGPLAN Notices*, v9, no. 4 (April).

Liskov, B. 1976. Discussion in the *Design and Implementation of Programming Languages* edited by John H. Williams and D. A. Fisher, p. 25, Springer-Verlag.

Mateti, P. 1979. Pascal versus C: A Subjective Comparison. *Proceedings of the Symposium on Language Design and Programming Methodology* (September). Also in *Comparing and Assessing Programming Languages* [Feuer and Gehani 1984]. Author expresses unhappiness over the presence of many potentially dangerous features in C that require programmers to use it with caution.

McGettrick, A. D. and P. D. Smith 1983. *Graded Problems in Computer Science*. Addison-Wesley.

McIlroy, M. D. 1960. Macro Instruction Extension of Compiler Languages. *CACM*, v3, no. 4, pp. 414-420. Classic paper in which the author discusses and advocates the use of macros in a high-level language as a language extension mechanism.

Morris, J. H., Jr. 1973. Types are not Sets. *ACM Symposium on Principles of Programming Languages*, Boston, MA. Introduces the notion that types are sets of values plus a set of operations.

Naur, P. 1963. Revised Report on the Algorithmic Language ALGOL 60. *CACM*, v6, no. 1 (January), pp. 1-17.

Phraner, R. A. 1983. Nine C Compilers for the IBM PC. *Byte*, v8, no. 8 (August), pp. 134-168. A discriminating look at the C compilers available for this lucrative market (taken from *Byte*).

Plum, T. 1983. *Learning to Program in C*. Plum Hall, Cardiff, N.J.

Pratt, T. W. 1975. *Programming Languages: Design and Implementation.* Prentice-Hall.

Pratt, V. 1983. Five Paradigm Shifts in Programming Language Design and Their Realization in Viron, a Dataflow Programming Environment. *Conference Record of the Tenth Annual ACM Symposium on Principles of Programming Languages* (January), Austin, TX.

Purdum, J. C. 1983. *C Programming Guide.* Que Corporation, Indianapolis, IN.

Richards, M. 1969. BCPL: A Tool for Compiler Writing and Systems Programming. *Proc. AFIPS SICC*, v34, pp. 557-566.

Ritchie, D. M., S. C. Johnson, M. E. Lesk and B. W. Kernighan 1978. The C Programming Language. *Bell System Technical Journal*, Part 2, v57, no. 6 (July-August), pp. 1991-2019.

Ritchie, D. M. 1980. The C Programming Language—Reference Manual. AT&T Bell Laboratories, Murray Hill, N.J. 07974. Revised version of the Reference Manual for the C Programming Language (as of September 1980).

Schwartz, J. T. 1975. On Programming—Interim Report of the SETL Project. Courant Institute of Mathematical Sciences, NY.

Sethi, R. 1980. A Case Study in Specifying the Semantics of a Programming Language. *Seventh Annual ACM Symposium on Principles of Programming Languages* (January), Las Vegas, NV. Specification of the semantics of C.

Sethi, R. 1981. Uniform Syntax for Type Expressions and Declarators. *Software—Practice and Experience*, v11, no. 6 (June), pp. 623-628. Author explains that type declarations in C are hard to read primarily because the operator for dereferencing is prefix instead of postfix. The author concludes by saying that "in declarations, a little bit of syntactic sugar makes a big difference".

Stroustrup, B. 1982. A Set of C Classes for Coroutine-Style Programming. Computing Science Technical Report No. 90, AT&T Bell Laboratories, Murray Hill, N.J. 07974.

Stroustrup, B. 1983. Adding Classes to the C Language: An Exercise in Language Evolution. *Software—Practice and Experience*, v13, pp. 139-161. The limited data structuring facilities in C are augmented by the addition of *classes*, a data abstraction facility. C's classes are based on the classes in Simula 67.

Stroustrup, B. 1984a. Data Abstraction in C. To be published. C++ is a superset of C with extensions such as the *class* facility, and function and operator overloading. The paper contains a detailed discussion of data abstraction using classes.

Stroustrup, B. 1984b. The C++ Programming Language—Reference Manual. Computing Science Technical Report No. 108, AT&T Bell Laboratories, Murray Hill, N.J. 07974.

Van Wyk, C. J., J. L. Bentley and P. J. Weinberger 1982. Efficiency Considerations for C Programs on a VAX 11/780. Technical Report CMU-CS-82-134, Dept. of Computer Science, Carnegie-Mellon University, Pittsburgh, PA 15213. Manual optimization of programs is a many step process. Here are some findings that may be used to optimize programs:

- It is always more expensive to operate on `char` or `short int` variables than on `int` variables. Use `char` or `short int` only where required semantically or where space is limited.

- It is always more expensive to operate on `float` than on `double` variables because of C's conversion rules. Use `float` only where required semantically or where space is limited.

- It is better to use increment operators (e.g., `+=`) than the assignment operator.

- Using arrays and array subscripts in loops can be more efficient than using pointers because it is possible to generate good code for arrays.

Welsh, J., M. J. Sneeringer and C. A. R. Hoare 1977. Ambiguities and Insecurities in Pascal. *Software—Practice and Experience*, v7, no. 6 (November), pp. 685-696.

Wirth, N. and C. A. R. Hoare 1966. A Contribution to the Development of ALGOL. *CACM*, v9, no. 6 (June), pp. 413-433.

Wirth, N. 1971a. The Design of a Pascal Compiler. *Software—Practice and Experience*, v1, pp. 309-333.

Wirth, N. 1971b. The Programming Language Pascal. *Acta Informatica*, v1, pp. 35-63.

Wirth, N. 1971c. Program Development by Stepwise Refinement. *CACM*, v14, no. 4, pp. 221-226. Classic paper on stepwise refinement. F. P. Brooks in his book *The Mythical Man—Month* calls stepwise refinement the most important programming formalization of the 1970s.

Wirth, N. 1973. *Systematic Programming: An Introduction.* Prentice-Hall.

Wirth, N. 1975. An Assessment of the Programming Language Pascal. *Proceedings—1975 International Conference on Reliable Software*

(April), Los Angeles, CA.

Wulf, W. and M. Shaw 1973. Global Variable Considered Harmful. *SIGPLAN Notices*, v8, n2, pp. 28-34.

Zahn, C. T. 1979. *C Notes: A Guide to the C Programming Language.* Yourdon Press, NY. Interesting comments that focus on many of C's implementation dependencies and semantic peculiarities.

# Index

# A

# B

# C

# D

# F

# K

# L

# M

# N

# P